The HTML of Cruciform Love

The HTML of Cruciform Love

Toward a Theology of the Internet

edited by
John Frederick
and
Eric Lewellen

James Clarke & Co

James Clarke & Co
P.O. Box 60
Cambridge
CB1 2NT
United Kingdom

www.jamesclarke.co
publishing@jamesclarke.co

Paperback ISBN: 978 0 227 17730 3
PDF ISBN: 978 0 227 90731 3

British Library Cataloguing in Publication Data
A record is available from the British Library

First published by James Clarke & Co, 2020

Copyright © Wipf and Stock Publishers, 2019

Published by arrangement
with Pickwick Publications

All rights reserved. No part of this edition may be reproduced, stored electronically or in any retrieval system, or transmitted in any form or by any means, electronic, mechanical, photocopying, recording, or otherwise, without prior written permission from the Publisher (permissions@jamesclarke.co).

This book is dedicated to the students who took my Christian Worldview and Media course at GCU in Phoenix in the Spring of 2017. Thanks for letting me think big thoughts with you about digital demons and other weird things. —JOHN

For Stephanie, Charlotte, and Audrey, whose unwavering support makes my participation in these projects possible. —ERIC

Contents

List of Contributors | ix

Preface and Acknowledgments | xi

Introduction: Toward a Theology of the Internet (John Frederick) | xiii

1. The Discipline of the Eyes: Reflections on Visual Culture, Ancient and Modern (Ben Myers and Scott Stephens) | 1

2. Interface Is Reality (Kutter Callaway) | 23

3. Cyber-Genesis of the Digital Self (John Frederick) | 39

4. The Bible Is Not a Database (T. C. Moore) | 52

5. See Me, Hear Me, Praise Me: An Internet for More than Vainglory (Chad Bogosian) | 62

6. A Theology of Work for a Virtual Age (Scott B. Rae) | 75

7. Mark's Jesus and the Internet: Exegetical Reflections on Authority, Identity, and Community (Jen Gilbertson) | 86

8. The Solomonic Temple: Technology and Theology (Walter Kim) | 101

9. The Internet Gaze (Eric Stoddart) | 117

10. Virtual Counterfeit of the Infinite: Emmanuel Levinas and the Temptation of Temptation (Donald Wallenfang) | 132

11. The Church and Electronic Media—Foundational Issues: Our Addiction to Efficiency and the Myth of Neutrality (Mark D. Baker) | 151

12. Crafting or Bearing the Present: Reflections on the Character of Christian Community (Clark Elliston) | 160

Subject Index | 175

Author Index | 179

Ancient Document Index | 183

List of Contributors

John Frederick is Lecturer in New Testament at Trinity College Queensland and Flinders University. His publications include *Worship in the Way of the Cross* and *The Enactment and Reception of Cruciform Love*.

Ben Myers is Director of the Millis Institute at Christian Heritage College in Brisbane and a research fellow of the Centre for Public and Contextual Theology at Charles Sturt University in Canberra. His publications include *Salvation in My Pocket* and *Christ the Stranger: The Theology of Rowan Williams*.

Scott Stephens is the editor of the ABC's Religion and Ethics website, and co-host (with Waleed Aly) of the radio program *The Minefield* on ABC Radio National. He is also specialist commentator on religion and ethics for ABC radio and television. He is currently completing a book entitled *Idiot Wind: The Media and Its Threat to the Moral Life*.

Kutter Callaway is Assistant Professor of Theology and Culture and Co-Director of Reel Spirituality at Fuller Theological Seminary, Pasadena. His publications include *Scoring Transcendence: Contemporary Film Music as Religious Experience* and *Watching TV Religiously: Television and Theology in Dialogue*.

T. C. Moore is Pastor of Roots Covenant Church in Saint Paul, Minnesota.

Chad Bogosian is Instructor of Philosophy at Clovis Community College in Fresno, California. His publications include "Impeccability, Consensus, and Trusting One's Moral Intuitions: Why Epistemic Might Doesn't Make Rational Right" in vol. 31 of *Southwest Philosophy Review*, and "Nussbaum On Forgiveness: A Christian Reply" in *Philosophy of Forgiveness*, Vol 4: *Christian Perspectives on Forgiveness*, edited by Gregory L. Bock.

Jen Gilbertson holds a PhD in New Testament from the University of St Andrews in Scotland. She is currently working in Student Development at Briercrest College and Seminary in Canada.

Scott B. Rae is Professor of Christian Ethics and Dean of the Faculty at Talbot School of Theology in La Mirada, California. His publications include *Moral Choices* and *Introducing Christian Ethics*.

Walter Kim is Pastor for Executive Leadership at Trinity Presbyterian Church, Charlottesville. His publications include contributions to Zondervan's *Archaeological Study Bible* and to the *Encyclopedia of Hebrew Language and Literature*. He serves on the Board of the National Association of Evangelicals.

Eric Stoddart is Lecturer in Practical Theology at St. Mary's College, University of St. Andrews in Scotland. His publications include *Theological Perspectives on a Surveillance Society: Watching and Being Watched* and "The Common Gaze" in *Mending the World? Possibilities and Obstacles for Religion, Church, and Theology*.

Donald Wallenfang is Associate Professor of Theology at Walsh University in North Canton, Ohio. His publications include *Dialectical Anatomy of the Eucharist: An Étude in Phenomenology* and *Human and Divine Being: A Study on the Theological Anthropology of Edith Stein*.

Mark D. Baker is Professor of Mission and Theology at Fresno Pacific Biblical Seminary in Fresno, California. His publications include *Proclaiming the Scandal of the Cross: Contemporary Images of Atonement* and *Ministering in Honor-Shame Cultures: Biblical Foundations and Practical Essentials*.

Clark J. Elliston is Assistant Professor of Christian Ethics at Schreiner University in Kerrville, Texas. His publications include *Dietrich Bonhoeffer and the Ethical Self: Christology, Ethics, and Formation* and *Theology and the Films of Terrence Malick* (editor).

Preface and Acknowledgments

It is with great joy and satisfaction that this volume has finally been brought to print in 2019. The project had its genesis four years ago when a group of friends and PhD students from the University of St. Andrews in Scotland held our second global webinar conference entitled "Ecclesia and Ethics II: Gospel Community and Virtual Existence." Following that conference, the organizers (of which the editors of this book were a part) decided to put the proceedings volume on hiatus because we had received only 5–6 submissions from among the plenary papers for publication. Several years later, however, we decided to return to the project. We strongly felt that the submissions we had by scholars such as Mark D. Baker, Clark Elliston, Ben Myers, Scott B. Rae, Walter Kim, and Donald Wallenfang were just too good to leave unpublished. In addition to the aforementioned pieces which were a part of the original conference, in 2015 we commissioned six new pieces from John Frederick, Kutter Callaway, T. C. Moore, Chad Bogosian, Jen Gilbertson, and Eric Stoddart to form a complete book.

Upon completing the project, we were truly surprised and encouraged to see how well the twelve pieces worked together in a single volume. In the view of the editors, the chapters function quite well as individual works, but also contribute to a cohesive conversation about the way in which the technology of the internet itself—even apart from its content—is a medium that is capable of cultivating communion or isolation, virtue or vice, incarnation or disembodiment, and presence or absence.

We, the editors, wish to thank the University of St. Andrews for their support of the Ecclesia and Ethics conference from its beginning in 2013. We're grateful to our colleagues John Anthony Dunne, Allen Jones, and

Janghoon Park for their integral work and involvement in the Ecclesia and Ethics conferences. Thanks go to the editorial team at Pickwick for taking on the project, and for being flexible, helpful, and a pleasure to work with throughout the entire process. Many thanks indeed to the scholars who were a part of the original conference but whose presentations do not appear in the current book including: Michael Bird, Bill Mounce, Loren E. Wilkenson, William M. Struthers, John Mark Reynolds, Brandon Cox, and Derek C. Schuurman. We're exceedingly grateful for all of the leaders, scholars, ministers, and congregants who attended the conference from all over the globe.

It is our sincere hope that this volume will be the beginning of a larger conversation in the church and in the academy that works toward a Christian theology and praxis of the internet.

John Frederick
Eric Lewellen
January 8, 2018

Introduction

Toward a Theology of the Internet

JOHN FREDERICK

This book is a collection of independent essays brought together into one volume focusing on a variety of themes revolving around a theology of the internet. There are at least two key common themes (and several sub-themes) that have emerged from the collection that are noteworthy and helpful to be aware of prior to reading the individual chapters, namely, the themes of *community* and *character*.

In regard to the theme of *community*, upon reading the collection of essays as a whole, we discovered a reoccurring focus on the nature and the type of community that is formed through the medium of the internet. Concerning the theme of *character*, we detected a nearly ubiquitous focus on the shaping power of internet behaviors and communities upon the formation of virtue and vice. In this brief introduction, I will highlight some of the instances of these themes—*community and character-formation*—as they appear in the content of the various chapters of this book. My goal will not be to summarize the chapters, nor will it be to offer a critique of them. Rather, I will aim to simply draw out the implications of the themes of *community* and *character* to provide a hermeneutical prolegomena and a coherent theological lens that can be used to assist the reader in assessing the individual chapters of the book, and the book as it works together in its various component parts.

The Internet and Community: Toward a Cruciform Network Sociality

The Digital Communion of the Saints

Central to most of the chapters in this book is a consideration, assessment, and critique of community that is created through the internet compared to community that occurs outside of the digital realm. It is worth bringing the voices of Myers/Stephens, Elliston, Frederick, Callaway, and Moore into constructive dialogue in order to assess the main points that have been made, and to consider how they can be synthesized to speak in a preliminary manner about the issue of community and the internet.

The two main currents that appear in this collection typically fall into opposing sides of the spectrum, namely, those which critique internet-based communities as in some sense deficient or problematic (Elliston, Frederick, Rae, and Gilbertson), and those which cast a more positive vision for the purpose and potential of internet communities (Myers/Stephens and Callaway). Of course, as the reader will discover, the actual positions of each author contain both positive and negative assessments of internet community. Yet, I am speaking here in general terms in reference to the main emphasis—whether positive or negative—in the particular essays of the authors in this book. For example, in my own chapter ("Cybergenesis of the Digital Self") I mostly focus on the negative potential for disastrous, communal and demonic activity through the medium of the internet. Yet, in stating negatively what is potentially dangerous about the medium, I have, through engaging with the other essays in this book, come to see how these same technologies can be used in a redemptive manner.

Myers's and Stephens's chapter focuses initially on exploring an ethics of seeing through parsing out a biblical and patristic visual-ascetic practice of the "fasting of the eyes" as it relates to the internet. However, its secondary point relates to the power of sacred images to create communities of proximity and sacramental presence. The idea is that the context for the celebration of the sacraments and the Christian visual experience is the community of the church. The implication and challenge—as I take it—seems to be in applying this patristic experience of transformative, communal "seeing" to our experience as a digital community, or what I would like to refer to as the "digital communion of the saints." The question becomes: In what sense can our cyber-praxis contribute to the experience of the proximity and presence of God through our own proximity to and presence with one another as a digital communion of believers?

While there seems to be great potential in the power of the internet as a medium for building community, Elliston in his chapter rightly wonders: Are the communities created by the internet able to operate as effectively as flesh and blood communities? Citing the inability of online communities to foster long-term friendships and the decreased function of burden-bearing in cyber-settings, Elliston focuses on the deficiency of the medium to compete with flesh and blood communities to produce true Christian presence and proximity. This resonates with Rae's suspicion that the move to virtual workplaces will result in a perceived lack of adequate human interaction leading to the feeling of a lack of belonging and identity in workers. He also keenly detects that the loss of a sense of the intrinsic goodness of work when it undergoes a shift into a merely instrumental role in its virtual instantiations could constitute a deficiency in the virtual workplace as a community.

In my view, both perspectives represent the reality of the potentiality, potency, and presence of cyber-communities. Unless it is recognized that the internet constitutes a different type of community than non-cyber social settings and mediums, there will always be an inherent deficiency in communities that have their genesis in the zeros and ones of the internet. As technology and communications expert Andreas Wittel has argued in his article "Toward a Network Sociality," internet existence is far less stable and coherent than life occurring outside of the net. Due to the ambiguous, often inflated and fabricated nature of online communication, community exists in the internet as a "network sociality," a unique communal phenomenon of community that is inherently fragmented and unreliable. While not using the term "network sociality," readers will find the concept of internet communication and community as a "network" taken up by Callaway in his chapter as a guiding metaphor for understanding digital engagement and culture. Likewise, Gilbertson, in her chapter, also draws attention to the network-based culture of the internet by exploring the loose nature of the communities they form. Thus, she too picks up on a common thread in cyber-studies, namely, that there is a potential and proclivity within the medium of the internet and its users to experience community as a network sociality typically characterized by fragmentation.

In a preliminary attempt to bring these diverse perspectives together, I would like to suggest that while it is true that "our cyber selves exist in a network sociality of fragmentation rather than a community of coherence,"[1] nevertheless, this is not a defect inherent in the medium of the internet. Rather, it is a problem that is derived from our sinful use of the medium. If the church is to embrace the internet as a mechanism of cultivation for the koinonia of the digital communion of the saints as the body of Christ, Christians must transform the phenomenon of a network sociality into something that exceeds the current modus operandi. What is required in order to redeem the medium so that it might be a sufficient generator of transformative Christian presence and proximity is a sanctification of cyber-community into a *counter-cultural, cruciform* network sociality. If the current trend in behavior of our network socialities is based on fragmentation, distance, and individualism, we must aim as the church to rebuke these anti-communal tendencies, replacing them with the virtues of coherence, presence, and burden-bearing communalism. To use Kim's framework, we can adopt the medium of the internet and network socialities, but we must become innovators and repudiators of them as well. The network sociality of the internet must be cruciformed in order to become a catalyst for the pneumatic power and presence of the digital communion of the saints.

Incarnation through Interface

While readers will likely agree that the above approach to online communities and networks is worth pursuing, it is less likely that there will be agreement on the question of whether the internet presents a medium that increases embodiment through incarnation, or if it is one that decreases embodiment through "excarnation."[2] Callaway argues that our interfaces become part of our embodied existence, thus extending our bodies by incorporating them into the technology of the internet. He helpfully compares this to the concept of the body of Christ in the New Testament in which human persons are envisioned as existing within an extended network. To Callaway: "Paul's understanding of the church hinges upon a conception of the human person not as body-bound but as extended."[3]

Moore's chapter likewise views our use of the internet as an "extension" of the human person. Yet, Moore keenly points out one potential problem with this reality, namely, the fact that human beings are sinful.

---

1. Frederick, *Cybergenesis of the Digital Self*, 42.
2. Callaway, *Interface is Reality*, 25–28.
3. Ibid., 35.

Thus, theological anthropology is a variable to consider when discussing the extended nature of our bodily existence through the internet. If we are sinful, then it stands to follow that our cyber-extension will also engage in sinful acts, and is susceptible to assault and damage from the sin of the cyber-extension of the Other.

In stark contrast to Callaway, Elliston argues that internet churches "can speak to the theological revolution enacted in the Incarnation, but cannot be incarnate for its members."[4] Here too, I think both sides of the coin are necessary. To point out, as Elliston has, that what essentially constitutes the phenomenon of internet community is more accurately designated as a "network sociality," is to highlight the current problem with the medium that really does hinder the full blessing and experience of embodied Christian communion. Yet, in my view, recognizing this problem does not delegitimize the medium. Nor does it disqualify it in any way from its cruciform consecration as a viable instrument for the digital communion of the saints. Rather, in recognizing the sinfulness of the humanity that is extended through interface (Moore), and reckoning with the flightiness and fragmentation that currently constitutes our often disembodied ecclesial social networks (Elliston), we can identify the very problems and sinful proclivities that must be eliminated in order for the presence of God to be manifested through a cruciformed community of incarnate, extended souls in communion with each other through the zeros and ones of the HTML of cruciform love.

The Internet and Character: Toward the Sanctification of the Saints through a Cruciform Network Sociality

Demonology of the Digital Self

The second major strand of cohesion that emerged from this collection relates to the formation of character and identity through our online engagement and patterns of behavior. It is generally recognized by all of the authors that the medium is capable—in varying degrees—of contributing to the formation of virtue or vice. Yet, within the individual essays (perhaps with the exception of Bogosian's which deals with the topic of virtue ethics) there is typically a tendency to emphasize either virtue or vice.

4. Ibid., 170.

In regard to vice, the most severe of the critiques is my own chapter which formulates a demonology of the digital self. The idea here is that our online engagements leave in their wake clusters of data which can be activated by others even after we unplug—indeed, even after we physically die! The activated—or to use the technical hermeneutical term "ideated"—result of our digital imprint, I argue, conjures up a residual narrative self that can become a negative phantom presence. Wallenfang's discourse on the "promiscuity of the self" created through the varying forms of self-presentation on the internet hits on this same point. The worlds and selves that we create through the internet are not *like* the real world; *they are, in some sense a real world*, with real effects, and real consequences. The picture of digital demonic gloom and doom that I paint in my chapter—while talking more about *the result* of our negative behaviors on the internet on others—connects substantially with the observations of Bogosian, Wallenfang, and Elliston who parse out *the particular behaviors* that lead to the creation of harmful, indeed demonic (in a phenomenological sense), digital content.

Bogosian, for example, focuses on the propensity of internet users to develop habits of vice through the practice of vainglorious online behaviors. This vainglory becomes ingrained in our being, our character, through our actions that are rooted in the misrepresentation of our social status, physical appearance, and our expertise. An instantiation of human pride and inauthenticity, these behaviors affect ourselves and others. In relation to my own thesis, these behaviors would affect not only ourselves and current users, but future users through their seemingly endless activation and ideation.

Resonating with Bogosian and my own observations are the contributions of Wallenfang who applies Levinas' idea of the "temptation of temptation" to our experience of internet search engines. The concept of an empty, blinking search engine bar itself represents a true invitation to either virtue or vice; that is, the medium itself, apart from its content, constitutes a tempting phenomenon. This is important, because as Marshall McLuhan and Jacques Ellul have famously argued, it is not merely the *content delivered* through mediums of technology, but the *mediums themselves* that constitute part of the impact and effect of the message. This point is well-delivered by Baker in his chapter which successfully brings this core idea to bear on a theology of the internet by keenly and carefully arguing that *efficient* mediums are not always the same as *effective* mediums.

Sanctification and the Digital Self

The positive counterpoint to the prophetic digital doom oracle that is my own chapter comes through the work of Myers/Stephens and Bogosian. Both chapters offer rich resources for the life of holiness and virtue in the digital realm, and both chapters drink deeply and impressively from the well of Scripture and the early church fathers. Myers/Stephens break new ground in applying the patristic emphasis on "the moral use of the eyes" and "visual asceticism" to a theological praxis to Christian life on the internet. In applying Clement of Alexandria's concept of a "systematic curriculum for the pedagogy of the eyes" to contemporary internet praxis, Myers/Stephens offer a new way forward for Christian spiritual formation in the cyber realm. It strikes me that most of the literature I have encountered concerning Christian behavior on the internet is reactionary rather than catechetical. What Myers/Stephens offer here should, in my view, be incorporated into the very fabric of contemporary catechesis in order that our approach to cyber-reality would be preemptive and formative, rather than primarily reactionary and restorative.

In the same manner, Bogosian's chapter is where the abstract theologizing of the book (which itself is necessary and good) hits the ground running. Bogosian offers the patristic practices of prayer, silence, and solitude as a framework for turning our engagement on the internet into an experience of virtue formation, character growth, and sanctification. Regarding transformative approaches to the internet, Stoddart's response to the dulling, capitalistic, consumeristic "internet gaze" makes a major contribution. He argues that the transition from a dulling "gaze" to a "caring gaze" will cultivate "connection and community." In my view, this type of community is precisely what we have previously labelled a cruciform network sociality for the digital communion of the saints.

Conclusion

Labelling this section a conclusion is, perhaps, deceptive. In all reality this book constitutes a truly collaborative beginning. In working toward a constructive, cruciform theology of the internet, there is much work to be done. The one conclusion I can make is that the topic of the internet, technology, the church, and the self is one that is vastly underrepresented in the literature at the time of this book's publication. It is certainly viewed as a "special interest" topic. Yet, it is evident to the contributors and likely to you as the reader that there is perhaps no topic more pertinent to our daily walk as contemporary followers of Jesus Christ than the theological implications and presuppositions of the internet. My hope is that what this book offers will be expanded, corrected, and supplemented by many other books, articles, sermons, catechetical materials, podcasts, and conversations to come. It is only when we come to terms with our existence as embodied persons connected through interface that we will begin to see the internet as more than a mere supplementary component to our personal lives, but a medium of vital connection for the digital communion of the saints through the HTML of cruciform love.

1

The Discipline of the Eyes

Reflections on Visual Culture, Ancient and Modern

BEN MYERS AND SCOTT STEPHENS

> "Like hospitality or any other virtue, the good gaze develops through practice." —IVAN ILLICH[1]

> "If your right eye causes you to sin, tear it out and throw it away." —MATT 5:29

Margaret Atwood's novel *Oryx and Crake* (2003) depicts a dystopian society dominated by images. Two boys, Jimmy and Crake, click idly back and forth between porn sites, animal snuff sites, and live coverage of executions and assisted suicide. They are fascinated in equal measure by images of sex and images of cats being torn apart by hand; by nude newsreaders and live beheadings in front of cheering crowds; by scenes of paedophilia and scenes of live open-heart surgery. The sex and brutality blur together,

> the body parts moving around the screen in slow motion, an underwater ballet of flesh and blood under stress, hard and soft joining and separating, groans and screams, close-ups of clenched eyes and clenched teeth, spurts of this or that. If you switched back and forth fast, it all came to look like the same event.[2]

---

1. Illich, *Rivers North of the Future*, 109.
2. Atwood, *Oryx and Crake*, 81–87.

All these images of sex and violence, however, are not "real" in any straightforward sense. The boys suspect that the Chinese beheadings and Middle Eastern stonings are probably filmed somewhere in California, with crowds of hired extras standing around cheering. The websites don't simply supply images of reality. Rather, reality is produced for the sake of the image. Just as porn actors fake arousal for the sake of the camera, so, in Atwood's dystopian cyberspace, "the guys being executed had started hamming it up for the cameras." In this dystopia, assisted suicide rates have skyrocketed as a result of the popularity of live suicide websites. "There was said to be a long lineup of people willing to pay big bucks for a chance to appear on it and snuff themselves in glory, and lotteries were held to choose the participants." Reality exists for the sake of the image, and the image exists to meet an insatiable demand: what the Bible calls "the lust of the eyes" (1 John 2:16).

The most disturbing thing about Atwood's dystopia is the fact that it is instantly recognizable as a parody of our image-saturated society. Christians today live in a society of the spectacle. Our lives are dominated to an unprecedented degree by images and by the moral act of looking at them.

The pages that follow will first explore early Christian thinking about the role of the eyes in the moral life. Early Christian teachers wrote and preached extensively about the moral and spiritual use of the eyes. They developed a thorough critique of the ever-popular public shows and commended visual disciplines as a normal part of the baptized life. One of the distinguishing marks of Christians was the way they used their eyes. Turning to an analysis of contemporary visual culture, we will argue that the prodigious consumption of online images has all but eviscerated the moral life, and that moral recovery might depend on a new practice of visual asceticism—the fasting of the eyes.

Early Christian Teaching on Public Spectacles

The one who looks—"merely" looks—is often assumed to be passive. But for early Christian teachers, looking was a moral act. More than that, it was a spiritual act that exposes a person's innermost being to external influences, whether malignant or benign. The eyes, along with the other senses, were considered to be gateways to the spiritual world.

Very early in the history of Christian thought, it became something of an ethical axiom that the eyes are instruments of moral agency. The second-century Athenian apologist, Athenagoras, pointed out that the chastity of Christians extends even to the functioning of their eyes.

> So far are we removed from promiscuity that we are not allowed even to look with passion upon another; for, as scripture says, "anyone who even looks with lust at a woman has already committed adultery with her in his heart." God made our eyes to be a light to us, and we may not use them otherwise.[3]

Likewise Christians take nonviolence so seriously that their eyes avoid violence. "We cannot bear even to see a person put to death," Athenagoras observes. And frankly admitting the appeal of the public shows, he says: "Who is not enthralled by armed contests and animal fights . . . ? But we have renounced such spectacles, judging *that to look on murder is much the same as murder itself.*"[4]

The baptismal language of renunciation is invoked to describe the stance of Christians towards the shows. Abstaining from public entertainments is assumed to be one of the marks of the Christian community. The eyes are not passive. They are moral and spiritual organs. They can commit adultery and murder. Or they can shine like lamps.

Writing a century later, the North African apologist Lactantius similarly described the moral agency of the eyes:

> What is so horrible, so foul, as the butchery of a human being? That is why our lives are protected by strict legislation; that is why warfare is so hateful. . . . If one's presence at manslaughter implies a consciousness of guilt, the spectator is equally guilty with the doer of the deed. Consequently in these gladiatorial butcheries the onlooker is no less sprinkled with blood than the butcher.[5]

Cyprian of Carthage condemned both the violence of the shows and the ocular violence of the spectators. He described the public entertainments in the great cities as "death processions" and lamented that the whole world seemed intoxicated by human blood.[6] At the games, he said, "a man is slain for human sport. The ability to kill is a skill, it is an exercise, it is an art. . . . The ability to destroy a man is a discipline." But the cruellest thing of all, in Cyprian's view, was not the armed gladiator but the spectator.

---

3. Athenagoras, *Embassy for the Christians*, 32.
4. Athenagoras, *Embassy for the Christians*, 35.
5. Lactantius, *Epitome of the Divine Institutes*, 63.
6. Cyprian, "To Donatus," 6–7.

After all, the supply of public violence is linked to demand. Were it not for the eager eyes of the spectator there would be no such violence: "The gladiatorial game is laid on so that the bloodshed might entertain eyes that reflect a merciless blood lust." Even the families of gladiators will pay an entrance fee to come and watch their loved ones battle to the death. By becoming spectators, Cyprian argues, such a family becomes guilty of parricide: "They do not stop to think that with their eyes they are murderers of their relatives."[7] It is not only the contestants who kill; the eyes of the spectators commit murder too.

John Chrysostom drew on the same moral principle of the complicity of the eyes in what they see. He instructed his catechumens about attendance at the public shows, telling them:

> Let there be no more talk about the hippodrome and the lawless spectacles of the theatre, for they provide the fuel for licentiousness. Let there be no talk of the cruel pleasure derived from the combats between wild beasts and men. For what pleasure is there in watching a fellow human, who shares in the same nature as yourself, being mangled by savage beasts? And are you not afraid, do you not shudder, for fear that a thunderbolt might fall from on high and set your head ablaze? For it is you, one might say, who sharpen the teeth of the beast. You, by your shouts, have a personal part in the murder, if not by your hand, at least by your tongue.[8]

In the same sermon, Chrysostom quotes Matt 5:28 as scriptural proof that the spectator is morally equivalent to an actor:

> He who has come under [Christ's] yoke ought to forget his old way of life and keep a close watch over his eyes. For the Master says, "Anyone who even looks with lust at a woman has already committed adultery with her in his heart." So we must put a guard on our eyes, that death may not enter through them.[9]

If an adulterous look is morally equivalent to adulterous behavior, then by the same logic the one who looks willingly on murder commits murder with the eyes. It was above all the enormous popularity of the Greco-Roman public shows that pressed Christian teachers to reflect on the morality of the eyes. Christianity had taken root in a society of the spectacle. In the great cities, public entertainments were an indispensable means of

---

7. Cyprian, "To Donatus," 7.
8. Chrysostom, *Baptismal Instructions*, 1.43.
9. Chrysostom, *Baptismal Instructions*, 1.32.

social cohesion. On feast days devoted to various gods, citizens flocked to the great stadiums to witness "the spectacles": athletic contests, wrestling, horse races, animal baiting, reenactments of famous battles, as well as thrilling gladiatorial contests.

The power of these shows may be judged by the way they continued to enthral Christian converts. If early Christian sermons are anything to go by, the public shows lost none of their appeal for most believers. The sermons of John Chrysostom seem to be forever explaining why Christians cannot take part in the "Satanic spectacles." Chrysostom complains bitterly about the continuing power of the shows over believers. Church attendance in Antioch would swell to bursting at the great feasts of Easter and Pentecost, and would decline just as dramatically on the pagan feast days. One Sunday, huge crowds would gather to hear the Logos and to partake of the body and blood of Christ, and the following week the same crowd would swarm into the hippodrome to witness the blood-sports in honor of Greek gods. One of Chrysostom's Lenten sermons begins with the melancholy report: "Again there are chariot races and Satanic spectacles in the hippodrome, and our congregation is shrinking." The same people who yesterday were in church fasting, he says, "have today rushed away." Under the circumstances, the ever-talkative Chrysostom confesses that he is nearly too depressed to preach at all.[10]

In the second century Tertullian had found it necessary to write a treatise explaining why followers of Christ should not attend the shows. His treatise, *On the Shows*, is interesting not only for its meticulous descriptions of the various forms of public entertainment but also for its frank acknowledgement of Christian attendance at the shows. Tertullian refers to theological arguments, both pagan and Christian, that were used to justify the shows. Some argued that the merely "external pleasures" of the ear and eye have no bearing on faith, since faith is internal and is untouched by the senses.[11] Others argued that the shows were celebrations of God's creation. It is an impressive argument; it has an almost Augustinian ring to it. Can the athletic contest be condemned when a man's physical strength is God's handiwork? Can the gladiatorial game be condemned when the lion is one of God's creatures? Even the physical environment, so the apologists of the shows argued, was all part of God's creation: the stones, the marble slabs,

---

10. Chrysostom, *Baptismal Instructions*, 6.1–2.
11. Tertullian, *De Spectactulis*, 1.3.

the towering columns.¹² What could be more innocent—indeed, more reverent and worshipful!—than gazing on God's creatures as they skillfully encounter one another in the arena?

The seriousness of this argument can be judged by the extreme care with which Tertullian dismantles it. He does not deny that the shows involve the gifts of creation. But he makes a distinction between creation and corruption. All God's creatures are good but they can all be perverted by misuse. "You see murder committed by iron, poison, magic incantation: but iron, poisonous herbs, demons are all equally creatures of God. Yet did the creator design those creatures for destroying human beings? Certainly not!"¹³

Tertullian points out that God's commandments are concerned with the misuse of good creatures. The human being was made in God's image, yet human nature has become corrupted through misuse:

> For we did not receive the eyes for lust, the tongue for evil speech, the ears for listening to evil speech, the mouth (together with the belly) for indulging in the sin of gluttony, the genitals for shameless excess, the hands for violence, and the feet to wander.¹⁴

In every instance sin occurs "through the medium of God's handiwork." Sin is nothing else than "the misuse of God's creation by God's creatures."¹⁵ This is one of the earliest and most precise formulations of the relation between creation and fall: a key doctrinal clarification that emerged from the church's struggle with the society of the spectacle.

Tertullian saw that the theological arguments used to defend the shows were a product, not the basis, of attendance at the shows. Once we have become addicted to a certain pleasure, we will tend to adapt our beliefs to justify the pleasure and to avoid cognitive dissonance. "How clever in argument human ignorance seems to itself, especially when it is afraid of losing something like this, some delight or enjoyment of the world!"¹⁶

Apparently baptized converts were in the habit of calmly pointing out that Scripture contains no direct prohibition against the Roman shows. There is no scriptural text that says: "Thou shalt not go to the circus," or

---

12. Tertullian, *De Spectactulis*, 2.1–2.
13. Tertullian, *De Spectactulis*, 2.8.
14. Tertullian, *De Spectactulis*, 2.10.
15. Tertullian, *De Spectactulis*, 2.11.
16. Tertullian, *De Spectactulis*, 2.2.

"Thou shalt not look at a contest or a gladiatorial spectacle."[17] Again, the seriousness of this argument is measured by the care and precision of Tertullian's response. If all God's commandments are intended to prohibit a certain misuse of creation, then the commandments can be extended to cover other areas of life as well. Scriptural prohibitions of idolatry, for example, should be extended to participation in public entertainments that involve the celebration of Roman gods. Commandments concerning lust should be extended to cover every kind of addiction to pleasure. The shows, Tertullian says, belong here as a species of lust.[18]

Tertullian also argues that the pleasures of the shows are at every point opposed to Christian piety. The one who is swept up in the ecstatic frenzy of the stadium cannot enjoy God's peace.[19] The one who cheers for the death of a gladiator cannot obey Christ's command to love our enemies.[20] The one called to a life of holiness cannot pursue purity while opening the gates of the eyes and ears to the polluting influence of the shows: "the ears and eyes are servants of the spirit, and the spirit cannot be clean when its servants are filthy."[21] Those who revel in "punches and kicks and blows and all the reckless use of the fist and every disfiguration of the human face, that is, of the divine image" cannot truly love humanity.[22] Those who sit "with their eyes fixed on the bear as it bites," stirred by a "murderous pleasure," cannot be stirred by pity.[23] Those who are called to the marriage supper of the Lamb cannot recline as guests at the devil's table, "stuffing themselves" with the devil's sweets.[24] In short, Tertullian makes a case that Christian faith is diametrically opposed to participation in the shows.

> What sort of conduct is it to go from the assembly of God to the assembly of the devil, from sky to sty [*de caelo in caenum*], as the saying goes? Those hands which you have lifted up to God, to tire them out afterwards applauding an actor? To cheer a gladiator with the same lips with which you have said "Amen" over the Most

---

17. Tertullian, *De Spectaculis*, 3.2.
18. Tertullian, *De Spectaculis*, 14.2–3.
19. Tertullian, *De Spectaculis*, 16.1–5.
20. Tertullian, *De Spectaculis*, 16.6.
21. Tertullian, *De Spectaculis*, 17.5.
22. Tertullian, *De Spectaculis*, 18.1.
23. Tertullian, *De Spectaculis*, 25.4.
24. Tertullian, *De Spectaculis*, 28.1.

> Holy? . . . For no one can serve two masters. What has light to do with darkness? What has life to do with death?[25]

Tertullian notes that even pagan citizens recognize renunciation of the shows as the main public mark of Christian conversion.

> Shall we ask the pagans for an answer? Let them tell us whether a Christian may go to the shows. This, above all, is how they understand that someone has become a Christian, that he renounces the shows. So to remove this distinguishing mark is a denial [of faith].[26]

Attendance at the shows, in Tertullian's view, is tantamount to a denial of baptism. It is sobering to recall that we are talking here about something one does only with the eyes. The Christian who attends the amphitheatre is seemingly passive. He is not, one might suppose, doing anything at all: he is only looking. But for Tertullian the eyes are servants of the spirit. When the physical eye looks, the spirit looks too.

Centuries later, Augustine's *Confessions* would dramatize this theme of the link between the eyes and the soul. In a celebrated scene,[27] Augustine describes his friend Alypius, who had renounced a fanatical love of the public games in order to pursue a philosophical life. But one day a group of revelling friends dragged him forcibly to the stadium in Carthage. He went unwillingly, protesting that he would sit there with his eyes shut. "You may drag my body into that place," he scolded, "but can you direct my mind and my eyes to the show?" They arrived and took their seats. Alypius "kept the gateways of his eyes closed." But then a huge roar rose from the crowd. Poor Alypius: his curiosity got the better of him. He decided he would take just one peek—strictly for the purpose of condemning whatever had occurred. "He opened his eyes," Augustine reports, "and suffered a more grievous wound in his soul than the gladiator . . . had received in the body." In a vivid metaphor, Augustine describes Alypius "falling" spiritually just as the gladiator has fallen in the arena. It is as if the soul of the spectator and the body of the contestant were linked by an invisible bond. As soon as Alypius saw the blood, his eyes "gulped the brutality" with a terrible thirst. He "fixed his gaze" on the contest. He could not look away. "What more needs to be said?" asks Augustine sadly. "He watched, he shouted, he grew hot with excitement." "No longer was he

---

25. Tertullian, *De Spectactulis*, 25.5—26.3.
26. Tertullian, *De Spectactulis*, 24.3–4.
27. Augustine, *Confessions*, 6.8.13.

the man who had joined the crowd; he was now one of the crowd he had joined." And all because he opened his eyes.

Fasting with the Eyes: Early Christian Visual Pedagogy

The enthralling nature of the public shows, and the power of the eyes to direct the spiritual life, gave rise to a substantial literature on visual asceticism. Already in the second century, Clement of Alexandria's treatise on divine education had developed a systematic curriculum for the pedagogy of the eyes. The eyes are to abstain from the public shows, from lustful ogling, and from immodest glances. "The eyes should be used sparingly," Clement says, "for it is better to slip with the feet than with the eyes."[28] The eyes should avoid hankering after the sight of brightly colored clothes (especially purple clothes, which incite lust).[29] They should be trained to avoid the darkening effects of excessive sleep.[30] Men should not let their hair grow down over the eyes.[31] Women should avoid painting and adorning the eyes.[32] The eye is God's sacred lamp; cosmetic additions only diminish its native beauty. At all times the eyes should be clear and uninhibited and "anointed by the Logos."[33] Tellingly, though Clement is fond of convivial wine-drinking, he objects to drunkenness in part because it impedes clarity of vision. Under the influence of too much drink, the eyes slide and roll about. Everything appears to be swimming, as if everything were submerged in wine. Even worse, Clement says, the eyes become bloodshot: their native brightness is traded for the dull stare of a corpse.[34] Prior to baptism, sin was an obscuring film that covered the eye. But now this film has been removed so that "the eye of the spirit is free and unimpeded and full of light."[35] The pedagogy of the Christian life involves a training of the senses and, in particular, a discipline of the eyes.

28. Clement of Alexandria, *Christ the Educator*, 3.11.
29. Clement of Alexandria, *Christ the Educator*, 2.11.
30. Clement of Alexandria, *Christ the Educator*, 2.9.
31. Clement of Alexandria, *Christ the Educator*, 3.11.
32. Clement of Alexandria, *Christ the Educator*, 3.2.
33. Clement of Alexandria, *Christ the Educator*, 2.13.
34. Clement of Alexandria, *Christ the Educator*, 2.2.
35. Clement of Alexandria, *Christ the Educator*, 1.6.

John Chrysostom similarly spoke of a visual fast in which the eyes are brought under Christ's discipline:

> Do you fast? Prove it by your works.... If you see a poor man, take pity on him. If you see an enemy, be reconciled to him. If you see a friend being honoured, don't envy him. If you see a lovely woman, keep walking! For it's not only the mouth that fasts, but also the eye, and the ear, and the feet, and the hands, and all the members of our bodies. Let the hands fast by being pure from plunder and the love of money. Let the feet fast by no longer running to the lawless spectacles. Let the eyes fast by learning never to fix themselves immodestly on lovely faces or to be preoccupied by strange beauties. For looking is the food of the eyes.[36]

Chrysostom links the discipline of the eyes to the sacraments. Participation in the holy mysteries helps to bring about a reorientation of one's gaze, a conversion of the eyes to divine realities. In baptism the eyes see the bath of water and the hand of the priest, but the "eyes of the spirit" must look upon the invisible realities. Believers train their eyes to see not just water but the grace of the Spirit; and not just the priest's hand, but the hand of Christ resting on the one who is being baptized. They see not just a bodily washing but a washing of the soul; not just a body emerging from the water but "the new human being come forth brightly shining from that sacred purification."[37] Chrysostom says all this in his instructions to the catechumenate. He is bringing their eyes under a sacramental discipline and teaching them how to see.

In another sermon to the catechumens, he speaks of a eucharistic discipline. Those who receive Christ's body in the hand may never again strike a human being in violence. Those who receive Christ's body in the mouth, whose tongues have been "purpled by a blood so precious," may never again use their mouths for blasphemy or perjury or abuse. Those whose ears have heard the mystic words of the sacrament may never again contaminate their ears with the songs of harlots. And last but not least, the eyes: "Do you not deserve the most extreme punishment if you use the same eyes with which you behold the ineffable and awesome mysteries to look upon harlots and to commit adultery in your heart?"[38]

---

36. Chrysostom, *Homilies on the Statues*, 3.11.
37. Chrysostom, *Baptismal Instructions*, 2.10; 11.12.
38. Chrysostom, *Baptismal Instructions*, 12.18.

The sacramental mystery trains the senses and reorients ordinary perception. When one has seen Christ and the Spirit in baptism, one begins to see everything else differently too. When one has looked upon the mystery of the eucharistic meal, all human beings begin to appear in a new light. The point is a pedagogical one that has little to do with medieval doctrines of sacramental efficacy. The church is a school of the senses. The liturgy is a training ground for perception.

The theological emphasis on the training of the eyes was part of a wider culture of "visual piety" in Christian antiquity.[39] By the fourth century, Christians were making pilgrimages to the Holy Land to gaze on sites from the biblical stories. Even more important were journeys to monastic settlements where devout pilgrims would seek to catch a glimpse of the holy faces and emaciated bodies of the famous ascetics. Accounts of the desert monks abound in descriptions of their faces and of the effect they had on pilgrims who came to see them. John Cassian describes the pedagogy of the faces of the monks: "Old age and holiness, in bodies now bent over, shine so brightly in their faces that the mere sight of them is able to teach a great deal to those who gaze upon them."[40]

The first monastic biography, Athanasius's *Life of Antony*, had dwelt at length on the visual piety surrounding Antony in the desert. "His face had a great and marvelous grace, and this spiritual favor he had from the Savior."[41] Athanasius describes the crowds of spectators who came to look at Antony. Young men reformed their lives merely by "looking at Antony." Many young women, "simply seeing Antony at a distance," resolved to enter the monastic life.[42] After the monk's death, his cloak and sheepskin were preserved among his followers. These items were prized as relics. The sight of them continued to convey virtue since, as Athanasius remarks, "even seeing these is like beholding Antony."[43]

Thus Christian antiquity witnessed the rise of a complex apparatus of visual discipline. The eyes were submitted to a process of training and purification: negatively through various visual renunciations, and positively by visual participation in the liturgy, in pilgrimage, and in the use of relics.

---

39. The term is from Georgia Frank's excellent study, *Memory of the Eyes*, 174.
40. Cassian, *Conferences*, 11.2.
41. Athanasius, *Life of Antony*, 67.
42. Athanasius, *Life of Antony*, 87–88.
43. Athanasius, *Life of Antony*, 92.

Such was the culture of Christian visual piety that emerged under the influence of—and in protest against—the ancient society of the spectacle.

Virtual Culture and the Discipline of the Eyes

Needless to say, there are considerable differences between the ancient society of the spectacle and our own visual culture. The Greco-Roman shows were tied to religious rites and traditions. They weren't merely public entertainments but represented religious assemblies convoked in honor of the gods. This is why early Christian critiques of the shows, like that of Tertullian, focused not only on the violence of these entertainments, but also—and sometimes primarily—on the problem of idolatry.

Moreover, public entertainment in antiquity was occasional and festive, whereas visual entertainment today is constant and pervasive. For the Roman citizen, entertainment was part of the rhythm of the calendar year. For citizens of our global city, every day is marked by the rhythm of visual entertainments—perhaps news clips in the morning, Facebook and Twitter through the day, a movie at night, a little porn before bed. For us, each day has become a little calendar with its own miniature festivals and cathartic releases. And although vast congregations assemble online for these festivals, the use of the screen to mediate presence creates the illusion of privacy and individuality.

The lack of any kind of physical assembly for our modern spectacles is significant in another way too. The ancient citizen could not watch a violent contest in the privacy of his own home. The whole city would assemble for those consoling entertainments. For Christians, therefore, withdrawal from the shows was motivated by concerns about the *public* witness of the faith. The church was seen as an alternative public assembly with its own festivals, its own entertainments and its own holy spectacles. That is why Tertullian insisted that Christians who went to the amphitheatre were publicly trading their allegiance to Christ for an alternative spiritual allegiance. It is why participation in the shows came so quickly to be viewed as a public renunciation of baptism. It is why many Christian authorities, including Augustine, imposed excommunication as a penalty for such attendance.

And yet, for all these differences, the distance that separates the Greco-Roman world from our own image-saturated age should not be overstated. One of the characteristics of our time that is often overlooked is the extent to which our consumption of images is underwritten by an ethical or quasi-religious justification. We rarely see ourselves as complicit in the way our eyes glide over the images that have come to dominate news sites and populate our social media feeds—whether it be scenes of carnage in Syria or starvation in Yemen, a cataclysmic weather event in the Pakistan or a made-for-media protest in London, some freakish happenstance on a highway in Los Angeles or the latest dalliance of the world's most glamorous in Paris. Neither the sheer number of images nor the vast moral disparity of their content, ranging as they do from the tragic to the utterly banal, gives us pause. This is due, in large part, to the dramatically altered status of images themselves. Whereas once photographs in the popular press might have functioned like windows on to the world in all its grim and dizzying variety, now images are more like slivers of *experience*—captured, commodified, offered for consumption. And whereas once the cost of film and the trained eye of photographers could not help but imbue photographs with a certain iconic or interpretative quality, now the ubiquity of camera technology no longer aims to make the world intelligible but to make the world sharable. The criterion of "sharability" is, of course, mercilessly indiscriminate because it is concerned only with the spectacle itself and its power of fascination, not with whether it is true, trivial, or manufactured.[44]

What gets lost in this transformation, as Susan Sontag brilliantly anticipated forty years ago, is an "ethics of seeing": the introspective pause after one encounters a deeply affecting image; the opportunity to subject one's "political consciousness" to the searing scrutiny of the image itself;

---

44. We are powerfully reminded at this point of Dwight MacDonald's searing critique in the 1950s of the "homogenized culture" of the modern West. In his 1956 essay "Masscult and Midcult," he holds up the example of the then fabulously popular *Life* magazine as emblematic of this process of homogenization: "*Life* is a typical homogenized magazine. . . . Its contents are as thoroughly homogenized as its circulation. The same issue will present a serious exposition of atomic energy followed by a disquisition on Rita Hayworth's love life; photos of starving children picking garbage in Calcutta and of sleek models wearing adhesive brassières; an editorial hailing Bertrand Russell's eightieth birthday . . . across from a full-page photo of a matron arguing with a baseball umpire . . . ; nine colour pages on Renior paintings followed by a picture of a roller-skating horse; a cover announcing in the same size type two features: a new foreign policy, by john foster dulles and kerima: her marathon kiss in a movie sensation. Somehow these scramblings together seem to work all one way, degrading the serious rather than elevating the frivolous." Some, admits MacDonald, defend magazines like *Life* as a valiant attempt at popular education. "Just think," he writes, "nine pages of Renoirs!" But then "that roller-skating horse comes along, and the final impression is that both Renoir and the horse were talented." He thus anticipated our debauched culture of "sharability" by half a century. See MacDonald, *Against the American Grain*, 12–13.

the willingness to suffer the image, as it were, but to transmute that suffering into redoubled conviction and thence genuine action.[45] Such an ascetic ordeal cannot but seem foreign to us now, in a time when truly *looking* has been replaced by *liking*, when the hard work of interiority has been swallowed up in our vast culture of publicity and self-promotion, when the capacity of iconic images to arrest and to invite a certain moral attentiveness that draws us nearer to the inextinguishable humanity captured by the photograph is lost amid a boredom whose inattentiveness is broken only by the intermittent compulsion to "share" something.

And yet, while these disturbing trends in our consumption habits of news and social media point to a de-moralization or hollowing-out of our practices of looking, such that images lose their already fragile ethical content and become merely pornographic—a matter of superficial fascination which is extinguished in the gratification of the nonplussed self—all this coincides with a residual if unformed and inconsistent sense of moral duty. The fact that the images we consume are now no longer mediated through magazines or newspapers but are seen, swiped, scrolled, shared on personal devices like smartphones and tablets has inadvertently reinforced an older notion of the function of images: that, phenomenologically, images bring the world close. They make the world both proximate and available, and with that availability comes both an expectation of transparency (we have the right to see) and an obligation to look. Sometimes this moral injunction to look is overt: just think of the thirty images of the tortured, maimed, destroyed bodies of victims of Bashar al-Assad that were smuggled out of Syria and publicly displayed in the halls of the United Nations building in New York City in March 2015, accompanied by the command "not to look away." Or consider the morally laden injunctions accompanying the "viral" image of the body of three-year-old Aylan Kurdi, lying face down on a Turkish beach.[46] Certainly in the post-Vietnam era, when human rights began to take hold in public and media discourse, the role of photographs in giving human rights ideals a human face was incalculable.[47] Images displayed in the media were a way of making nations accountable to international norms, and a way of stigmatizing perpetrators

---

45. See Sontag, "On Photography," 529–45.

46. There is no space here to explore just how problematic is this notion of "virality"—suffice it to say it is the final expression of the pornification of the image in a social-media age, and, as such, is one of the more perfidious forms of our modern idolatry.

47. Such is the argument of Linfield in *Cruel Radiance*.

of human rights abuses. Thus looking came to be —even if only tacitly—as an act of popular surveillance.

But in order truly to understand how an act of relatively cheap consumption could acquire the status of an ethical act, we need to go back earlier than the human rights era. Søren Kierkegaard was perhaps the first to recognize, in 1847, a strange logic that the popular press had begun to exert on the world: the very act of expanding citizens' sphere of awareness, of bringing the world close, had the effect of contracting and ultimately flattening out the moral responses available to them. The newspapers and periodicals that by mid-century had become staples of bourgeois society had wrested people out of a state of innocence "in which they were by no means obliged to have an opinion" and forced them into what Kierkegaard calls a "condition of guilt" in which they were forced have an opinion.[48] For the first time, merely possessing an opinion became a moral thing to do, because it was the only response available to those newly in possession of this expanded awareness of the world.[49] It is no wonder that, just to the extent that journalists became the purveyors of opinion, the act of buying newspapers quickly acquired an ethical status as well. And yet, as Kierkegaard insisted, this cannot help but debauch the nature of ethical responsibility. For by substituting that sense of responsibility which is only forged in interiority and silence for irresponsible "chatter" (Kierkegaard's derisive term for opinion quickly gained and

48. Quoted in Graff, *Søren Kierkegaard*, 471.

49. This already highly commercialized sense of duty was tainted from the beginning by a kind of bourgeois fashionability. Kierkegaard wrote scathingly of that form of "opinion which despite its insubstantial quality is nonetheless put on and worn as—a necessary item." But it was his Parisian contemporary, Gustave Flaubert, who was most carefully attuned to the way in which fashion and a certain moral pretense went hand-in-hand in the popular press. In his unforgettable instruction of the proper use of newspapers, for example, Flaubert writes, "You must leave them about in your drawing room, taking care to cut the pages open beforehand. Marking certain passages in blue pencil is also impressive. In the morning, read in article an one of those grave and solid journals; in the evening, in company, bring the conversation around to the subject, and shine." See Flaubert, *Dictionary of Accepted Ideas*, 67. It is also mercilessly portrayed in his novel, *Madame Bovary*. Just consider the way Emma, in her restless narcissism, devours magazines like *Corbeille* and *Le Sylphe des Salons* and she longs for her name to be "repeated in newspapers," even as "she would talk to [Charles] about the things she had read, such as a passage from a novel, a new play, or the *high society* anecdote being recounted in the paper." Or Monsieur Homais's own lust for renown, which produces a kind of obsession with newspapers ("they would talk about what was *in the newspaper*. Homais, by that time of day, knew it all by heart; and he would replay it in its entirety, including the editorials and the sorties of each and every catastrophe that had occurred in France or abroad"). See Flaubert, *Madame Bovary*, 49–50, 52–53, 85.

cheaply held), and by replacing what he calls *intensity* (which knows and consistently holds to only some things) for a more superficial and necessarily contradictory *extensity* ("which chatters about anything and everything and continues incessantly"), ethics becomes less a matter of the soul and more a performance of the narcissistic self.[50]

But with the collapsing stocks of the print media over the last decade—both figuratively and literally—and in a time defined by incommensurable disagreement and hyper-partisan suspicion, it is small wonder that the moral centre of gravity has shifted from opinions to images. Long gone are the days when a newspaper's seriousness was inversely proportional to the number of images it printed to embellish its content. As words have steadily lost their potency, images have shrugged off their traditional subservient role as mere adornment of the text and have gained moral force as indices of the real.[51] Amid the cacophony of contested narratives and competing interests that clutter the modern media landscape, we have come to believe that images bypass thinking and touch us directly at the level of feeling. Images, unlike words, are capable of piquing our attention and arousing our sentiments. They can galvanize a sense of shared outrage and give a human face to otherwise complex and intractable conflicts.

It is for all these reasons that we no longer think there is anything morally problematic about our constant consumption of images. And so Hilaire Belloc's 1929 jeremiad against the popular press, that its "orgy of pictures and headlines" prevents thinking and engenders an unreflective stupor, now sounds alien to our ears.[52] So too does Sontag's warning that images of wartime atrocity might transfix but they also anesthetize, and that the "concerned" photography of the Vietnam era had "done at least as much to deaden conscience as to arouse it."[53] For us, images promise more than information. They offer proximity, immediacy: experience. At a time when the rest of the world has moral weight only to the extent that it *can* be experienced, images bring the world within reach by transforming it into so many discrete objects to be consumed, shared, and then quickly discarded when we are done with them.

50. Kierkegaard, "Two Ages," 265.

51. Facebook and Twitter were originally platforms for short-burst, text-based communication. Now the role of text on both platforms is negligible, as they have transformed themselves over the last four years into bearers of images, moving and still. From memes to emojis, what text there is seems increasingly to function as a kind of pictograph.

52. Belloc, *Survivals and New Arrivals*, 127.

53. Sontag, "On Photography," 542.

To just this degree, all images today are pornographic: they arouse—but without danger, obligation, or contamination. The ubiquitous screens that bear the images to us are our moral prophylactics. We are brought close to the experience of others, but not too close. The illusion of personal connection is an ersatz placebo. As Darian Leader has suggested, the introduction of touch technology into our use of visual media, like the screens of smartphones and tablets, becomes one more form of our alienation from an authentic proximity to others.[54]

There is a disturbing yet instructive illustration of this in the work of Swiss provocateur and darling of the Kunsthalle circuit, Thomas Hirschhorn. Hirschhorn is well known for his use of images of death and dismemberment. Magazine clippings and photocopies of scenes of human carnage have been a staple ingredient in his sprawling, frenetic collages. But in a more recent video piece titled *Touching Reality*, Hirschhorn depicts a hand interacting with a series of images of mangled bodies, cracked and crushed heads, severed limbs and mounds of unidentifiable viscera, all through the medium of some sort of tablet. The images themselves are grainy and indistinct, evidently taken by amateurs or bystanders on whatever device was at hand. Most, perhaps all of them would appear to have been retrieved directly from the internet. The poor quality of the images, however, has the perverse effect of luring viewers into a discomfiting cycle of revulsion and macabre curiosity, just to the extent that what appears on the screen is often hard to make out. Hirschhorn insists that the prominence he gives to images of "destroyed human bodies" is neither meant to be sensationalist nor merely aesthetically transgressive. Rather, they pose a form of resistance to what he calls the media's "iconism": the undue privilege accorded to images deemed more newsworthy, more *iconic*, than others. Hirschhorn thus disavows any pretension to artistic agency, that he somehow mediates "the Truth" in deference to what he deems to be the moral character of the images themselves. They present a reality ("Truth") obscured by the media's official *mediating* function. For Hirschhorn, reality exceeds verifiability or the status of factuality:

> I am interested in Truth, Truth as such, which is not a verified fact or the "right information" of a journalistic story. . . . Truth is irreducible; therefore the images of destroyed human bodies are irreducible and resist factuality. . . . The habit of reducing things to facts is a comfortable way to avoid touching Truth, and

---

54. Leader, *Hands*, 107.

to resist this is a way to touch Truth. Such an acceptance wants to impose on us factual information as the measure, instead of looking and seeing with our own eyes. I want to see with my own eyes. Resistance to today's world of facts is what makes it important to look at such images.[55]

In *Touching Reality*, the hand interacting with the tablet is white, female, and impeccably manicured. It manipulates the images with a disturbing and incurious remove, pausing occasionally to inspect some object that happens to grab its attention—charred remains of a limb, a sign, a mobile phone, a bystander's expression, a hideously damaged face—as though it were shopping online or browsing an issue of *Vanity Fair*. By contrast, the images portray dead or mortally wounded male bodies from undifferentiated zones of conflict in the Middle East, South Asia, and North Africa. In the very interaction between this hand and these images, the gap that separates the two remains inviolable, unmediated. Rather than touching reality, the hand in fact touches *nothing*, is moved by nothing. For the problem with the dead and damaged bodies scattered across Hirschhorn's work is not that they offend the effete sensibilities of Western viewers by presenting too much, but rather that they are incommunicable. They are what Augustine called *inanibus phantasmibus*,[56] hollow images that can neither mediate real contact nor point beyond themselves. They can only fascinate or horrify. In this sense, Hirschhorn's corpses are *anti-icons*: "a nonpresence or a presence of the negative," as Rowan Williams put it describing Hans Holbein's unnerving *The Body of the Dead Christ in the Tomb*.[57]

Such modern anti-icons contrast starkly with the Christian use of images of suffering, where Christ and the saints are depicted both as objects of veneration *and* as invitations to draw near, to discover the peace of God in the midst of inhumanity, humiliation, and death. As Paul Griffiths writes:

> A human nature in this calamitously damaged world could not be hypostatically unified with the divine unless it underwent damage of just this sort. This is why Christians venerate Christ's wounds; it is also why the sufferings of the martyrs and saints, and of the groaning mass of humanity in general, constantly tortured, eviscerated, raped, burned, and consumed by painful disease as it is, can be, according to the extent of their participation

---

55. Hirschhorn, "Why Is It Important," 102.
56. Augustine, *True Religion*, 51.100.
57. Williams, *Dostoevsky*, 53.

in Christ's sufferings, iconic arrays for Christians. Depicting and ruminating the wounds of Christ, or the arrows piercing St. Sebastian's body, or the death of St. Catherine on the wheel, or the consuming of Perpetua and Felicity by the beasts of the arena, or the execution of Maximilien Kolbe in Auschwitz, is not, then, an exercise in morbidity but rather an accurate perception simultaneously of what is wrong with the world (that it is a place where such things happen) and what is right with it (that it is a place where such things happen).[58]

Matthias Grünewald's *Isenheim Altarpiece* provides an especially potent iconic counterpoint to Hirschhorn's sterile images of "destroyed human bodies." The outermost scene of the unfolding altarpiece portrays the crucifixion in infamously bleak fashion. Set against the darkened sky of his dereliction, Christ's body is stretched taut across the beams. His hands and feet are twisted cruelly around three unyielding nails. Christ's "fleshy heaviness" is disproportionately prominent.[59] His large body overwhelms the painting, bending the cross-beam and repelling even the most devoted companions by the sheer weight of his suffering. The imposing size of Christ's body—accentuated by the size of the altarpiece itself—renders the violence visited upon it all the more distressing. Christ's flesh is lacerated, punctured, and pocked; his wounds and lips are tinged with necrosis. Death and disease hang heavily upon him.

In her classic study of the Isenheim Altarpiece, Andrée Hayum drew attention to the interlocking liturgical and hospital setting for which these images were intended.[60] Early in the sixteenth century the Order of Hospitalers of St. Anthony commissioned the altarpiece for the hospital chapel in their monastery in Isenheim. Those suffering from disease—including a debilitating form of gangrenous ergotism that become known as *ignis sacer* or "St. Anthony's fire" due to the particular care provided by the Antonites—would ostensibly derive comfort from the reassurance that they were sharing in Christ's sufferings, and thus could hope to share too in his resurrection.[61] This is doubtless correct, given the symmetry of the

---

58. Griffiths, *Intellectual Appetite*, 194.
59. Baldwin, "Anguish, Healing and Redemption," 83.
60. Hayum, *Isenheim Altarpiece*.
61. Thus, Pope Emeritus Benedict XVI: "Though Grunewald's altarpiece takes the realism of the Passion to a radical extreme, the fact remains that it was an image of consolation. . . . The images are consoling, because they make visible the overcoming of our anguish in the incarnate God's sharing of our suffering, and so they bear within them

appearance on the left panel of St. Sebastian whose wounds echo those of Christ. But it overlooks the more immediate liturgical implications of the altarpiece. The visual logic of Grünewald's *crucifixion* (from Christ's heavily hanging head, to the flow of blood from his side and feet, to Mary Magdalene's exemplary supplication at the foot of the cross, whose blood-red sash mirrors Christ's blood and that of the lamb flowing into the chalice) directs the eyes of worshippers down toward the predella at the base of the altarpiece. There, the tender proximity of St. John to Christ's deceased body is surely addressed, not to those suffering from *ignis sacer*, but to the Antonites themselves. So too the image of St. Antony on the right panel, who, unlike St. Sebastian, addresses himself directly to those praying before the altar. Through their patient and prayerful proximity to the dying, and their receipt of the Eucharist alongside them, the Antonites were truly sharing in the suffering of Christ.

Thus, unlike the incommunicable images of destroyed bodies of Thomas Hirschhorn and the sterile scenes of human devastation peddled by the media, *sacred images* and *images viewed sacredly* have the potential to compel us truly to touch the reality to which these images direct us.

It may well be that one of the tasks for Christians today is to rediscover the primacy of proximity in an image-saturated age, to displace our now corrupted habits of sight by means of the recovery of the moral importance of those senses more attuned to the presence of the neighbor: smell and touch.[62] After all, the power of sacred images lies in their capacity to draw their viewers into an unbearable—and, precisely as such, ethical—nearness to their object. Sight thus mediates the exercise of the more ethically demanding senses that register and respond to the sheer bodily reality of the neighbor.

And perhaps we can recover the early Christian confidence that the training of the eyes is possible—that we can learn how to look, and to refrain from looking, even in a culture of visual promiscuity. Do Christian communities still believe it is possible to cultivate visual disciplines, and periods of visual asceticism, as necessary parts of the spiritual life? Do we recognize the moral value of providing havens from the dominance of the image, while also nourishing alternative traditions of perception? Do we offer catechesis in the use of holy images, whether these are works of art or the faces of living saints? Recent years have seen a growing appreciation for

---

the message of the Resurrection." See Ratzinger, *Theology of the Liturgy*, 78–79.

62. See Kearney and Treanor, *Carnal Hermeneutics*.

the spiritual importance of silence—the fasting of the ears—in a world of constant noise. Is it too late today to recover the ancient Christian practice of the fasting of the eyes?

Bibliography

Athanasius. *The Life of Antony and the Letter to Marcellinus*. Translated by Robert C. Gregg. New York: Paulist Press, 1980.
Athenagoras. *Embassy for the Christians*. Translated by Joseph Hugh Crehan. Ancient Christian Writers 23. New York: Newman Press, 1956.
Atwood, Margaret. *Oryx and Crake*. London: Bloomsbury, 2003.
Augustine. *Confessions*. Translated by Maria Boulding. Hyde Park: New City Press, 1997.
———. *True Religion*. In *On Christian Belief*, edited by Boniface Ramsey. Hyde Park: New City Press, 2005.
Baldwin, Robert. "Anguish, Healing and Redemption in Grünewald's Isenheim Altarpiece." *Sacred Heart University Review* 20.1–2 (2000) 80–91.
Belloc, Hilaire. *Survivals and New Arrivals*. New York: Macmillan, 1929.
Cassian, John. *The Conferences*. Translated by Boniface Ramsey. Ancient Christian Writers 57. New York: Paulist Press, 1997.
Chrysostom, John. *Baptismal Instructions*. Translated by Paul W. Harkins. Ancient Christian Writers 31. New York: Paulist Press, 1963.
———. *Homilies on the Statues*. In *Nicene and Post-Nicene Fathers* 9. Edinburgh: T. & T. Clark, 1889.
Clement of Alexandria. *Christ the Educator*. Translated by Simon Wood. Washington, DC: Catholic University of America Press, 1954.
Cyprian. "To Donatus." In *On the Church: Select Treatises*. Translated by Allen Brent. Crestwood: St. Vladimir's Seminary Press, 2006.
Flaubert, Gustave. *The Dictionary of Accepted Ideas*. Translated by Jacques Barzun. New York: New Directions Books, 1968.
———. *Madame Bovary*. Translated by Lydia Davis. London: Penguin, 2010.
Frank, Georgia. *The Memory of the Eyes: Pilgrims to Living Saints in Christian Late Antiquity*. Berkeley: University of California Press, 2000.
Graff, Joakim. *Søren Kierkegaard: A Biography*. Translated by Bruce H. Kirmmse. Princeton: Princeton University Press, 2005.
Griffiths, Paul J. *Intellectual Appetite: A Theological Grammar*. Washington, DC: The Catholic University Press of America, 2009.
Hayum, Andrée. *The Isenheim Altarpiece: God's Medicine and the Painter's Vision*. Princeton: Princeton University Press, 1989.
Hirschhorn, Thomas. "Why Is It Important—Today—to Show and Look at Images of Destroyed Human Bodies?" In *Critical Laboratory: The Writings of Thomas Hirschhorn*, edited by Lisa Lee and Hal Foster, 99–104. Cambridge: MIT Press, 2013.
Illich, Ivan. *The Rivers North of the Future: The Testament of Ivan Illich*. Edited by David Cayley. Toronto: Anansi Press, 2005.
Kearney, Richard, and Brian Treanor, eds. *Carnal Hermeneutics: Perspectives in Continental Philosophy*. New York: Fordham University Press, 2015.

Kierkegaard, Søren. "Two Ages—The Age of Revolution and the Present Age: A Literary Review." In *The Essential Kierkegaard*, edited and translated by Howard V. Hong and Edna H. Hong, 252–68. Princeton: Princeton University Press, 2000.

Lactantius. *Epitome Institutionum Divinarum*. Edited by E. H. Blakeney. London: SPCK, 1950.

Leader, Darian. *Hands*. London: Hamish Hamilton, 2016.

Linfield, Susie. *The Cruel Radiance: Photography and Political Violence*. Chicago: University of Chicago Press, 2010.

MacDonald, Dwight. *Against the American Grain*. New York: Da Capo, 1983.

Ratzinger, Joseph. *Theology of the Liturgy: The Sacramental Foundation of Christian Existence*. Edited by Michael J. Miller. Translated by John Saward, Kenneth Baker, S.J., Henry Taylor, et al. Collected Works 11. San Francisco: Ignatius Press, 2008.

Sontag, Susan. "On Photography" (1977). In *Essays of the 1960s and 70s*, 529–45. New York: Library of America, 2013.

Tertullian. *De Spectactulis*. In *Apology and De Spectactulis; Mincius Felix*. Translated by T. R. Glover. Loeb Classical Library. Cambridge: Harvard University Press, 1931.

Williams, Rowan. *Dostoevsky: Language, Faith and Fiction*. Waco: Baylor University Press, 2008.

2

Interface Is Reality

KUTTER CALLAWAY

My children have never known a world without screens they could touch. They love to swipe through pictures and videos on my cell phone. They navigate the apps on our family's Kindle with far more aplomb than I do. And they frequently hear their father explain that, unlike most of their electronic devices, his laptop does not have a touchscreen. So hands off!

But it wasn't until recently that I recognized the ways in which my daughters' touchscreen understanding of the world significantly departed from my own. My five-year-old and I were sitting on the couch, trying to find a suitable program on Netflix that both she and her sister could watch during their allotted "screen time." As the father, I of course have exclusive rights to the remote control, so I began navigating the various columns and rows of shows provided by the Netflix app just as one might imagine.

In short order, my daughter was able to identify the icon of the show that she wanted to watch. Unfortunately, I had already passed it, so she desperately tried to point me in the right direction. She kept saying "Daddy, go up! No, I said *up*! Up, Daddy, up. Why won't you go *up*!"

Being the eternally patient father that I am, I conveyed my levelheaded take on the situation with a reply that was equal parts calm and rational: "I *am* going up! This is up!"

As is often the case with a five-year-old, we were at an impasse. But it was not until we reached this critical juncture that I finally noticed what she was doing. She was standing in front of the TV screen, using her entire body in an effort to communicate to her (completely dumbfounded) father.

I had originally thought that she was *pointing* up. But what she was actually doing was *swiping* up. And she wanted me to swipe up too.

Take a moment to visualize this. If we want an image or text on a touchscreen to move up, we physically touch the screen and swipe our hand up. It makes perfect sense. In fact, it happens so intuitively we don't even think about it. But if we are using a remote or the arrows on a keyboard to control an on-screen cursor, we actually move these same images up by pressing the "down" button. And vice versa.

When I finally realized the source of our shared frustration, it became obvious that my daughter and I weren't simply miscommunicating. In fact, both of us were being quite clear (not to mention, loud). Instead, it was as if we inhabited entirely different worlds—worlds where "up" and "down" didn't just mean different things, but operated according to completely different logics. To be sure, we were engaged with the exact same digital content, which was instantly available to us via any number of internet-based streaming services. But it was the particular interface with which each of us was most familiar (for her, a touchscreen and, for me, a remote control) that structured our basic awareness of how these digital and physical worlds worked and interacted. Or to put it somewhat differently, for my daughter and me, interface was reality.

In the pages that follow, I explore the theological significance of these interfaces. That is, I consider the ways in which our vision of the world, the human person, and ultimately, God, is shaped by how we touch (or don't touch) our digital environment—how we daily relate to it, encounter it, and otherwise become involved in its numerous goings on. Of course, in a book of essays about the internet, it might seem odd to focus so much attention on that which we physically touch, but in truth, without some kind of interface, the "internet" is purely conceptual—a vast network of ones and zeroes suspended in the digital ether. So to speak of this digital world without making any reference to the various mediums by which we access it would be to reify an abstraction.

In this essay, then, I want to suggest that our concrete, physical encounters with the internet bear theological significance. Indeed, the basic claim I am putting forward is that the interfaces we employ to connect with our digital environments provide us with both a model and a means for being and becoming more fully human. And perhaps even more scandalously (for theologians anyway), I also want to suggest that, if we have any desire for theology to be coherent or intelligible in the age of the internet, we would do well to draw upon these interfaces as necessary resources for constructive theological reflection.

Needless to say, conceiving of interfaces in this way is difficult enough, but it will be altogether impossible if the theological tradition is unwilling to adopt a fundamentally different model for understanding the human, which is why it is vital for us to interact with and learn from a more diverse set of conversation partners. It is for this very reason that, in what follows, I attend primarily to the insights of the psychological and cognitive sciences (in addition to media studies and theology). In doing so, I hope to offer a more robust accounting of the ways in which digital interfaces not only shape our awareness of the world and connect us to our broader social networks, but also become an integral part of who we are as human beings.

Excarnation and the Problem with Bodies

These claims are hardly uncontroversial. Indeed, space will not allow a comprehensive listing of every theologian who might disagree with the ideas I am putting forward here. However, a common concern shared by those whose views differ from my own has to do with the theological significance of our bodies. For instance, in his *iPod, You Tube, Wii Play*, Brent Laytham rightly suggests that any theological conversation about our digital lives must take seriously the doctrine of the incarnation:

> [T]he Christian doctrine of the *incarnation* means that bodily life is good, something to be embraced and enjoyed. Our hope in Christ is not that we can finally escape the limitations of bodiliness for the freedom of a purely mental or "spiritual" existence. It is rather that we might be freed from death and sin for a resurrected bodily life that enjoys God forever.[1]

Here, Laytham is correct. Bodies matter. And any attempt to reduce, diminish, or escape our bodies is to take a decided step away from the historic Christian understanding of the human person. But from Laytham's perspective, the contemporary cultural imagination, which has become captivated by a vision of "excarnation," stands in stark opposition to an incarnational view.[2] Indeed, for Laytham, the various digital interfaces

---

1. Laytham, *iPod, YouTube, Wii Play*, 120 [emphasis original].

2. By employing the term "excarnation," Laytham is drawing explicitly on the work of philosopher and social theorist Charles Taylor in *Secular Age*.

that connect us to the World Wide Web (e.g., iPods, YouTube apps, and video game consoles like the Nintendo Wii) necessarily involve "powerful trajectories of excarnation precisely because they locate [our] actions and identities in a virtual—that is, non-bodily—realm."[3] As a consequence, our interactions with the digital world can never be anything other than an attempt to overcome our bodily limitations and perhaps even escape the body altogether.

In contrast to an embodied, incarnate life, says Laytham, our online lives are de facto *dis*-embodied and *ex*-carnate. As such, to affirm them is to advance a theology that is at best sub-Christian and, at worst, heretical.[4] And if this is indeed the case, then the way my young children have come to see and understand the world is not simply different than my own. It's much worse than that. Their "touchscreen-shaped imagination" is in fact mal-adaptive and de-formative because it is a subversion of the Christian understanding of the incarnation. Without even knowing it, they have been co-opted by the forces of excarnation, seduced by flickering pixels into disregarding their bodies.

Oddly enough, even in those cases where new media are creating space for a more fully embodied encounter with the digital world, Laytham still interprets this movement in entirely negative terms. Responding to a piece I wrote in which I identify the interface of the Nintendo Wii as representative of the contemporary cultural impulse toward more somatic, holistic, and affective interactions with the virtual world, Laytham demurs:

> But there's the rub! There's no ball to rub, hold, swing, and hurl with a Wii, only a weightless simulacrum on a high-definition screen. Though a fuller range of motion is involved, the Wii and its imitators continue the trend of excarnation precisely by substituting virtual images for material objects, a virtual environment for real space, and an avatar for me—that is, for my body.[5]

---

3. Laytham, *iPod, YouTube, Wii Play*, 121.

4. Laytham interacts with a number of the contributors to *Halos and Avatars*, finding the majority of them to be theologically questionable. But he reserves his most critical assessment for Craig Detweiler's conclusion to the volume. Laytham suggests that Detweiler's understanding of Jesus as an avatar is antithetical to the incarnation. Even worse, this move verges on heresy: "Detweiler is an example of what it looks like when the world absorbs the text, a danger that began, ironically, with gnosticism." Laytham, *iPod, YouTube, Wii Play*, 124, n. 30.

5. Laytham, *iPod, YouTube, Wii Play*, 122–23. Here, he is interacting with and quoting from Callaway, "Wii Are In*spirit*ed."

In other words, even when a digital interface like the Wii remote is designed for the express purpose of incorporating the whole of our bodies into its basic operations, the fact that virtual (i.e., digital) representations are also present somehow negates the very embodied agents who make this digital/human interaction possible in the first place. For Laytham, when the virtual world augments physical reality, the human body is simply eliminated from the equation.

Laytham is certainly not alone in raising concerns about how our bodies relate to digital environments.[6] But I mention his work in particular for two primary reasons. The first is to point out the importance of not confusing the *internet* (or any other virtual realm for that matter) with the *interfaces* that serve as our concrete point of contact with the digital world.[7] Whether it's a touchpad on a laptop, a Kinect sensor for Xbox One, a Roku remote, or the touch-screen of an iPad, interfaces are neither "weightless simulacrum" nor "virtual imitations" of material objects. They are themselves material objects, which connect other material objects (i.e., people) to digital environments through a kind of "soft-assembly."[8] What is more, the representations that make up this digital realm are just that—*re*-presentations. That is, they are not substitutes, but are in fact virtual duplications of physical reality. The images displayed on our screens exist *in addition to* the bodies that generate them. Which means that there are *more* bodies in play here—both digital and physical—not less. Indeed, at the level of the interface, it's not that virtual bodies are replacing our physical bodies. Rather, it is here that our bodies are augmented and extended.

This notion of extension leads to the second reason for interacting with Laytham, and it has primarily to do with the question of how broadly we are willing to understand the human person. Where does the body and, by extension, the human begin and end? And how are the (digital) tools that humans use and the (digital) environments they inhabit implicated (if

---

6. In their helpful book *Networked Theology*, Heidi Campbell and Stephen Garner classify Laytham's line of thinking as "technological pessimism" (as opposed to "technological optimism" or "technological ambiguity"). They include in this category other theologians and media critics such as Jacques Ellul, Sherry Turkle, and even the Pontifical Council for Social Communications.

7. For the sake of clarity, I will be adopting Haugeland's definition of interface: "a point of interactive 'contact' between components such that the relevant interactions are well-defined, reliable and relatively simple." Haugeland, "Mind Embodied," 32.

8. I am borrowing this term from Andy Clark, whose work we will consider more below. See Clark, *Supersizing the Mind*.

at all) in this formulation of personhood? It's important to point out that the different answers Laytham and I might provide in response to these questions aren't necessarily the result of theological or doctrinal differences. After all, we share nearly identical understandings of the incarnation and its significance for Christian life and practice. However, the way we interpret the theological significance of digital life is quite different, and the main reason is because we are operating with divergent pictures of what it means to be a human being. Thus, what Laytham sees as digitally mediated disembodiment, I see as the embedding of our bodies in digital environments. And where Laytham sees excarnation, I see extension.

Extension and Embodiment

To be clear, I do not intend to suggest that life as it is lived online is entirely uncomplicated or makes physical life somehow "better" in an unqualified sense.[9] Technology (digital or otherwise) is no more capable of creating utopia than any other modern endeavor. I am suggesting, however, that our involvement with digital environments is not *inherently* deficient, destructive, or dehumanizing, as Laytham and others seem to suggest. Put more positively, I would go so far as to say that, rather than moving us either out of or even away from our bodies (i.e., "excarnation"), digital interfaces can be highly incarnational insofar as they become incorporated into our bodily schema and serve as extensions of our bodies through their constant negotiation (and renegotiation) of the boundaries between self and world. Or to borrow a turn of phrase from the philosopher and cognitive scientist Andy Clark, rather than lead us away from our bodies, digital interfaces represent the very machinery that constitutes us as "profoundly embodied creatures."[10]

Much of Clark's work is rather technical, so we need not unpack it all here. However, one of his primary contentions is that the reigning models of human cognition too clearly separate our minds from our bodies and the world. Rather than a "brainbound" model, Clark advocates for an "extended" model of cognition—one in which "at least some aspects of human cognition [are] realized by the ongoing work of the body and/or the extraorganismic

---

9. This, of course, is the claim many Transhumanists make, which is somewhat ironic, given that its utopian vision of humanity's technological future—although explicitly non- or anti-theistic—is structurally identical to dispensationalist theology.

10. Clark, *Supersizing the Mind*, 43.

environment."¹¹ In other words, humans just are the kind of creatures that make the most of their bodies and their environments in their ongoing interactions with the world. Thus, people constantly (even promiscuously) incorporate and exploit external tools and environmental resources into their intentional, problem-solving regimes—a "profoundly embodied" activity that involves the intimate intermingling of human agents and the various interfaces that serve as their point of contact with the world:

> What makes such interfaces *appropriate* as mechanisms for human enhancement is, it seems, precisely their potential role in creating *whole new agent-world circuits*. But insofar as they succeed at this task, the new agent-tool interface itself fades from view, and the proper picture is one of an extended or enhanced agent confronting the (wider) world.¹²

For Clark then, it is this picture of an "extended" or "enhanced" agent—a "new systemic whole" created by the agent-tool interface—that offers the best model for understanding what it means to be human.¹³ And if correct, then Clark's notion of "extension" bears directly upon our theological understanding of what it means to interface not only with physical environments, but digital ones as well. This is especially the case in the midst of a highly technologized culture where digital interfaces are becoming increasingly incorporated into daily life and, as a result, their operations ever more obscured:

> As we move toward an era of wearable computing and ubiquitous information access, the robust, reliable information fields to which our brains delicately adapt their inner cognitive routines will surely become increasingly dense and powerful, perhaps further blurring the boundaries between the cognitive agent and his or her best tools, props and artifacts.¹⁴

---

11. Clark, *Supersizing the Mind*, 82.
12. Clark, *Supersizing the Mind*, 31.
13. Clark, *Supersizing the Mind*, 39.
14. Clark, *Supersizing the Mind*, 41. It is important to note that, for Clark, not all interfaces and/or tools are incorporated into one's cognitive system. Some are simply "used" and, as such, should not be considered as an "extension" of the agent. He identifies four criteria for inclusion: (1) the resource must be "reliably available and typically invoked"; (2) any information retrieved must be "more or less automatically endorsed" and not "subject to critical scrutiny"; (3) information should be "easily accessible as and when required"; and (4) it should be "consciously endorsed at some point in the past." As Clark outlines these criteria, he specifically mentions "mobile access to Google" as failing

From this perspective, the operations of the mind bleed into the surrounding world to such a degree that it becomes difficult to distinguish between human agents and their most useful technologies (digital or otherwise). Yet, for all this talk about *cognition* and *the mind*, Clark's central concern is really the mind/body/world relationship.[15] To be sure, his notion of extended cognition begins with the assumption that the mind is essentially a thinking or representing thing, but at its core, Clark's philosophy of mind seeks to capture the fundamental nature of the human person as a whole. That is to say, even though his concept of cognitive extension reconceives of the human being as an agent augmented by nonbiological media (e.g., digital interfaces), personhood for Clark always remains "anchored" in the body.

Bodies Embedded in Emergent Systems

Interestingly enough, Clark's seemingly holistic formulation (i.e., cognition as extended *and* embodied) can still carry with it an implicit dualism—one in which the "mind" is some kind of "inner agency" that resides within but is nevertheless distinct from the body. Given the theological difficulties this kind of anthropological dualism presents (e.g., "excarnation"), Warren Brown and Brad Strawn (the former a neuroscientist and the latter a clinical psychologist and ordained minister) have proposed a model that builds upon Clark's notion of extended cognition, but seeks to address both the implicit dualism of his model and the conceptual simplicity of others. They refer to their view as Complex Emergent Developmental Linguistic Relational Neurophysiologicalism (CEDLRN):

> From this viewpoint, personhood is constituted by emergent properties which are the product of self-organizing processes within the hypercomplex neurophysiological systems of human

---

to qualify according to conditions 2 and 4. I think his assessment was correct in 2011, but given the rapid rate at which mobile technology and broad-band internet access has proliferated, "mobile access to Google" is now "automatically endorsed" and "consciously endorsed in the past" by almost every person who has a smartphone and/or a social media profile. The sharing of "fake news" through social media is evidence of this kind of "automatic endorsement." That is, it demonstrates "the potential role of nonbiological media as support for an agent's dispositional beliefs." Clark, *Supersizing the Mind*, 79–81.

15. Indeed, the title of an earlier book in which he begins to work out some of these concepts is *Being There: Putting Brain, Body, and World Together Again*.

beings, and which come about progressively over a long period of developmental, linguistic, and relational history.[16]

Although Brown and Strawn admit that their long list of descriptors is a bit cumbersome (CEDLRN!), there is much about their model that is helpful in describing and characterizing our interactions with the digital world. Three elements are particularly salient for our purposes. First, theirs is an irreducibly *embodied* picture of personhood—one that is not merely physicalist or even biological, but neurophysiological (N). This way of framing things intentionally underscores the sheer complexity (C) of human biology and, thus, avoids an overly simplistic notion of embodiment that often conceals more than it reveals.

Second, to focus attention on the neurophysiological nature of embodiment is to call out the ways in which human nature *emerges* (E) from complex, dynamic, and interactive systems. Like other complex dynamical systems, the human being emerges through a relational (R) process of self-organization. That is, "the elements of the system come to work together in a coherent or coordinated manner to create a larger-scale functional system that can adapt to the demands of the physical, social, or cultural environment in complex and subtle ways."[17] As a result, the system as a whole (especially at higher levels of complexity) can have properties that do not (and cannot) exist within the elements that make up that system.

Third, because this highly complex biological system adapts, interacts, and receives feedback from the environment, human persons are not simply embodied and emergent, but embedded as well.[18] The capacity for language (L) is perhaps the most significant example of how personhood develops (D) over time as we actively encounter, respond to, and attempt to make sense of the world into which we have been thrown. But language is just one of the more prominent examples. As Clark has suggested (and as Brown and Strawn would agree), embodied persons, who are highly complex, emergent systems themselves, are always already embedded in, and thus, intimately intermingled with the larger emergent systems of which they are a part. In other words, rather than a reductive physicalism that equates the core of the human person (or even the mind) with "the brain,"

---

16. Brown and Strawn, "Self-Organizing Personhood," 3.
17. Brown and Strawn, "Self-Organizing Personhood," 5.
18. I am indebted here not only to Brown and Strawn's CEDLRN model, but also to their earlier work on embodied and embedded models of theological anthropology, specifically Brown and Strawn, *Physical Nature of Christian Life*.

the CEDLRN model implies that peripheral systems (both biological and non-biological) are necessarily implicated in the emergence of human personhood. As a result, this model doesn't collapse all distinctions between the person, the interface, and the world, but it certainly blurs the boundaries in a helpful (albeit ever-more complex) way.

Interfacing With and As the Body of Christ

But what, exactly, does all this mean theologically? If my opening anecdote is to be taken seriously, it seems clear that the ongoing emergence of my daughter's personhood is intimately bound up with the various interfaces she employs to interact with, adapt to, and experience the increasingly digital environment in which she is embedded. It's not simply that she has no access to much of her world in the absence of her Kindle Fire or my iPhone or our family's Netflix app. It's that she cannot help but imagine the world and her life in it through any other means. Both her awareness of reality and her very sense of self—her thoughts, emotions, memories, and experiences—have developed (and continue to develop) in relationship to these non-biological media. And my daughter is not alone. The same could be said of her entire cohort—a generation of digital natives who have never known any other world.

Here, then, we return to our central question: is this phenomenon evidence of excarnation or, rather, extension? In other words, is our interaction with the digital world an escape from our bodies—a modern form of Gnosticism that the Christian community ought to critique and condemn on theological grounds? Or is it an (not uncomplicated) expansion of what it means to be a fully embodied human being living in a digital age?

One of the primary claims I have put forward in this essay is that the way in which we answer these questions has less to do with doctrine and more to do with the models we employ for understanding the human person. In turn, these models direct (and in some cases determine) our theological reflection. For instance, critics like Laytham start with a rather "body-bound" picture of the human person and, thus, a "body-bound" notion of the incarnation. Given the anthropological model he employs, it is perfectly logical that he construes our encounters with the digital world as indicative of a move toward excarnation. Because all digital interfaces exist "outside" the bounds of the body's physical structures, our interactions with them must be understood necessarily as dis-embodied and ex-carnate.

However, if we adopt a different model for understanding the human person—one that accounts for our complex, emergent, developmental, linguistic, relational, neurophysiology—we are able to reconceive of these very same digital interfaces in terms of their theological possibilities rather than their inadequacies. And while this move certainly encourages a more charitable take on digital life, the theological implications of adopting a "body-centric" rather than "body-bound" model are more than merely interpretive. Indeed, to conceive of digital interfaces as extensions of our bodies is to suggest that every point of contact with the digital world has the potential for providing us with both a model and a means for becoming more fully human.

Thus, I'd like to consider three key ways in which an embodied, extended, emergent, embedded model of the human person might allow us to reconceive of digital interfaces as helpful resources for constructive theological reflection.

An Anthropological Model

In their aptly titled *Networked Theology*, Heidi Campbell and Stephen Garner propose the "network" as a guiding metaphor to understand digital culture, primarily because it characterizes the contemporary situation so well: "Indeed, many have argued that we now live in a network society, in which new social, economic, political, and cultural structures are emerging from an increasingly wired and global world."[19] This is neither to celebrate nor to condemn networked society, but simply to describe the facts on the ground. For good or for ill, modern humans are embedded simultaneously in digital and physical environments, which operate according to the logics of highly complex, emergent, dynamical systems.[20] And the point of contact between these emergent systems is of course the interface, which functions as both the site where the physical and digital worlds meet and the medium by which individual persons are extended into their broader social networks.

---

19. Campbell and Garner, *Networked Theology*, 3.

20. "Through networked community we see that people online live simultaneously in multiple social networks that are emergent" (Campbell and Garner, *Networked Theology*, 77).

What is more, the ongoing interaction that takes place between online and offline systems (i.e., "networks") does not entail a flight from the body, but rather an expansion of bodily, physical life:

> Because the Internet has become increasingly assimilated into daily routines, researchers have recognized that patterns of Internet use often arise out of users' offline patterns of behavior and beliefs. Such findings challenge concerns that online practices might supplant engagement in offline groups or routines. Instead, Internet-based social activities frequently serve as an extension or supplement to offline engagement and in some cases may stimulate rather than reduce social interaction.[21]

If we imagine the human person to be fundamentally body-bound, then there is simply no way to account for this phenomenon in positive terms. However, if being a human means that we are extended bodies who are embedded in a vast network of emergent systems, then we can say with some confidence that digital interfaces are not standing in the way of our humanity, but are in fact helping us be and become more fully human. Digital life is of course far from perfect, but it does provide us with unique possibilities for extending ourselves into broader networks of relationality that are "profoundly embodied" and, thus, quintessentially human. In an important sense, it is through the digital interface that our bodies become incorporated into an expansive network of humanity and, at the same time, that network becomes a part of us.

So rather than simply decry the contemporary impulse to extend our physical lives through digital interfaces, we would do well to consider the ways in which this augmented reality might present us with a more robust picture of the human person. Indeed, it may very well be that we are only ever fully human—ever fully alive—when we are extended in this way, which is why both lay and professional theologians would benefit from reflecting upon what it looks like for humans to flourish in and through these digitally mediated environments, and then to take the next step of actively encouraging that kind of flourishing.

---

21. Campbell and Garner, *Networked Theology*, 77.

An Ecclesiological Metaphor

Truth be told, the Christian tradition already has a metaphor for extended, embodied life.[22] The "Body of Christ" that Paul describes in 1 Cor 12:12–30 has long served as one of the central images for understanding the structure of the community of faith:

> For just as the body is one and has many members, and all the members of the body, though many, are one body, so it is with Christ.... Indeed, the body does not consist of one member but of many.... Now you are the body of Christ and individually members of it. (1 Cor 12: 12, 14, 27)

Paul knew nothing of digital interfaces or the internet. Nevertheless, it is not incidental that the primary image he deploys to speak of the Christian community is a body comprised of numerous individual bodies who are extended into a larger, higher level network of bodies. Each member has his or her role to play, but the system as a whole (i.e., "the body of Christ") has properties that do not (and cannot) exist within the elements that make up the system. In other words, Paul's understanding of the church hinges upon a conception of the human person not as body-bound but as extended. Or, to put it in the terms we have been using, the Christian community itself is a complex, emergent, developmental, linguistic, relational, neurophysiological organism. Thus, from a theological perspective, for our bodies *not* to be extended into the hyper-complex organism known as the body of Christ is to live not simply in destructive isolation, but in a sub-human state.

If this is indeed the case, could it be that the various media by which we connect to the digital world are in fact necessary for contemporary Christians to enact Paul's vision of embodiment? Are these interfaces perhaps offering the community of faith a way of being and becoming the body of Christ that was entirely inaccessible before? Again, as Paul knew full well, the church will always be comprised of faulty members, so no form of communal interaction will ever be perfect, just as no method of interfacing with others will ever be flawless. But if we refuse even to consider the possibility that digital interfaces have the capacity to extend our bodies into a larger communal network, we run the risk of overlooking (and disregarding) one

---

22. Here again, the work of Brown and Strawn has proven instructive for my thought. I am thankful for their ongoing willingness to engage in dialogue around these topics. They specifically explore the notion of the Christian life as an extension into the body of Christ in their forthcoming book *Supersizing the Christian Faith* (IVP Academic).

of the primary avenues by which the people of God might actually become the body of Christ in the midst of our digital age.

A Theological Metaphysic

Finally, I want to conclude on a more speculative note. What follows is highly provisional and is meant to be more suggestive than anything else, but it does reflect a question (or series of questions) that I could not seem to shake as I formulated the central components of this essay. Namely, what if the extended model of the human person and, by extension, the body of Christ is more than a model? What if it's more than a helpful metaphor that Paul used to illustrate some other (i.e., more "real") reality? What if it has some kind of metaphysical purchase?

If so, then it stands to reason that our online interactions, mediated as they are by digital interfaces, are capable of doing far more than connecting us to various social networks, with the church being but one of many others. Indeed, we could go so far as to say that, if the Christian community is not just a generic social body, but is in fact the body of *Christ*, then the means by which we in-corpor-ate our individual bodies into the complex dynamical system known as the "church" is the very same means by which Christ is made manifest in our midst. In other words, the extension of our bodies (through digital and physical means) into the body of Christ creates the necessary conditions for Christ to be present—real, actual, effective—in the first place. "For where two or three are gathered in my name, there am I in the midst of them" (Matt 18:20). Thus, whether its members gather online or offline, the church is not merely the *metaphorical* body of Christ. It *is* the body of Christ—extended, embodied, embedded, and emerging in those very spaces where the digital and physical worlds meet.

But if this "presencing" of Christ does indeed take place in and through the extension of our bodies (digitally or otherwise), then the inverse must be true as well. That is, the incarnation itself might best be understood as the extension of divine personhood by means of a complex, emergent biological system otherwise known as Jesus' human body. Jesus "took on flesh" (John 1:14, Heb 2:14) and, in doing so, incorporated material reality into the divine life. Thus, even the hypostatic union develops and emerges through a process of self-organizing personhood, the sum of which cannot be reduced to its constituent parts. Likewise, the resurrected Christ now takes on a human body insofar as the community of faith enacts or realizes itself as the body of Christ. And in even broader, more cosmic terms, the entire created order might be seen as an extension of this same incarnational impulse—an ongoing, dynamic process of emergence in which God is embodied, embedded, and extended in and through the world.

None of this is meant to suggest that the created order is to be equated with God. But neither is creation wholly separate from God. Rather, the immanent order of creation is an embodiment and extension of the transcendent God. Both God and the world create the conditions for the o/Other to emerge, which is why the apostle Paul can say, "for from him and through him and to him are all things" (Rom 11:36), and that God will one day be "all in all" (1 Cor 15:28).

From this view, God is neither "inside" nor "outside" the world. Instead, in the words of Mark C. Taylor, the extension of God "names the unnamable 'outside' that is 'inside' every system, structure, and schema as its necessary condition. As such, it is the irreducible trace that marks and remarks the openness and incompletion of seemingly closed systems. . . . [It] is neither transcendent nor immanent but is an immanent transcendence that disrupts and dislocates systems, structures, and schemata that seem to be secure."[23] If this is indeed true, then we might even say that the material world itself is the interface where the divine and the human encounter and disrupt one another through a near-chaotic but infinitely creative process. And just as anyone with a five-year-old already knows, interface is reality.

Bibliography

Brown, Warren S., and Brad D. Strawn. *The Physical Nature of Christian Life: Neuroscience, Psychology, and the Church*. New York: Cambridge University Press, 2012.

———. "Self-Organizing Personhood: Complex Emergent Developmental Linguistic Relational Neurophysiologicalism." In *The Ashgate Research Companion to Theological Anthropology*, edited by Joshua Ferris and Charles Taliaferro, 91–102. Burlington: Ashgate, 2016.

Callaway, Kutter. "Wii Are In*spiri*ted: The Transformation of Home Video Consoles (and Us)." In *Halos and Avatars: Playing Video Games with God*, edited by Craig Detweiler, 75–90. Louisville: Westminster John Knox, 2010.

Campbell, Heidi A., and Stephen Garner. *Networked Theology: Negotiating Faith in Digital Culture*. Grand Rapids: Baker Academic, 2016.

Clark, Andy. *Being There: Putting Brain, Body, and World Together Again*. Cambridge: MIT Press, 1997.

---

23. Taylor, *After God*, 127. Even though he is exploring the value of religion in a post-secular world, the concept of God's "immanent transcendence" is not original to Taylor. Indeed, Jürgen Moltmann articulated a strikingly similar concept in *Spirit of Life*.

———. *Supersizing the Mind: Embodiment, Action, and Cognitive Extension*. New York: Oxford University Press, 2011.

Haugeland, J. "Mind Embodied and Embedded." In *Having Thought: Essays in the Metaphysics of Mind*, edited by J. Haugeland, 207–40. Cambridge: Harvard University Press, 1998.

Laytham, D. Brent. *iPod, YouTube, Wii Play: Theological Engagements with Entertainment*. Eugene, OR: Cascade, 2012.

Moltmann, Jürgen. *The Spirit of Life: A Universal Affirmation*. Minneapolis: Fortress, 1992.

Taylor, Charles. *A Secular Age*. Cambridge: Harvard University Press, 2007.

Taylor, Mark C. *After God*. Chicago: University of Chicago Press, 2007.

3

Cyber-Genesis of the Digital Self

JOHN FREDERICK

Proto-Genesis: Primordial Theopoetics

My beginning has already occurred. That is, my first beginning. Thirty-six years ago to be exact. New beginnings have occurred along the way. They will continue to occur. Revolutions and rebirths, seasons of reinvention that ebb and flow between the dialectical waves of popular culture and pure chance, between the inscrutability of providence and its immanent appearance as abject absurdity. But still I remain, tethered to memories of who I once was, racing toward the future, hopeful and terrified of who I might become. Gripped by the profundity of this terrible, beautiful world[1], I press on. Gaze upon me! You will no doubt encounter the face of a man who shuns regret but regrets everything, and then apologizes instantaneously for the harshness of that regretful hyperbole. A man who exudes confidence but is confidently unsure about everything, and that in perpetuity! A man who is not his own creator, who played no role in his own proto-genesis, but who is chief architect of his second genesis.

Ashes to ashes, dust to dust; absent from the body, present with the Lord; absent from the body, I will be a presence through my words. While who I am will be hidden in Christ, who I will become will be determined by my reader. For while the soul of my proto-genesis will reside with God, there are other versions of "me" that will digitally dwell elsewhere; versions of which I am the sole author. Beautiful versions and sinister ones, textual

---

1. The phrase "terrible, beautiful world" is taken from the title of the Decemberists 2015 album entitled *What a Terrible World, What a Beautiful World*.

versions and visual ones. They are the sum total of my cyber existence which will outlive and surpass the impact and presence of my physical bodily existence. Who I am will be hidden with God in Christ, but who I am becoming will dwell in the zeros and ones of the Hades of HTML. I am he who has been created, I am he who is creator; creator of the data that comprises my digital selves which exist in a state of cyber-immortality and virtual potentiality. *We* exist, we *will* exist, and we are legion. Wretched man that I am! Who will deliver me from this body of death? Answer: on the one hand Jesus, and on the other, your local internet service provider.

Cyber-Genesis: Preliminary Theotechnics
Search Engine Schemata and the Residual Narrative Self

Residing in the pages of history and fiction are a host of characters representing everything from sinners to saints, from superheroes to sluggards. Whether "real," in the sense of having existed as an actual historical human being in the flesh, or "fictional," having existed only as a character in a literary work, both exert a form of "real presence" through our engagement with them in the present as the culmination of a gestalt of textual schemata. In the act of reading we conjure up the personae of various characters through the schematized aspects about them that we have at our disposal through written words and other forms of digital media. Oftentimes—as is the case with some historical works—these texts are composed by the character herself. As Wolfgang Iser has argued, when we engage with the schemata and instructions of a text put in place by the author, we the reader ideate and make present the characters and meaning of a text.[2] This experience creates an encounter, a "dynamic happening,"[3] and a "living event"[4] in which we actually participate in the text, and are "caught up in the very thing we are producing."[5] Through our entanglement with the characters and scenarios that we ideate from the text, our perspectives are changed, our world is changed; *we* are changed. When applying this theory of reader-response hermeneutics to history and literature, we find that characters who are wholly absent (and, in the case of most historical figures, typically

---

2. Iser, *Act of Reading*.
3. Iser, *Act of Reading*, 22.
4. Iser, *Act of Reading*, 128.
5. Iser, *Act of Reading*, 127.

deceased), are once again made present to us through the process of ideation which takes place in reading.

In the same way that characters of fiction and history experience a textually-ideated presence to future audiences through the activation of their literary schematized aspects, we must begin to think of our own internet exchanges as the authorial creation of cyber content which function as the schemata of our residual narrative selves. Our internet activity leaves in in its wake narrative codes, segments of text, data, and information that— when ideated by future readers— creates a residual narrative self that may be different than the bodily self of non-cyber reality. This alternate digital self becomes a presence and a power when the recipient of the text, data, information, and media schemata pieces together the various component parts thus conjuring up a phantom presence, a residual narrative self. This is cause for alarm rather than celebration.

The best of us live forever on the internet; and so do the worst of us. Fred Phelps, the infamous hate preacher and former leader of the Westboro Baptist Church no longer preaches homophobic sermons or protests the funerals of fallen soldiers; he is dead, yet he lives! The digital schemata of Fred Phelps will haunt the Hades of HTML for a contingent eternity. An eternity, that is to say, that is contingent upon the internet itself. So long as there is an internet, Fred Phelps lives; and so do you, in the gloomy chambers of digital code databases. In the case of Phelps, no matter what the context, his words and teachings will always show themselves to be instantiations of hate and evil, for there is no context in which anything the man said could ever be considered righteous or justified. For average internet users, however, the vast majority of whom are not abjectly evil hate preachers, residual narrative selves will exist as ideated phantom selves, often detached from ostensible reference, constructed and ideated by whomever compiles them from a host of disconnected and incomplete search engine or social media schemata. Even for the most pure hearted blogger (if such a category exists) and conscientious social media user, this reality will lead to the ideation of a being that is independent of our physical bodies and control, an alternate, residual self—encoded and ensouled in the zeros and ones of the digital main frame of the internet. There will be as many of us as there are interpreters and ideators of us. We will exist as cyber shadows of our former selves, as fragmented texts waiting to be read, with the power to cause either cruciform blessing or catastrophic destruction.

Network Sociality and the Residual Narrative Self

The residual narrative self is indeed organized according to a *narrative*. Yet, unlike traditional theories that incorporate the idea of narrative as a central component of selfhood, residual narrative selves created and ideated online do not exist in the context of true communities but within a network sociality. As Wittel has argued, true communities exhibit "stability, coherence, embeddedness and belonging."[6] They are characterized by "strong and long-lasting ties" and a "common history" which provides coherence and identity to its various members.[7] In contrast, a network sociality is "not rooted in a common and shared history" which results in a "disembedded intersubjectivity" that is characterized by fragmentation and disintegration.[8] Residual narrative selves derive their cyber genesis from within the context of a network sociality. Their very existence as phantom digital selves relies upon the activation and ideation of a host of fragmentary, decontextualized elements of data which together lead to the construction and conjuring up of a residual self.

However, since these cyber selves exist in a network sociality of fragmentation rather than a community of coherence, the narrative aspect to the self is provided only partially by the author and is primarily constructed by the reader. In most theories of selfhood which utilize the concept of narrative it is the unity and constancy of the narrative that make a self coherent and recognizable, both to oneself and to others.[9] Yet, our ideated digital selves are narrival not as a result of coherence and permanence in a narratival community in the present, but rather through their construction and plasticity as they are ideated by another user in order to become a presence. The coherence of a residual narrative self is provided by the reader, the ideating one, and is not present in the fragmentary schemata of the potential digital self. Thus, the residual narrative self differs from both actual physical human selves and from imaginary fictional characters in stories. In the case of actual physical human selves, existence and identity formation take place within a community, while imaginary fictional characters come to us

---

6. Wittel, "Toward a Network Sociality," 51.
7. Wittel, "Toward a Network Sociality," 51.
8. Wittel, "Toward a Network Sociality," 51.
9. MacIntrye, "Virtues, the Unity of a Human Life," 91. He argues that "the concomitant concept of selfhood [is] a concept of a self whose unity resides in the unity of a narrative which links birth to life to death as narrative beginning to middle to end."

with a ready-made context in which their identity can be ascertained and as a result of which their actions are intelligible.

Residual narrative selves by their very nature lack sufficient authorial metanarratives within which individual selves can cohere and be identified by others. It is this very fragmentation and lack of additional contextual data that cause residual digital selves to be experienced as a phantom presence acting through an instance of parasocial interaction.[10] As has been similarly shown to be the case with television viewers in their interaction with TV personalities, subjects often react to persons mediated solely via telepresence in a way that mirrors live, geographically-resident human interactions. In these parasocial interactions, as Lombard notes, "media users respond to social cues presented by persons they encounter within a medium even though it is illogical and even inappropriate to do so."[11] These parasocial cyber presences bear some resemblance to us but are more like the unfeeling, gloomy ghosts of Hades than the imprints of our earthly identity that Christians imagine to exist in heaven. As Marshall McLuhan prophetically wrote in *The Global Village*, separate from our bodies, our minds will "float out into the electronic void, being everywhere at once in the data bank."[12]

Like Homer's Hades, the Hades of HTML is occupied by residual narrative selves which lack consciousness.[13] Stephen Crites has rightly noted that both consciousness and memory are necessary components for coherence to occur within the human experience of identity.[14] Our postmortem digital selves are incapable of both because as pure schemata they derive their entire existence and impact through ideation. Nevertheless, though residual selves exist contingently and only through ideation it would be a

---

10. Cf. Lombard, "At the Heart of It All," 8.

11. Lombard, "At the Heart of It All," 8.

12. McLuhan and Powers, *Global Village*, 97.

13. On the scope of thought and nature of Hades see Wright, *Resurrection*, 32–45. Wright sums up the Homeric view of the dead as: "shades (skiai), ghosts (psychai), and phantoms (eidola). They are in no way fully human beings, though they may look like them; the appearance is deceptive, since one cannot grasp them physically" (43). Comparably, the residual narrative self is an ideated shade or ghost of our former physical self. It exists as schemata waiting to be activated in the halls of an HTML Hades.

14. Crites, "Narrative Quality of Experience," 73: "Without memory, in fact, experience would have no coherence at all. Consciousness would be locked in a bare, momentary present, i.e., in a disconnected succession of perceptions which it would have no power to relate to one another." Cf. Fornaciari, "Language of the Technoself," 68.

mistake to deny them the quality and capability of presence.[15] Ratan (citing Lee) is helpful here. He argues that:

> presence [is] a psychological state in which virtual objects, social actors, or virtual selves are experienced in sensory and non-sensory ways [and that they] . . . can be either para-authentic, having real-world correlates, or artificial, without real world correlates.[16]

Thus, it is the nature of the internet itself as a network sociality and the ontology of residual narrative selves as contingent schematic ideated beings that leads to their phantom-like quality. Furthermore, the sociological atmosphere of the internet as a network sociality lends to the proliferation of selves which are characteristically distinct from our physical bodily selves. This results in the creation of a multiplicity of schematic clusters that provide the digital DNA for future ideations of a plurality of residual selves.

Anonymity, Multiplicity, and the Residual Narrative Self

As a network sociality, the internet provides a safe and powerful medium for experimentation and identity formation. Users are free to post, comment, and generally interact in most virtual communities with varying degrees of anonymity. Yet, while there are many positive benefits to this element of the internet (such as the ability to investigate and experiment with different aspects of one's sexuality, personality, and social skills) the anonymity and disembodied nature of cyber reality often leads to behavior which is uncharacteristic of our embodied selves. A misinterpreted phrase or statement, which in real life can easily be corrected via physical and verbal gestures may well remain unclear in cyberspace.[17] Likewise, even in settings that are not anonymous it is common for individuals to purposely suspend and even sever the connection with the coherence and character of their physical self, opting instead to create a supplementary persona

---

15. Cf. Barker, "Social Networking and Identity," 478: "Although this philosophical viewpoint creates confusion around the terms virtual, actual and real, Styhre (2003, p. 21) explains . . . that the domain of virtual reality "reproduces the 'real' through technology which creates 'reality' through technology-mediated images and perceptions in cyberspace."

16. Ratan (citing Lee 2004), "Self-Presence, Explicated," 323.

17. Geyer, "Virtual Communities in Cyberspace," 61. Cf. Wynn and Katz, "Hyperbole over Cyberspace," 319.

that is incommensurate with the idem structure of their bodily identity.[18] Renowned MIT professor and researcher Shelly Turkle has argued that in cyberspace millions of users create "online personae" and form "multiple identities"[19] such that "any notion of a real and unitary self" is lost; indeed, lost in the "virtual worlds" of the internet.[20] The internet, along with many other places in our contemporary society encourages us to think of ourselves as "fluid, emergent, decentralized, multiplicitous, flexible, and ever in process."[21] There are many benefits, indeed, to conceiving of identity as a progressive dialectic as Ricouer has well demonstrated.[22] Yet, when considering the schemata that comprise the DNA of our residual digital selves, what is surely a strength and positive instrument of identity formation and personal growth for our physical selves can become the encoding of evil for future ideations of our digital selves.

A lesson learned through rash or verbally abusive behavior online loses its positive instrumentality and function when it is detached from ostensible reference and inserted—or better, hyperlinked—into a new language game which is incommensurable and disconnected from its original context. Polkinghorne expounding Wittenstein's theory of language games explains:

> The Wittgensteinian language position denies [the existence of] an underlying transcultural logic. There, what is reasonable and sensible is a function of the context of each particular language game. Language games are *not commensurate*, and *meaning cannot be translated across games*. We are all boxed in by the rules of the games in which we participate. We have no way to get outside a game in order to understand, for *understanding is created only within a game*.[23]

When decontextualized schemata reemerge in an incommensurable new linguistic environment, even the well-intentioned holy benedictions of a

---

18. Wynn and Katz, "Hyperbole over Cyberspace," 303. On the concept of "idem identity," see Ricouer, *Oneself as Another*. Ricouer describes the self as a dialectic between idem and ipse identity. Idem identity is conceived of as "sameness (Latin idem, German Gleichheit, French mêmeté)" while ipse identity refers to selfhood (Latin ipse, German Selbstheit, French ipséité)," 18, 116 respectively. For Ricouer, selfhood, ipseity is determined "by way of its dialectic with otherness," 297.

19. Turkle, *Life on the Screen*, 267–68.

20. Turkle, *Life on the Screen*, 268–69.

21. Turkle, *Life on the Screen*, 263–64.

22. Ricouer, *Oneself as Another*.

23. Polkinghorne, *Narrative Knowing*, 142.

saint can turn into the profane imprecations of a demon. In the network sociality of the internet, the schemata of our future ideated residual selves are the result of anonymity, multiplicity, and a willed plurality of personae. The cumulative data that constitutes the DNA of these digital selves are often times the result of a warped self-presentation caused by deindividuation. Anonymity and the camaraderie wrought by the digital realm has been shown to lead to this deindividuated state. According to McKenna, the deindividuation leads to

> a weakened ability for an individual to regulate his or her own behavior, reduced ability to engage in rational, long-term planning, and a tendency to react to immediate cues or based largely on his or her current emotional state. Furthermore, an individual will be less likely to care what others think of his or her behavior and may even have a reduced awareness of what others have said or done. These effects can culminate in impulsive and disinhibited behaviors (Zimbardo, 1970).[24]

McLuhan spoke similarly about the effect of anonymity and the telephone. Writing before the advent of the internet, McLuhan noted that the anonymity available through telecommunication led to the creation of disincarnate, uncontrollable "phone poltergeists" and "acoustic ghosts."[25] Now with the revolution of telecommunication through cyberspace, the sonic spirits of McLuhan have evolved into the ideated phantoms of the residual narrative self. Just as fictional characters and works of art possess the power to spark revolutions, incite riots, and inspire paradigm shifts in personal and societal life, so too are our ideated residual narrative selves capable of significant influence. Thrones, dominions, rulers, authorities, the cosmic powers of the world— these exist not merely as personal demonic beings or as the personification of sinful structures of human power.[26] Rather, the *stoicheia* ("elemental spirits") exist as the cumulative effect of the search engine

---

24. McKenna and Bargh, "Plan 9 from Cyberspace," 61.
25. McLuhan and Powers, *Global Village*, 124.
26. Cf. Wink, *Naming the Powers*, 15: "The language of power in the New Testament is far too rich and complex to reduce either to the human structures and institutions of the liberation theologians or to the spiritual beings of traditional theology. What is needed is an interpretive framework that can do justice to the loose way the ancients could refer to these powers as now human, now structural, now heavenly, without feeling any apparent need to indicate specifically which they had in mind."

schemata of our digital selves. They exist through their activation and ideation by present and future inhabitants of the new sacred, the internet.[27]

Simul Sanctus et Stoicheia: "At Once Saint and Cosmic Power"

As both physical narrative selves and digital narrative selves, human beings (and Christians in particular) exist as Simul Sanctus et Stoicheia, that is, "at once holy and cosmic Power."[28] The New Testament proclamation concerning the phenomena of thrones (θρόνοι), dominions (κυριότητες), rulers (ἀρχαί), authorities (ἐξουσίαι), and the cosmic powers of the world (τὰ στοιχεῖα τοῦ κόσμου) refer not only to personal spiritual beings and human institutions—they refer to the schematized aspects of the ideated digital self. Elsewhere, employing Walter Wink's phenomenological reading of the powers, I have argued that "blogs, the virtual self and other cyber realities are legitimate powers—outward manifestations of an inner ethos or spirit."[29] This means that—in some sense—the biblical teaching about the spiritual realm applies to us: we are the powers, we are the principalities; we are the digital instantiation of the rulers and authorities, a "legion" of cyber-ideated stoicheia dwelling in the Hades of HTML.

While many traditionalists would likely balk at the idea of including a digital component to the category of the "demonic," (perhaps casting it off as a novel concept), Wink's exegesis has already effectively unraveled the convincingness of any critique that constrains the scriptural talk about the powers to purely personal malevolent demonic beings. Referring to the discussion of the powers in Col 1:16, Wink points out that the powers are *specifically described* by the biblical author as representing both "earthly *and* heavenly, visible *and* invisible" phenomena. Therefore, he rightly concludes that—whatever the powers are metaphysically—we should "expect them to include human agents, social structures and systems, and also divine powers."[30] Furthermore, if, as Col 1:16a states, "all things were created *by*

---

27. Ellul, *New Demons*, 145: "modern man set up technology as a sacred."

28. The phrase "Simul Sanctus et Stoicheia" is a play on the well-known phrase associated within Lutheran theology, "simul iustus et peccator" ("at once righteous and sinner").

29. Frederick, "Discerning, Disarming," 154–55.

30. Wink, *Naming the Powers*, 11. Cf. *Engaging the Powers*, 8, where Wink notes that he is taking a phenomenological approach rather than a metaphysical approach

him (ἐν αὐτῷ)" and "all things were created *through him* (δι' αὐτοῦ) and *for him* (εἰς αὐτὸν)" we must also conclude that the powers, whether earthly or heavenly, have their genesis in Christ through the creative power and prerogative of God. The evil that a power exhibits, then, is not a result of an intrinsic malevolence inherent in the spiritual being, institution, or force. Rather, the demonic status of a power as evil is a result of its corruption and contamination through its cooperation with human sinfulness, and its collusion with and contribution to the sinful structures of the world. The wickedness of the demonic is not a result of ontology; it is a result of idolatry.[31] Far from being totally depraved by nature: "The Powers are good. The Powers are fallen. The Powers must be redeemed."[32]

Wink has argued that all powers have both an inward spirituality and an outward external form. Thus, for example, in the New Testament, personal demonic beings must possess human beings in order to operate.[33] Likewise, in contemporary society, references to the "spirit" of an institution (such as a corporation or political party) or public office (e.g.; the position of governor, mayor, or president) demonstrate this two-fold phenomena of an inner spirituality made tangible through external outward forms. In regard to the relevance of this to the residual narrative self, I propose that the inner spirituality of our residual cyber selves is created and embodied in the digital schemata that becomes a presence through ideation.

While our physical bodily self dies in Christ, the manifold residual narrative selves that we have authored through our online activity live in a state of contingent ideated immortality. These virtual selves can be ideated and activated as either hostile or holy powers, capable of being the digital bearers of either inspirational benefit or catastrophic calamity, blessing or

---

to addressing the biblical concept and language about the powers. Thus, he chooses to "[bracket] the question of the metaphysical status of the Powers."

31. Cf. Wink, *Engaging the Powers*, 65. I am convinced of Wink's assessment that the evil aspect of the Powers "is not intrinsic, but rather the result of idolatry." Contra Arnold, *Colossian Syncretism*, 255, who interprets the rulers and authorities in Colossians to be references to "angelic beings in league with the authority of darkness (1:13), foes of God and his son Jesus Christ." While personal angelic beings are certainly to be included in the list of possibilities here, I find Arnold's specific argument against the admission of the category of "impersonal forces" in regard to the powers to be without warrant and unconvincing. Wink has demonstrated in *Naming the Powers* (see esp. 10–100) that rulers, thrones, dominions, and authorities more often refer to human institutions, structures, and individuals than to personal demonic spiritual beings.

32. Wink, *Engaging the Powers*, 10.

33. Wink, *Unmasking the Powers*, 4. Cf. *Engaging the Powers*, 3, 8.

curse—indeed, even life or death. Prayer, holiness, and gospel ministry can be the result of the schemata that make the residual self a powerful phantom presence, but so can body shaming, homophobia, and hate speech. The power of digital communication to lead a weary soul struggling with their sexual orientation, depression, or loneliness to a place of self-harm has—time and time again—shown itself to be a medium loaded with poisonous and destructive potential. The words of a racist do not die with the racist; they live forever in the ideation of a racist residual narrative self. While the "real life racist" might have lived in a small town, and kept relatively to himself, his racist schemata, posted on social media, blogs, and message boards could potentially reach thousands. When his residual self is ideated—potentially thousands of times in perpetuity—a legion of demonic residual selves haunt the halls of the cyber Hades wreaking havoc on new generations of human beings made in the image of God long after his body is dead. What's more: imagine that this cyber racist is—in so-called "real" life—actually a *former* racist, having repented, become a Christian, and spent the last years of his life combating the destructive, hateful, bigotry of his earlier years. Even with the celebration of a racist turned penitent the residual power of his ideated words invoke an eternal phantom presence detached from ostensible reference to his entire life story and his repentance. Existing in fragmentary textual form, this man is at once "holy and corrupt cosmic power." He is Simul Sanctus et Stoicheia . . . and in all likelihood, so are you.

Cyber-Conflagration: Pyrotechnic Epilogue

The ancient Stoics believed that the universe proceeded in repetitive cycles, always ending in an apocalyptic conflagration in which the entire cosmos was consumed.[34] After the conflagration, the universe would begin again from scratch, continuing on until the next conflagration, repeating itself ad infinitum. The only souls thought to (possibly) have survived

---

34. On the idea of conflagration in the Stoics see Baltzly, "Stoicism": "God is identified with an eternal reason (logos, Diog. Laert. 44B) or intelligent designing fire (Aetius, 46A) which structures matter in accordance with Its plan. This plan is enacted time and time again, beginning from a state in which all is fire, through the generation of the elements, to the creation of the world we are familiar with, and eventually back to fire in a cycle of endless recurrence. The designing fire of the conflagration is likened to a sperm which contains the principles or stories of all the things which will subsequently develop (Aristocles in Eusebius, 46G)."

the consuming flames were those of the wise men, the Stoic sages. These men represented an infinitesimally small portion of humanity. Unlike the Stoic sages, the volume of residual narrative selves are legion. However, like the Stoic universe, the cybergenesis of the digital self is a conflagratory pyrotechnic affair. The technologically-contingent existence of the digital self is annihilated in a pyroclastic manner, breaking apart in the cyber fire and settling back into the unideated data of the Hades of HTML. While the real presence of the residual self vanishes in the pyrotechnic conflagration after ideation, the effects of its carnage remain in the memories of its co-creators, its readers, its users. In the case of demonic residual selves, the idolatries and ideologies of evil then become intertexts in the schemata of other users; a true computer virus spreading through the medium of words and infecting not only software but hardware. Real, bodily humans—made in the image of God, of infinite value and worth, are broken down by the virtual presence of those whose digital imprint lives on in cyber-immortality. We comfort our children back to sleep from nightmares under the false pretense that "monsters aren't real." How could we utter such nonsense? Monsters exist, demons exist, evil beings exist. We are constantly creating them. We *are* them.

Bibliography

Arnold, Clinton. *The Colossian Syncretism: The Interface Between Christianity and Folk Belief at Colossae*. Tübingen: Mohr Siebeck, 1995.

Baltzly, Dirk. "Stoicism." In The Stanford Encyclopedia of Philosophy, edited by Edward N. Zalta. https://plato.stanford.edu/archives/spr2014/entries/stoicism/.

Barker, Rachel. "Social Networking and Identity." In *Handbook of Research on Technoself: Identity in a Technological Society*, edited by Rocci Luppicini, 474–501. Hershey, PA: IGI Global, 2012.

Crites, Stephen. "The Narrative Quality of Experience." In *Why Narrative? Readings in Narrative Theology*, edited by Stanley Hauerwas and L. Gregory Jones, 65–88. Eugene, OR: Wipf and Stock, 1997.

Ellul, Jaqcues. *The New Demons*. New York: Seabury, 1975.

Fornaciari, Federica. "The Language of Technoself: Storytelling, Symbolic Interactionism, and Online Identity." In *Handbook of Research on Technoself: Identity in a Technological Society*, edited by Rocci Luppicini, 64–83. Hershey, PA: IGI Global, 2012.

Frederick, John. "Discerning, Disarming, and Redeeming the Digital Powers—Gospel Community, the Virtual Self, and the HTML of Cruciform Love." In *Ecclesia and Ethics: Moral Formation and the Church*, edited by E. Allen Jones III et al., 153–63. London: T. & T. Clark, 2016.

Geyer, Felix. "Virtual Communities in Cyberspace." *Kybernetes* 25 (1996) 60–66.

Iser, Wolfgang. *The Act of Reading: A Theory of Aesthetic Response*. Baltimore: John Hopkins University Press, 1978.

Lombard, Matthew. "At the Heart of It All: The Concept of Presence." *Journal of Computer-Mediated Communication* 3 (1997) 0. doi:10.1111/j.1083-6101.1997.tb00072.x

MacIntrye, Alasdair. "The Virtues, the Unity of a Human Life, and the Concept of a Tradition." In *Why Narrative? Readings in Narrative Theology*, edited by Stanley Hauerwas and L. Gregory Jones, 89–110. Eugene, OR: Wipf and Stock, 1997.

Markus, Hazel. "Self-Schemata and Processing Information About the Self." *Journal of Personality and Social Psychology* 35 (February 1977) 63–78.

McKenna, Katelyn Y. A., and John A. Bargh. "Plan 9 from Cyberspace: The Implications of the Internet for Personality and Social Psychology." *Personality and Social Psychology Review* 4 (2000) 57–75.

McLuhan, Marshall, and Bruce R. Powers. *The Global Village: Transformations in World Life and Media in the 21st Century*. Oxford: Oxford University Press, 1989.

Polkinghorne, Donald E. *Narrative Knowing and the Human Sciences*. New York: SUNY Press, 1988.

Ratan, Rabindra. "Self-Presence, Explicated: Body, Emotion, and Identity Extension into the Virtual Self." In *Handbook of Research on Technoself: Identity in a Technological Society*, edited by Rocci Luppicini, 322–36. Hershey: IGI Global, 2012.

Ricouer, Paul. *Oneself as Another*. Translated by Kathleen Blamely. Chicago: University of Chicago Press, 1992.

Turkle, Sherry. *Life on the Screen: Identity in the Age of the Internet*. New York: Touchstone, 1995.

Wink, Walter. *Engaging the Powers: Discernment and Resistance in a World of Domination*. Minneapolis: Fortress, 1992.

———. *Naming the Powers: The Language of Power in the New Testament*. Minneapolis: Fortress, 1984.

———. *Unmasking the Powers: The Invisible Forces that Determine Human Existence*. Minneapolis: Fortress, 1986.

Wittel, Andreas. "Toward a Network Sociality." *Theory, Culture & Society* 18 (2016) 51–76.

Wright, N. T. *The Resurrection of the Son of God*. Minneapolis: Fortress, 1994.

Wynn, Eleanor, and James E. Katz. "Hyperbole over Cyberspace: Self-Presentation and Social Boundaries in Internet Home Pages and Discourse." *The Information Society* 13 (1997) 297–327.

4

The Bible Is Not a Database

T. C. Moore

Introduction

Not that long ago, I misplaced something at home. When normally I would begin trying to remember where last I was and what I was doing, instead, I instinctually thought: "I'll just run a search for it." The thought felt so natural that it was as if I subconsciously believed the whole world was indexed in a database somewhere to which my brain was wirelessly connected, and with a few mental keystrokes I could locate my missing object. That moment signaled to me something significant. The technology I use every day is not just *helping* me to think, it's shaping *how* I think. Since I use databases every day, I now think the world is a database I can quickly search with simple combinations of keywords. I use this technology so often that thinking my search queries will return the results I'm seeking has become second nature. The relationship between the tools I use to navigate the world and how I conceptualize the world is merging.

Since I'm both a tech geek and a pastor, this experience got me thinking about the way I and others are now accessing the Bible. In my experience, gone are the days when, in some worship gathering, I might have heard the ruffling of paper pages when a Bible reference was given. Fewer and fewer people are using printed translations of the Bible in the worship gatherings I lead or attend. Instead, I've noticed far more people accessing digital translations of the Bible on mobile devices like phones and tablets. Admittedly, the convenience of having the Bible at one's fingertips to a mother wrangling three small children is quite understandable. I even have some personal hang-ups and stigma that I attach to people wielding big Bibles at church. But it does raise this question in my mind. How does the use of this new technology shape the way we think about the Bible?

We may learn some things about how this new digital medium might be changing the biblical message from considering how another seismic media shift changed the message of the Bible. I'm referring, of course, to the invention of the printing press. However, to appreciate how radically the printing press reframed our understanding of the Bible, fundamental beliefs some of us hold uncritically are likely to be challenged. In many Western traditions of Christianity—particularly the Protestant varieties—it's assumed that an individual is able and encouraged to read the Bible for themselves. Even more specifically, such a conclusion is probably self-evident to most of those in America who call themselves "Evangelical." My guess is, it would likely come as a shock to them that this belief is relatively new. And it might be even more shocking that such belief is at least as much a product of *technology* as *theology*.

People of the Book

As a means of introducing the significance of the shift occasioned by the printing press, let us consider the words of Shane Hipps:

> Protestant Christianity is a by-product of a single medium—the printed Bible. Without printing, no one could have challenged the authority of the pope. How disconcerting to have a faith yoked so closely to a medium that is now in the dusk of its life, at least its life as we currently know it. Our culture has a shrinking preference—and even aptitude—for reading books, especially complex ones. If the Bible is anything, it is complex, so it should not surprise us to see a growing biblical illiteracy in the electronic age. The Bible is an extraordinarily demanding library of books. The stories, letters, and laws are shrouded by the fog of time. The thick dusty languages of ancient Greek and Hebrew convey the message through cumbersome translations. The books were born in civilizations and cultures alien to us, and the assumptions and attitudes of the original authors often escape us entirely. In many cases, excavating meaning requires the fortitude, patience, and discipline of an archeological dig.[1]

---

1. Hipps, *Flickering Pixels*, 146–47.

When the printing press made it possible for an individual to possess their own, personal copy of a Bible translation—in their own language, no less—the way people accessed and interacted with the Bible was fundamentally altered. Rather than most often, or perhaps even exclusively, hearing Scripture read aloud in a corporate worship context, a person could read the Scriptures apart from any worship environment and apart from the input of clerics or biblical scholars. It should come as no surprise, then, that some began to read the Bible as merely a collection of ancient literature, no different from other literature from antiquity. The technological advancement of printing simultaneously advanced textual criticism simply by placing a copy of the Bible in the hands of individuals apart from a worshiping community.

> By the 17th century, the [printed word] had become the dominant means of communication. These conditions embedded the bias of the printed medium deeply into the Western worldview and gave rise to the modern mindset that represented a dramatic departure from medieval European thought. This newly entrenched worldview was characterized by a strong emphasis on individualism, objectivity, abstraction, and reason, in contrast to the medieval worldview characterized by an emphasis on tribal, mystical, and sacramental experiences.[2]

What a person expected of the Bible changed. Rather than expecting biblical interpretation to be conducted corporately in a worshiping community with clerics and biblical scholars while inextricably linked to application, the expectation emerged that the individual is empowered to interpret the Bible for her or himself and apply their interpretation individually, or not at all. Private interpretation was powered by the technological advancement of printing, which served to radically transform the message of the Bible. From that point on, the very message of the Bible was expected to be individualistic.

This is not to say that the Reformers naively advanced a pure democratization of biblical insight. As Mark Labberton, president of Fuller Seminary, has written,

> The apparent democratizing of divine knowledge that the perspicuity of the Bible provided for was affirmed by the Reformers, but the priesthood of all believers did not mean the equality of all readers. Calvin could imagine Bible reading occurring only

---

2. Hipps, *Hidden Power*, 51.

in the context of Christian community and not by isolated readers on their iPhones between dumbbell sets at a 24-hour fitness club. This shift would have been literally unimaginable for the Reformers, because for them, reading was a communal act that extended back in time through history (including biblical history) and encompassed all its many members and readers. In the "proper pasture" Calvin envisioned, the sheep did not find the pasture or graze there alone.[3]

Nevertheless, Calvin's own work of translation served to undermine even his noble ideal of communal interpretation by assuring Bible-readers that having the Scriptures translated into their native language would ensure their understanding of the gospel.

> Calvin, like many of the Reformers, spoke confidently about "the perspicuity of Scripture." He was convinced that just as the gospel of Jesus Christ is available for every kind of person, so the Bible, which proclaims this good news, must be as well. This double conviction is evident from his very first Reformed writing, the preface to Olivétan's New Testament. He explains that the fulfillment of the Old Testament law and the reconciliation of God in Christ "is what is stated plainly in the [New Testament] and set forth there openly." The purpose of the translation is "to enable all Christians, men and women, who know the French language, to understand and acknowledge the law they ought to obey and the faith they ought to follow." Scripture makes plain both our human need and God's way for salvation; this is the core of the claim of perspicuity.[4]

Instead of making the Bible easier to understand and accessible to all, personal translations of the Bible changed the message of the gospel and multiplied interpretations of it exponentially. Now, there are millions of people who are confident they have received God's unmerited grace by faith, but are much less confident that they need to participate in meaningful Christian community or love their neighbor by seeking justice for the oppressed. Individualistic interpretation of the Bible has given rise to many potentially destructive forms of "Christianity," not least of which are the so-called "Prosperity Gospel" and the concept of "personal salvation" that's focused solely on a blissful afterlife.

The technological development of printing simultaneously developed alternative expectations of the printed Bible's message and application in

---

3. Labberton, "The Plain, Difficult Sense of Scripture."
4. Labberton, "The Plain, Difficult Sense of Scripture."

the hands of individuals. People shaped the tool of the personal, printed Bible and then the tool of the personal, printed Bible shaped them.

Personalized Search

Today, the technological advancement of the web has introduced a new dimension to this shift. Not only can the Scriptures be read and interpreted privately and applied personally, without either the insight of biblical scholars or the guidance of pastoral leaders, they can also be rapidly and precisely searched. The database is now a fixture of our digital lives, whether we realize it or not. It's running in the background of all our most beloved online destinations and mobile apps. It powers our digital quests for both enlightenment and entertainment. This hidden dimension of the web is what enables us to quickly access information that we would otherwise never unearth. We no longer have to read off long URLs when we want to direct people to a particular page of a website. We simply direct them to the site's home page and recommend some concise keywords (e.g., "For more information, go to NPR.org keyword 'Fresh Air'"). Or, one doesn't even need to bother requesting the particular domain, when one can simply start from a search engine like Google. In fact, we no longer "search" for pages on the web, we "google" them. What formative power does this new practice (empowered by the database) have on our way of thinking? How has the shaping of databases shaped us?

For one thing, it makes us "queriers." When a person submits their keyword search into the search field of a database-driven site, they are "running a query." The user has a question and the magical database elves run around finding the answer. You and I come to the database with our questions, and we have faith that the database has the answer. How self-centered this process is can be easily overlooked. Who we are has more to do with the questions we're asking than the text from which we're seeking answers. Our social locations are constraints upon the range of subjects with which we'll concern ourselves.

For example, among many other subjects, Martin Luther was embroiled in discussion of how the Lord's Table should be theologically conceptualized. What do Christians mean by Christ's "presence" in the bread and cup? This is no doubt an important subject, since it has to do with a Christian tradition that is taught in Scripture and practiced by all Christians everywhere. But, as Dr. James Cone powerfully points out, our social locations play an important role in the theological questions we ask.

> I respect what happened at Nicea and Chalcedon and the theological input of the Church Fathers on Christology; but that source alone is inadequate for finding out the meaning of black folks' Jesus. It is all right to say as did Athanasius that the Son is *homoousia* (one substance with the Father), especially if one has a taste for Greek philosophy and a feel for the importance of intellectual distinctions. And I do not want to minimize or detract from the significance of Athanasius' assertion for faith one iota. But the *homoousia* question is not the black question. Blacks do not ask whether Jesus is one with the Father or divine and human, though the orthodox formulations are implied in their language. They ask whether Jesus is walking with them, whether they can call him up on the "telephone of prayer" and tell him all about their troubles.
>
> To be sure Athanasius' assertion about the status of the Logos in the Godhead is important for the church's continued christological investigations. But we must not forget that Athanasius' question about the Son's status in relation to the Father did not arise in the historical context of the slave codes and the slave drivers. And if he had been a black slave in America, I am sure he would have asked a different set of questions. He might have asked about the status of the Son in relation to slaveholders. Perhaps the same is true of Martin Luther and his concern about the ubiquitous presence of Jesus Christ at the Lord's Table. While not diminishing the importance of Luther's theological concern, I am sure that if he had been born a black slave his first question would not have been whether Jesus was at the Lord's Table but whether he was really present at the slave's cabin, whether the slave could expect Jesus to be with him as he tried to survive the cottonfields, the whip, and the pistol.[5]

The questions that drove the early church councils, and the questions that drove Luther's discussion of the Lord's Table, were occasioned by their social locations. The questions with which we approach the Bible are shaped by the social locations from which we approach it, which in turn shape the answers we expect to find. Eighteenth century American Southerners arrived at far different conclusions regarding what the Bible has to say about slavery than do Twenty-first century American Southerners. The text of the Bible has not changed, but the society around the Southerners

---

5. Cone, *God of the Oppressed*, 14.

has. They now stand in a different social location as if the ground beneath their feet had shifted.

Furthermore, N. T. Wright has warned Protestants against remaining trapped in a Reformation time capsule, by continuing to ask the questions that were relevant then, instead of conducting a fresh investigation of what the Bible's ancient message means for a postmodern world. "For too long we have read Scripture with nineteenth-century eyes and sixteenth-century questions. It's time to get back to reading with first-century eyes and twenty-first-century questions."[6]

In his book, *iGods*, Craig Detweiler comments on Google's service of "personalized search."

> Google offers different search results depending on where we are, what it knows about our interests. When we arrive in Portland or Miami, Google knows we're there—and our local news shifts to match our locale. It is nice to get news tailored to our favorite teams or our most pressing issues, but it is somewhat creepy to consider how our location is targeted so invisibly. Pariser understands why we embrace personalized recommendations: "Our media is a perfect reflection of our interests and desires. By definition, it's an appealing prospect—a return to a Ptolemaic universe in which the sun and everything else revolves around us." This is the iGods' alluring and dangerous promise—to place us at the center of our own self-reflexive universe. But what if we don't necessarily know what is best? What if our limited experiences are further delimited by our choices so far? Instead of expanding our world and understanding, we could become consumed by what we already see and hear.[7]

Technology, as an extension of ourselves, is limited by our limitations. It is by nature self-centered. How ironic is it that the message of a book that is thought by many to teach people how to be less self-centered, can be so changed by how we access it that it makes us more self-centered?

Losing the Plot

This new and convenient way of tailoring our study of the Bible to the questions which are relevant to us poses a serious problem for how we

---

6. Wright, *Justification*, 37.
7. Detweiler, *iGods*, 122.

understand its purpose. Approaching the Bible like a database fundamentally misunderstands Scripture as a repository of data in search of queries. But the Bible does not promise to answer our every question. In fact, the Bible has its own agenda and isn't particularly interested in catering to our whims. The Bible is a story. How we conceptualize the nature and purpose of the Bible will affect how we engage with it and seek to apply its teaching. Instead of thinking of the Bible as a warehouse of information that we digitally access with search terms, as if there were digital forklifts that we program to scour the aisles stacked high with words in order to return to us a palette of verses, perhaps we could think of the Bible as a ride at a theme park. The creators of the ride have a goal for those who experience it. Maybe the ride is based on a movie. So, the ride's creators want to introduce you to the setting of the movie by taking you around in a boat beside various animatronic figures who act out scenes from the movie with a backdrop from the movie. Then, the ride takes you through some obstacles that simulate conflict from the film. Lastly, the ride resolves just as the movie had, with the hero victorious.

Like all stories, the biblical canon has a beginning, a middle, and an end. It has a rising action, a climax, and a falling action. Together, the Hebrew Bible (or Old Testament) and New Testament tell one, overarching narrative. That narrative has been systematized and cataloged many times and in many different ways. The canon of Scripture follows the pattern of a story rather than an encyclopedia of answers. Therefore, the very medium of a biblical database can contribute to misunderstanding the Bible's character.

Imagine someone picking up a novel and looking for the search field. They say, "I don't want to read this whole book. I'm not interested in the plot, or the story the author is trying to tell. I just want to know the age of the main character. Why can't I just 'google' the answer to my question?" Well, the reason one cannot simply "google" the answers to one's Bible queries is because the Bible may not be answering those questions. Just as *Animal Farm* was not addressing how to make popcorn or *Twilight* answering the question of how to make "insanely great" deals, the Bible isn't necessarily going to contain answers to our personalized queries. This could be very frustrating to those who assume the purpose of the Bible is to return results that are helpful to their self-centered goals. This contributes to the cultural trope that the Bible is no longer "relevant." If what is meant by relevance is whether or not the Bible can supply advice that is tailored to the interests or desires of those querying it, then the trope is correct. The Bible has no interest in being "relevant" in that way. However, the story the Bible tells is incredibly relevant to all human beings since it is the story of humanity's Creator and the Creator's redemption of creation. In order to grasp the relevancy of the Bible, however, one must actually know the story the Bible is telling.

Asking the Wrong Questions

Perhaps much of our frustration over theological divisions is due to the way we have come to conceptualize the Bible. Many of the current controversies that threaten to divide denominations center around contemporary cultural phenomena that did not exist when the Bible was written. Those who view the Bible as the highest authoritative arbiter on matters of ethics or church practice approach the Bible seeking answers. They might query: "What does the Bible say about same-sex marriage?" Or they might run a search with this question: "What does the Bible say about abortion?" As the story of humanity's Creator and that Creator's redemption of all creation, certainly the story the Bible is telling is relevant to these subjects. But there is no "abortion" or "same-sex marriage" encyclopedia entry in the Bible. It will also not suffice to find every verse which contains the word for which one searches. Finding every instance of "pig" in *Animal Farm* tells one nothing about the book's message.

The only way Bible-readers will be able to discover the teaching of the Bible is to know the story. And the only way Bible-readers will become those who apply the teaching of the Bible in their lives is by becoming part of that story. To do this will require resisting the way our accessing of the Bible via digital databases seeks to shape how we conceptualize its character. And as we resist the database conception of Scripture, retaining its narrative constitution, we must also resist the temptation to see ourselves as the ones around whom the story revolves—becoming its main character. The Bible is not a database. Instead, the Bible is the story of the Creator God redeeming creation. All human beings are invited to find themselves in that story, to be caught up in it, through the Author, Main Character, and through God's story-shaped people.

Bibliography

Cone, James. *God of the Oppressed*. San Francisco: Harper, 1978.

Detweiler, Craig. *iGods: How Technology Shapes Our Spiritual and Social Lives*. Grand Rapids: Brazos, 2013.

Goheen, Michael, and Craig Bartholomew. *The True Story of the Whole World: Finding Your Place in the Biblical Drama*. Grand Rapids: Faith Alive, 2009.

Hipps, Shane. *Flickering Pixels: How Technology Shapes Your Faith*. Grand Rapids: Zondervan, 2009.

———. *The Hidden Power of Electronic Culture: How Media Shapes Faith, the Gospel, and the Church*. Grand Rapids: Zondervan, 2005.

Labberton, Mark. "The Plain, Difficult Sense of Scripture." *Christian Century*, March 30, 2017. https://www.christiancentury.org/article/plain-difficult-sense-scripture.

Wright, N. T. *Justification: God's Plan & Paul's Vision*. Downers Grove, IL: InterVarsity, 2009.

5

See Me, Hear Me, Praise Me

An Internet for More than Vainglory

CHAD BOGOSIAN

Introduction

Over the past three decades, the internet has woven its way into the substance of our daily lives. It offers new avenues for human connection, business and commerce, as well as the transmission of knowledge. But these prospects bring with them the possibility for misusing the internet. Recently our Philosophy Club organized an interdisciplinary panel discussion about how technology is affecting our understanding of what it means to be human. As we explored some of the prospects and pitfalls of technology, the conversation landed on the use of social media. One panelist asked the audience the following question: "How many of you think people you see on social media are narcissistic?" The majority of hands went up. The same panelist followed up with this question: "How many of you consider yourself narcissistic?" Not a single hand was raised. Laughter erupted as most immediately realized the problem. Do you ever use the internet to strategically craft a particular image (personal or professional), one that's inauthentic but praised in other's eyes? Do you use social media with the hope of getting lots of "likes" or seeing your video go viral? Do you ever feel slighted when people criticize your blog posts or pictures or web content?

These kinds of questions can induce moral discomfort, and it's tempting to redirect the conversation to how the internet benefits our lives. If we're honest, however, we can admit (as my students often do) that we don't always use the internet in ways that promote the good of everyone. We choose, rather, to use it in ways that cultivate character dispositions that adversely affect our love for God and others.[1] The Christian tradition is replete with analyses of the various vices and their contrasting virtues, and many Christians have gone to great lengths to include a diagnosis of so called "deadly sins." While Protestants have not historically drawn on this rich literature to develop a moral theology and a virtue ethics, there's been a positive change in this direction over the past few decades. In this paper, I want to join this recovery by bringing the classic and contemporary work on virtues and vices to bear on how we use the internet. The internet is an arena where virtuous character can be formed and put on display, yet this opens us up to the potential for vicious character to be formed or put on display as well. In this essay, I shall explore how the vice of vainglory is pursued through our internet activity, how vainglory, while rooted in pride, is distinct from pride, and how vainglory disrupts the proper flow of love of God and others. I shall conclude by identifying spiritual practices that can help us move from vainglory to truthfulness and love.

Vainglory: What's Wrong (and Right) with Glory-Seeking?

We live in a culture obsessed with projecting and maintaining a particular image of oneself in the interest of earning praise or glory. From professional athletes like LeBron James in his "Decision," to popular musicians such as Lady Gaga on her album *The Fame*, to scholars working for their reputation through shameless self-promotion, we see social influencers and thought leaders model ways to get noticed and glory in it. Philosopher Alvin Plantinga offers an important warning to young philosophers in this regard:

> Current philosophical culture encourages us to practice our craft in a sort of individualistic, competitive, and even egotistical style. Philosophers have a great interest in ranking each other with respect to dialectical and philosophical ability, deciding who is really terrific, who is pretty good, who is okay, and who is a real dog. (Those who do well in this derby sometimes remind me of

---

1. I understand virtues and vices to be traits or dispositions of character, where character includes thought, feeling, and motivation. Thought and feeling are here intended to encompass both intellectual and moral virtues, while this chapter is focused more on moral-spiritual dimensions of virtue and vice.

Daniel 8:8—"And the he-goat magnified himself exceedingly.") It's as if your worth—at any rate, qua philosopher—depends on your ranking; it's as if your main job is to try to achieve as high a ranking as possible.... Of course, a mere moment's reflection reveals the foolishness of that idea: Philosophy is not an athletic competition, and success as a Christian philosopher is not an individualistic matter of doing well in the intellectual equivalent of a tennis tournament. Christian philosophers are successful, not when they achieve a "reputation," but when they properly play the sort of role I've described above, in service to the Christian community. Philosophy is not without its dangers. But of course, the same goes for everything worthwhile, including worship, mother love, prayer, and humility. So welcome to the world of philosophy—and work at it with joy and enthusiasm![2]

Lest we leave anyone out, even parents and churchgoers struggle with vainglory. Parents often strive to maintain the images of being good parents and having perfect children (whatever that means), while churchgoers may project an image of being religiously put together. In the end, "Vainglory is a vice for us all—as tempting now as it was in the fourth century. Love of fame may be the most obvious or extreme form of this vice, but the truth is, we can *all* be overly attached to how we appear to others and are acknowledged and approved by them."[3]

But is it always wrong to value our good being on display and recognized by others? Scripture and the Christian tradition are in agreement that the answer is "no." Glory is good when it is pursued properly. In Matthew's Gospel, Jesus invites all to enter his good and beautiful Kingdom by following him into a life of ongoing interactive communion with God and his readily present Kingdom (Matt 5–7). The person who does so is "blessed" or "well off"—they have a good life. Moreover, a good person is one who's character (i.e. "heart") dispositions of thought, feeling, and motivation are "committed to promoting the good of everyone they deal with—including, of course God and themselves."[4] Embodying this kind of life is good and worthy of being recognized as such. However, along the journey we will face traps that threaten to derail us, interrupt our communion with God, and therefore our thriving as a person in every dimension of life. Such

---

2. Plantinga, "Letter."
3. Aquinas, *On Evil*, Q IX.1.ad3 and IX.2.ad9.
4. Willard, *Divine Conspiracy*, 187.

traps present themselves in the form of desires that bear the resemblance of something good, yet something is off.

One such trap is *respectability* whereby our performing of actions aims to elicit the response of praise without any concern for the heart (i.e. motives) from which the action springs. Jesus cautions his listeners by saying the scribes and Pharisees "do everything they do *with the aim* of being noticed by others. They enlarge the religious symbols on their clothing. They like to have the most prominent seats at dinners and in the synagogues. They relish loudly respectful greetings in malls and public places, and being called 'Professor' or 'Doctor' (Matt. 5:14–16 and 23:5–7)."[5] Religious activity done for the sake of respectability reveals our *motive or intent* of being noticed for the activity, and this fits our definition of *vainglory*. So while religious activities and being known are not wrong in themselves, the problem arises when our intentions are either to be seen for the activity or to be approved for our actions. Both intentions reveal that our heart is not to living for "the audience of one."[6]

Thomas Aquinas has this to say about human goodness on display: "It seems to belong to a natural appetite that one wish one's goodness to become known. . . . [W]e can rightly . . . desire to please other human beings."[7] If human nature has a built in desire for others to affirm one's goodness, then recognition of one's goodness on display can be appropriate if it is assigned and sought properly. It is sought properly when it reflects the Creator's goodness on display whereby he naturally radiates his loving character as a gift for our good; and in so doing his beauty draws us into a life-giving relationship. We cross the line into *vainglory*, however, when we get caught in "the excessive and disordered desire for recognition and approval from others. . . . We want acclaim too much, so much, that we accept it whether it is deserved or not."[8] In short, glory is "vain" when our pursuit of this good is empty or disordered.

One way our glory can be vain in the context of the internet is when we fake our expertise, social standing, or attractiveness. We do these things in numerous ways. Perhaps we name-drop scholars or influential people on a topic we're debating on a blog or social media sight in order to look well-read or intelligent. Perhaps we show off what we purchase or what

---

5. Willard, *Divine Conspiracy*, 188, emphasis added.
6. Willard, *Divine Conspiracy*, 189–90.
7. Quoted in DeYoung, *Glittering Vices*, 60.
8. DeYoung, *Vainglory*, 19.

places we frequent to appear well off or fashionable when in reality we are amassing debt and feel insecure about our attractiveness. Or perhaps we only post pictures in order to be seen at our best or go further to photo shop pics in order to make ourselves, friends, and family look more "beautiful" and acceptable. In the end, these fake and fluffy maneuvers are *superficial goods* and therefore not worthy of glory.[9] Superficial goods cut off mutual love since the relationship is based on deception instead of honesty. How can someone love me if they fail to know the real me?

Another way glory can be vain is when the goods for which we receive glory are *genuine goods*, however our attachment to the glory received runs amok. Suppose you have finished a graduate degree, earned an award for excellent service to your profession, or exemplified virtue in noticeable ways. These are all good things and worthy of praise for their goodness in your life and the lives of others. Now suppose you post updates about these on social media or your website and others praise you for said accomplishments. How might this go wrong if you are praiseworthy for these genuine goods? Well, if we update others simply to be praised for the accomplishment rather than to share this good with God who has given one the gifts to get there, then one is more attached to the praise than to the good itself or to reflecting God's goodness, beauty, and glory.[10]

Desert Father John Cassian explains how one might progress from being praised for a genuine glory-worthy good to embodying vainglory: "We shall lose the fruits of all the works that we have accomplished at the behest of vainglory [because] we wronged God by preferring to do for the sake of human beings what we should have done for his sake. [Thus we are] convicted by him who knows what is hidden of having preferred human beings to God, and the glory of the world to the glory of God."[11] In my view, Cassian is too strong to claim we lose any progress in spiritual formation if we fail to give God glory for spiritual progress. However, there is an important truth here: posting internet updates about our moral or professional successes for the sake of being known, without a concern for God being known for making it all possible, is a disordered or vainglorious praise. In sum, when we embellish or behave inauthentically on the internet for the sake of gaining people's approval, we are thereby using it vaingloriously.

9. DeYoung, *Vainglory*, 27–28.
10. DeYoung, *Vainglory*, 30–31.
11. Quoted in DeYoung, *Vainglory*, 31.

By now, we should see why the early desert fathers thought vainglory was one of "the capital vices" or "deadly sins." Evagrios the Solitary I, for example, puts vainglory in the top three in his list of eight vices (i.e. "evil thoughts" or "passions"). With the temptations of Christ in Matt 4 and Luke 4 in view, he says "Of the demons opposing us in the practice of the ascetic life, there are three groups who fight in the front line: those who are entrusted with appetites of gluttony, those who suggest avaricious thoughts, and those who incite us to seek the esteem of men. All the other demons follow behind and in their turn attack those already wounded by the first three groups."[12] The top three vices of gluttony, pride (avarice), and vainglory (esteem of men), are *capital vices* precisely because they are the commanding source of other vices, and since they disrupt our love for God. Vainglory leads us to seek happiness in glory for our goodness on display on the internet instead of finding our happiness in God alone.

Here it is important to say a few words about the difference between vainglory and pride, since up to this point it could appear as if they are one and the same. Pride, however, is one of the roots of vainglory and not simply the vice under another name. Rebecca Konyndyk DeYoung helpfully distinguishes the two as follows: "Pride excessively concerns excellence itself. . . . Vainglory, by contrast, concerns primarily the display or manifestation of excellence. . . . Pride is a desire for genuine status; vainglory, a desire for recognition and acclaim."[13] From this we can see that either vice aims to find happiness in something other than union with God. However, the difference is vainglory seeks happiness in the show or reputation. It's clear that one would not be motivated to seek the show if they were not also prideful, hence pride is a root of vainglory. Prideful-vainglory shows up in our internet use in all the ways mentioned above, but here it's worth emphasizing ways in which theologians, philosophers, and religious leaders might be especially tempted. Blogs, special topics websites, and social media can be used as a way to "one-up" our perceived interlocutors or competitors through publishing "replies" or "critiques" of books, articles, or interviews. Of course, what passes for these things is often little more than an exertion of one's intellectual savvy or power over another, an effort to defend one's views at any cost, or striving to show our knowledge and prowess in our areas of expertise. After all, one is an expert and thinks she should be known

---

12. Palmer, Sherrard, and Ware, *Philokalia*, 127.
13. DeYoung, *Glittering Vices*, 62.

as such. In the end, prideful-vainglory is in full operation, and our glory-worthy selves have distorted our love for God and others.

Another possible root of vainglory is *fear*.[14] Using the internet to build one's brand or image is often rooted in fear of what others will think if they knew the truth about us. We cannot imagine life with others if they knew who we really were, shortcomings and all. What if I'm not really as fiscally well off as they think? What if my faith community doesn't see me as spiritually mature? What if others expose my lack of knowledge in my field or on a topic I care about? What if my politician of choice really is a weak candidate for office? Our answers to these and similar questions can easily reveal why we behave vaingloriously on the internet. In the end, we fear what others think of us so much that we craft a fake or embellished image to get them to love us. We are like St. Augustine, "ambitious to win human approval . . . [because] we love to be loved,"[15] however, we cannot see that love has not come to the internet when we use it this way. Love, instead, has been traded in for a cheap substitute.

A Remedy for Vainglory: Truthfulness

Part of the problem with vainglory and why it distorts love is that we are dishonest in our dealings with others. Projecting a fake or embellished self is false, and we cannot flourish without a high regard for truthfulness. In Matthew's Gospel, Jesus discusses how *hypocrisy* is an off-spring vice of vainglory. Those who perform religious deeds for the show "do as the hypocrites do," and this is centered in a deceitful heart (Matt 6:2). At the end of the day, recognition for these acts is short-lived and the only praise one receives. For this reason, the desert father Evagrius cautions us: "Do not sell your labours for people's esteem, nor hand over the future glory for the sake of paltry fame, for human esteem settles in the dust (cf. Ps. 7:6) and its reputation is extinguished on earth, but the glory of virtue abides for eternity."[16]

The remedy for this condition is to "not let our left hand know what our right hand is doing" (Matt 6:2). Philosopher Dallas Willard offers a helpful explanation: "The kind of people who have been so transformed by their daily walk with God that good deeds naturally flow from their

---

14. See insightful comments on the nature of this root in DeYoung, *Vainglory*, 47–52.

15. Quoted in DeYoung, *Vainglory*, 48–51.

16. DeYoung, *Glittering Vices*, 69.

character are precisely the kind of people whose left hand would not notice what their right hand is doing . . . because of what they are pervasively and internally." Of course, they are this way due to God's graciously acting in their lives to do what they cannot accomplish on their own. However, we must make an effort to enter into and join with his grace for it to do its full work: "[Those who do] are people who do not have to invest in a lot of reflection of doing good for others . . . or they are absorbed in the love of God and those around them. . . . And because they really are looking toward God and living toward God, God responds to them: 'Your Father, the one who sees in secret, will reward you' (6:4)"[17] In short, we become virtuous by intentionally performing virtuous actions; we learn to glory well by practicing truthful display of one's goodness while relying on God's grace for help.

It is at this point we encounter an important objection from critics of the virtue and vice tradition in Christian ethics. Suppose we are to become a person who loves God with our entire being, and this means we have to work with God to overcome vainglory in our lives. The main way to do so on this account, with God's help, is to intentionally practice contrasting virtues that are not yet settled dispositions of thought, feeling, and action. Inevitably we will fall short in our attempts and do other than what we believe and claim that this is what Jesus wants of us (i.e. we'll act vaingloriously even though we say it's wrong). But this is hypocritical because it is an example of "faking it to make it" in which we pretend to be someone other than our true self.

In response to this objection, New Testament theologian N. T. Wright argues that while we often use the phrase "putting on" to mean "pretending," not every case of "putting on" is a form of hypocrisy. For example, when the Apostle Paul tells us to "put on the new self" and to "clothe yourself with Christlikeness," he goes on to give us an extensive list of virtues we are to intentionally acquire in our ongoing life with God: kindness, compassion, faithfulness, patience, gentleness, and love.[18] When we intentionally act as if we are kind in order to become kind, the *telos* of these actions is the eventual settled disposition of our character. "Part of Paul's point, which is utterly characteristic of 'virtue ethics' is that you have to go through that stage if you're going to go anywhere."[19] Crucial here, however, is what *motivates*

17. Willard, *Divine Conspiracy*, 192.
18. Wright, *After You Believe*, 144–47.
19. Wright, *After You Believe*, 146.

one's action. The aspiring artist or athlete acts out of a motive to become what they ought to be not out of a motive to dupe or fake out onlookers. This is a normal part of process of moral-spiritual formation just as it is for any other kind of formation.

What matters most for the person trying to overcome the vice of vainglory is to act *according to* the virtue of truthfulness in order to become the kind of person who eventually will, more often than not, act *from* the virtue of truthfulness. Truthfulness should not be thought of merely as speech acts but as an entire way of being towards others. This includes the image we project to them through all we say and do as we use the internet. Truthful persons neither over-communicate out of pride nor under-communicate out of fear.[20] They don't use the internet to convey words, actions or postures that present a skewed or false self. Becoming a truthful person takes time, patience, and practice; but the process is worth the reward of thriving relationships. What kinds of practices might we engage in to become a truthful, loving person who seeks glory well?

Spiritual Practices for Moving from Vainglory to Truthfulness, Love, and Glorying Well

In this section, I will focus on two kinds of practices: inward and outward. I understand spiritual practices to be activities we can engage in with God to open ourselves up to the character-transforming power of God. These are God-ordained tools we must use, because God will not impose his will and character upon us, nor can we by direct acts of will make ourselves be less vainglorious in our use of the internet.

Jesus, in his sermon, instructs the disciples to *pray* in non-showy ways (Matt 6:14–15). By conversing honestly with God *in secret* about our vainglorious uses of the internet, we open ourselves to receive God's truthfulness and love in us. As a result, we become in our use of the internet who we are in prayer: "[Jesus] teaches us how to be in prayer what we are in life and how to be *in* life what we are in prayer."[21] And we might add here that it's probably counterproductive to take to social media sites to invite the online world to help you pray about this. Employing the discipline of secrecy here is essential. A helpful tool for prayer that Jesus himself teaches his early apprentices is the Lord's Prayer (Matt 6:9–13). One might slowly read

---

20. DeYoung, *Vainglory*, 70–71.
21. Willard, *Divine Conspiracy*, 195.

and meditate on each line of this text daily while including some thoughts about one's image-shaping, attention-seeking, and vainglorious use of the internet. For example, "Jesus, always near me as I post on the internet today, let your name be made great through my actions; let your will be done on the internet as it is in heaven; forgive us as we forgive those who post and say things we feel are a slight to us; guard us against attack; may your truthful, good, and beautiful kingdom come in and through me . . . yours is the power and *glory* forever."[22]

The desert fathers highlight the power of *prayer* to purge and transform us into humble, loving beings like the Christ we follow: "It is through unceasing prayer that the mind is cleansed of the dark clouds. . . . When it is cleansed, the divine light of Jesus cannot but shine in it, unless we are puffed up by self-esteem and delusion . . . and so are deprived of Jesus' help. For Christ, the paradigm of humility loathes all such self-inflation."[23] Not only can prayer bring humility to counteract pride (one root of vainglory), it can open us to being formed by love for love: "Whatever a man loves, he desires at all costs to be near to continuously. . . . He who loves God also desires always to be with him and to converse with him. . . . The man who cries to God at dawn has withdrawn his intellect from every vice and clearly is wounded by love."[24] We typically think of wounds as bad, but here wounding is medicinal and therapeutic. Divine love wounds so we can become like Christ in our entire being, and this is what it means to become virtuous. As we become virtuous (more truthful and loving), we will be disposed to use the internet for good glory instead of vainglory.

Prayer leads to silence and solitude; and as we'll see, silence and solitude lead to prayer. So one might see these as mutual reinforcing practices. *Silence* is a powerful antidote to constant internet "chatter" that temps us to vainglory. It can be practiced in a number of ways both on and off the internet. Being in quiet on a weekend retreat (without internet access) is one way to power down in order to power up, so to speak. One can also practice silence by refraining from speaking about one's own needs, activities, disenchantments, or accomplishments online. How about starting small and devoting one or more days each week to refrain from "talking" about yourself on the internet? This can go a long way toward truly hearing

---

22. Adapted from Willard's paraphrase of the Lord's Prayer in *Divine Conspiracy*, 269.

23. Palmer, Sherrard, and Ware, *Philokalia*, 77.

24. Palmer, Sherrard, and Ware, *Philokalia*, 88.

others: "Only [the one] who is silent can hear."[25] Silence will also help one see the fluff and fakery for what it is, and to hear God on matters related to good and vainglory. In short, silence is a way to freedom and genuine mutual love, and it opens us up to prayer.

Solitude also helps us repel vainglory by denying "ourselves not speech but an audience."[26] Going for a walk or hike outside without the usual internet distractions will open you up to God's movements within you. Here we learn that God's attention is always loving, merciful, and enough. We don't need to perform to receive it. We only need to be. Richard Foster explains, "Solitude . . . frees us from the panicked need for acclaim and approval . . . [enables us to] lay down the crushing burden of the opinions of others."[27] By releasing ourselves from these burdens we open ourselves up to the audience of one, for his beauty to flood and animate our lives. We come to *know* by experience that we are loved unconditionally and this gift is enough. Receiving this gift enables us to live out "the most comprehensive [command]" which "is to love God and our neighbor. This love is made firm through abstaining from physical things, and through stillness of thought."[28] Like silence, solitude and stillness open us to hearing God and prayer.

Our pursuit to acquire a proper view of glory is not only a matter of private interior work. Rebecca DeYoung poignantly states: "Vainglory is a social vice; it's pollution is the very air we breathe."[29] As such, we need to consider a few practices we can engage on the internet to help us glory well. First, practice sharing the glory. If you accomplish something, it's likely that others helped make that possible even indirectly. Make that known by expressing gratitude for their involvement. When someone makes an insightful comment on a blog or social media site, affirm that person and express gratitude. Be quick to listen and slow to respond when someone challenges something you say. Be willing to say you'll think about it and get back to them, because this isn't about you showing them your intellectual chops but seeking truth together. Second, practice spiritual friendship by inviting others to lovingly point out your vanity. Invite them to ask you "Are you being genuine?" or "Why did you post that picture or make that statement

---

25. Pieper, *Four Cardinal Virtues*, 20.
26. DeYoung, *Vainglory*, 97.
27. Foster, *Freedom of Simplicity*, 68.
28. Palmer, Sherrard, and Ware, *Philokalia*, 165.
29. DeYoung, *Vainglory*, 117.

about yourself?" To take it a step further, you can practice responding well to criticism from those you barely know. Finally, practice praising others for the good you find in their lives. Don't flatter, just point out your excitement for the good you see. Conversely, allow others to point out the good you do, thank them for acknowledging and participating in those goods, and then praise God for those goods.

St. Augustine struggled with vainglory throughout his life, and here's how he responded to his congregation for their praise of his priestly work among them:

> We have our fellow poor to feed today . . . the rations I provide for you, though, are these words. I lack the means to feed everyone with visible tangible bread. So I feed you on what I am fed on myself. I am just a waiter, I am not the master of the house; I set food before you from the pantry which I too live on, from the Lord's storerooms, from the banquet of the householder who "for our sakes became poor, though he was rich, in order to enrich us from his poverty" (2 Cor 8:9).[30]

Here you can see that he shares the glory with God, genuinely acknowledges that he has some good to offer them, and he praises their sharing of this good with him. He's simultaneously engaged in all three practices mentioned. In the end, "Our goodness is from God and for God. . . . Our goodness is real and really ours, a gift of love from the source of all genuine goodness, which means we need not be slaves to human opinion and falsity and fakery characteristic of vainglory's fearful form."[31] But that's not all, because "our goodness is from him and for him. . . . We can display, celebrate, and share our good gifts with others without the puffed-up-self-promotion of vainglory's prideful form."[32] May we work within our faith communities to become people who radiate proper goodness, love, and beauty on the internet so that light of Christ would shine bright in that space.

Bibliography

Aquinas, Thomas. *On Evil*. Translated by Richard Regan. New York: Oxford University Press, 2003.

30. DeYoung, *Vainglory*, 105.
31. DeYoung, *Vainglory*, 105.
32. DeYoung, *Vainglory*, 105.

Aristotle. *Nicomachean Ethics*. Translated by David Ross. Oxford: Oxford University Press, 1988.

Cassian, John. *The Institutes*. Translated by Boniface Ramsey, O.P. Mahwah: Newmanm, 2000.

DeYoung, Rebecca Konyndyk. *Glittering Vices: A New Look at the Seven Deadly Sins and Their Remedies*. Grand Rapids: Brazos, 2009.

———. *Vainglory: The Forgotten Vice*. Grand Rapids: Eerdmans, 2014.

Foster, Richard. *Freedom of Simplicity: Finding Harmony in a Complex World*. San Francisco: HarperOne, 1973.

Palmer, G. E. H., Philip Sherrard, and Bishop Kallistos Ware, translators. *Philokalia: The Eastern Christian Spiritual Texts*. Woodstock: Skylight Path, 2012.

Pieper, Josef. *The Four Cardinal Virtues*. Translated by Clara Winston et al. Notre Dame: University of Notre Dame Press, 1966.

Plantinga, Alvin. "Letter to a Young Philosopher." Comment, March 1, 2011. https://www.cardus.ca/comment/article/4537/letter-to-a-young-philosopher.

Willard, Dallas. *The Divine Conspiracy: Rediscovering Our Hidden Life in God*. New York: Harper Collins, 1998.

Wright, N. T. *After You Believe: Why Christian Character Matters*. New York: HarperOne, 2010.

6

A Theology of Work for a Virtual Age

Scott B. Rae

Introduction: Changes in the Landscape of Work

Paula is a graphic designer who had been working steadily for her company for the past few years. Her work has received good reviews and she considers herself fairly secure in her job. So it came as quite a surprise when her company announced it was restructuring and that her position was being eliminated. She tried for months to find a new job, unsuccessfully, and eventually decided to try the world of free-lance work. She registered to become an "e-lancer" and worked through a web-based business that brokers a wide variety of free-lance work, connecting companies that need work done with the right people available to take it on.

Others find themselves more intentionally in this new employment arrangement, growing out of a desire to be on their own, with increased flexibility for family (either taking care of children or aging parents) and an overall job market that is still struggling. My son, for example, works as a freelance film editor and director, and he shops his services to production companies. Estimates are that by 2015 there will be close to 15 million fulltime and home based "indies," or independent contractors. When part time workers are included, some estimates suggest that up to 25–30 percent of all American workers are indies. In some areas of California, surveys show that as few as one third of workers actually hold traditional full-time jobs. Companies such as Elance, oDesk, and LiveOps, are just a few of the examples of the numerous brokerages that connect companies and indies.

The trends of outsourcing, downsizing, and advances in technology have all helped to drive the changes in the landscape for work in the past 30+ years. Companies are constantly working to become leaner and more responsive to the pace of change in the marketplace, hiring more temporary teams instead of full-time employees, a trend exacerbated by the Affordable Care Act. We're now seeing companies increasingly keeping employees hours under the 30 hour/week threshold for legally mandated health care benefits. With the dramatic advances in technology, it is now possible to have virtual corporations, and these are becoming more popular in some of the fastest growing and most innovative fields such as telecommunications, biotechnology, and entertainment.

These new arrangements raise new questions about work and how it is regarded by those in the marketplace today. Specifically, what happens to a person's sense of community and identity that is derived, in large part from one's work? Has work become only a means to the end of getting a paycheck and supporting oneself and one's dependents? Or are there ways to appreciate the intrinsic value of work, even in the midst of the more temporary and independent nature of work in a virtual world?

Though it is true that in many areas of the workplace, work is only seen as having instrumental value, a theologically informed view of work would suggest that all legitimate work has more than that—it has intrinsic value, both to God and the community which is served by one's work. To see work in its full theological framework is the place to begin. Then we will apply this framework to some of the trends that the virtual world are bringing to us.

Work was Instituted Before the Entrance of Sin

Work has great value because God ordained it *prior* to the entrance of sin/evil into the world. In the Genesis account of creation, God commanded Adam and Eve to work the garden *before* sin entered the picture (Gen 2:15). God did not condemn human beings to work as a consequence of Adam and Eve's decision to disobey. Work is not a punishment on human beings for their sin. To be sure, work was affected by the Fall, making it more arduous, stressful, and less productive, but that was not the original design (Gen 3:17–19). God's original idea for work was that human beings would spend their lives in productive activity, with regular breaks for leisure, rest, and celebration of God's blessing (Exod 20:8–11). Even in the pre-Fall paradise, God put Adam and Eve to work. Work was a part of God's original design for human beings from the beginning, and because of that it has great value to God.

Work will also be a part of the world in the fullness of God's Kingdom. The prophet Isaiah envisions such a world as one in which nations "will beat their swords into plowshares and their spears into pruning hooks" (Isa 2:4). The obvious point of the passage is to show that universal peace will characterize the kingdom when it is fulfilled. But what often goes unnoticed is that weapons of war will be transformed *into implements of productive work* (plowshares and pruning hooks). That is, there will still be productive work as part of the program when Christ returns to bring his kingdom in its fullness. So work has high value because it was ordained before the Fall and will be a part of life when the kingdom comes in its fullness. In the paradise settings at the beginning and end of human history, God ordains work.

Work and the Dominion Mandate

What makes work so valuable to God is its connection to another mandate from creation, the command to exercise dominion over the earth. God both commanded and empowered human beings to be responsible stewards over creation (Gen 1:28). They were to function as trustees of the earth, its resources, and the environment. They had authority over creation to use it for their benefit, and responsibility for managing creation for the common good. The Bible is clear that God embedded his wisdom into the creation (Prov 8:22–36) in order to enable human beings to more effectively exercise dominion.[1] God makes his wisdom known through the world, in part, by means of general revelation and common grace. For example, technologies and other discoveries that improve the lot of human beings and help alleviate the effects of the entrance of sin are the result of God's common grace to human beings. They are utilizing God's common grace to fulfill the mandate to exercise responsible dominion over creation with greater effectiveness.

In the Genesis account, human beings are given the opportunity and responsibility to be trustees over creation. The means by which human beings would fulfill their obligation as stewards over creation was, in part, through work. Adam and Eve worked the garden in order to reap its fruits

---

1. The Bible is also clear on the notion that God also uses creation to proclaim His glory (Ps 19).

and put it to their productive use. In doing so, they were fulfilling the dominion mandate of Gen 1:28. The other means by which they would fulfill this mandate was through procreation, by establishing a human community that together would serve as trustees over creation.

Work is intricately bound up with the dominion mandate over creation. God ordained work so that human beings could fulfill one of the primary roles for which they were created. Work is not something that we do just to get by, or to finance our lifestyles. It is not a necessary evil that will be done away with at some point. Work is not what we do just so that we can enjoy our leisure. Work has great dignity because it is the way God arranged for human beings to fulfill a part of their destiny on earth, that of exercising responsible stewardship over creation. That mandate is still in effect today and God is still empowering human beings to be effective trustees of his world. Thus, work has substantial value because of its connection to the dominion mandate. Adam and Eve were doing God's work in the world by tending the garden and doing their part to be responsible trustees over creation. We do God's work in the world in our jobs because our vocations are connected with the task assigned to all human beings to exercise dominion over the world.

Some use the term co-creation to describe how our work fits with the dominion mandate and to indicate the nobility of work.[2] Though the view we argue for here has much in common with this notion of co-creation, namely that it involves "working with and under God to care for the creation,"[3] the term may be somewhat misleading. British novelist Dorothy Sayers suggests that our work is a "medium of divine creation," appearing to make it analogous to God's original creation.[4] Some might conclude that this is far too high a view of human beings in the process of creation care. We would suggest that we *cooperate* with God in the advance of his dominion over the creation, which after the Genesis account of the Fall also involves alleviating the effects of the entrance of sin (evil) into the world.

To be sure, work seems to have lost much of its original dignity. The brokenness of the world results in jobs being dehumanizing, alienating, and actually destroying creation instead of protecting and restoring it. Sin made most work a mixed blessing, a way to honor God but fraught with numerous

---

2. Meilander, *Working*, 2–6.
3. Meilander, *Working*, 2.
4. Quoted in Meilander, *Working*, 45. However, we concur with much of Sayers's view of the intrinsic value of work, based on human beings being made in God's image.

and varied possibilities for wrong-doing.[5] In addition, instead of work always being fulfilling and enjoyable, it became arduous and stressful.

Sin brought a profound change in the nature of work. It brought alienation, from one's work and the process of work, in which people feel that they are simply cogs in a corporate machine. It brought a sense of frustration to work, in which a person's hard work could amount to little. And it brought a sense of corruption by introducing work that is degrading and dehumanizing, which tarnishes the image of God in human beings. Sin also brings ethical dilemmas and temptations to cut corners to the workplace. Sin brought about industries and businesses that contribute nothing to the common good. Sin also introduced the prospect for work to be a mixed blessing too, with some beneficial aspects combined with significant social and personal costs.

So far, I have focused on how work and the dominion mandate relates to the order of creation. But how might it relate to the order of redemption, or to the new creation that God is in the process of bringing? Theologian Miroslav Volf has extended the idea of the work and the dominion mandate to give it an eschatological dimension.[6] He sees work as one of the places where you can use your spiritual gifts, bringing a pneumatological component to work. He suggests that the New Testament idea of spiritual gifts is not limited to what he calls "ecclesiastical activity," or those activities that we commonly refer to as church work. Volf argues that in the New Testament era, God has "gifted" individuals to prepare his people for works of service (Eph 4:11–12, 1 Cor 12:7), both for the church and for the common good, and that those works of service cannot be limited to those that occur within the boundaries of the church. Thus, all of the people of God are gifted by the Spirit for specific works of service, both in the church and in the world, of which work is a primary arena. We cooperate with the Spirit in work, analogous to how we cooperate with the Spirit in the rest of our spiritual lives. Volf extends this notion by arguing that the Spirit "who imparts gifts and acts through them is a guarantee (2 Cor. 1:22; cf. Rom. 8:23) of the realization of the eschatological new creation."[7] If this is true, then work is actually cooperation with God in his eschatological transformation of the

---

5. See Grudem's work for more discussion of this point. He argues that business is both a means to honor God and a source of temptation, as a result of both the original goodness of work and the reality of sin affecting work. See e.g., Grudem, *Business for the Glory of God*.

6. Volf, *Work in the Spirit*, 114–18.

7. Volf, *Work in the Spirit*, 115.

new creation. Volf summarizes it like this: "As Christians do their mundane work, the Spirit enables them to cooperate with God in the kingdom of God that completes creation and renews heaven and earth."[8] Thus, work is not only a fulfillment of the dominion mandate, but also an act of cooperative service with God in the transformation of the world. In other words, work is transformational service to God in His new creation too.

God as a Worker

Thus, work has nobility because it was created before the entrance of sin and is the means by which we cooperate with God in the exercise of dominion over the creation. But a more foundational reason for the value of work exists, namely the fact that God is a worker and human beings are workers by virtue of being made in God's image. In other words, we work because that's who God is and who we are in his image. Of course, God is much more than a worker and so are we. But God mandates work because that's a part of who he is and part of who he made us to be in his image.

Look carefully at the way God is portrayed when it comes to work. One of the first portraits of God in Genesis is as a worker, fashioning the world in His wisdom. God is portrayed as a creative God in Gen 1–2, with initiative, ingenuity, passion for creation, and innovation all included as a part of his work in creation. God is portrayed with what we might call "entrepreneurial" traits in Gen 1–2. From the beginning of the biblical account, God is presented as engaged in productive activity in fashioning and sustaining the world. He is portrayed as creating good from the beginning of creation. At the end of the creation account, Gen 2:2 gives the Sabbath model as a day for God to rest "from *all his work.*" God blessed the Sabbath because "he rested from *all the work of creating* that he had done" (Gen 2:3). The pattern for the Sabbath was to rest because God rested (Exod 20:11), and conversely, to work because God worked in creation (Exod 20:9). The pattern for creation became the pattern for human beings. They worked six days as God did, and rested one day as God did. We work to create good because it is part of what it means to be made in God's image and to be like him. Whenever human beings work to create good, they are imitating God, who fundamentally creates good in all he does.

The poetic and wisdom literature describe the process of God's work in creation guided by wisdom (Prov 8:22–31). The Psalmist describes the

---

8. Volf, *Work in the Spirit*, 115.

work of God in creation as the pattern for His ongoing work of providing for the world (Ps 104). He refers to God's past work in creation and the flood (Ps 104:4–9), then praises God for His work in taking care of His creation (Ps 104:10–31). God is the one who provides water and food for both animals and human beings, giving them stable sources of sustenance and security in his world. The psalmist summarizes this putting it this way, "the earth is satisfied by *the fruit of his work*" (Ps 104:13). The psalm ends with the phrase, "may the Lord rejoice *in all his works*" (Ps 104:31). God is seen as a God who works diligently to care for his creation—that's a significant part of who he is. As people made in his image, that is a significant part of whom we are too.

This theme is carried on through the New Testament. In one of Jesus' many disputes with the religious leaders, Jesus heals a man on the Sabbath and receives heavy criticism for violating the Pharisees' traditions about the Sabbath, though not the Sabbath command itself. Jesus makes this remarkable statement that further inflamed the religious leaders when he said, "My father is *always at his work* to this very day, and I, too, am working (John 5:17). Jesus teaches that God is continually at work doing his work in the world, accomplishing His purposes. Further, Paul affirms that Jesus is both the creator and sustainer of the creation today, similar to the description of God in the Old Testament (Col 1:15–17). It is a part of who he is. We work because that's who God is, and whom we are as made in His image. Dorothy Sayers put it this way: "work is the natural exercise and function of man—the creature who is made in the image of his Creator. Work is not, primarily, a thing one does to live, but the thing one lives to do."[9] Or as Chuck Colson puts it, "We are indeed 'hardwired' for work," by virtue of being made in God's image.[10]

Work is immensely valuable to God because it was instituted before the Fall into sin, it is the means by which human beings partner with God in exercising dominion over the world, and it is a fundamental part of who God is and who we are as creatures made in His image. This is why Ecclesiastes can proclaim the goodness of work in the following ways: "A man can do nothing better than to eat and drink and *find satisfaction in all his work*. This too, I see, is from the hand of God, for without him, who can eat or find enjoyment?" (Eccl 2:24–25); "That everyone may eat

---

9. Sayers, *Creed or Chaos?*, 72–73.

10. Colson and Fickett, *Good Life*, 89. See also Stevens, *Other Six Days*; Stevens, *Doing God's Business*; Grudem, *Business for the Glory of God*.

and drink, and *find satisfaction in all his toil*—this is the gift of God" (Eccl 3:13); "So I saw that there is nothing better for a man *than to enjoy his work*, because that is his lot" (Eccl 3:22); "Then I realized that it is good and proper for a man to eat and drink, *and to find satisfaction in his toilsome labor* under the sun during the few days of life God has given him—for this is his lot. Moreover, when God gives any man wealth and possessions, and enables him to enjoy them, to accept his lot and *be happy in his work*—this is a gift of God." (Eccl 5:18–19).[11]

All legitimate work has great value to God, and no valid occupation has any more value to God than any other. There is no hierarchy of vocations in God's economy. The work of the plumber, child care worker, salesperson, executive, auto mechanic, and the pastor are all of great value to God because in their work they are fulfilling the dominion mandate over creation and expressing the image of God.

Work as Service to God

Regardless of how it feels, the Bible teaches that your work can be an aspect of your service to God in the world. The building site for the construction worker, the day care center for the day care worker, the office for the administrative assistant, the classroom for the teacher, the pulpit for the pastor, the laboratory for the scientist, and the restaurant for the chef are all places where people offer themselves in service to God. All valid work is sacred to God and is a place of sacred service to Him. This is the point Paul was making in his charge to believers in the workplace when he said, " *whatever you do*, work at it with all your heart, as working for the Lord, not for men. . . . It is the Lord Christ you are serving" (Col 3:23). It's important to note that the context of Paul's teaching here is that of slavery—encouraging slaves to render faithful service to their masters because they were ultimately serving Christ. That is, they were serving Christ in the mundane, menial work to which slaves were assigned. Even in the dreary and monotonous work of slaves, they were serving Christ.

You serve Christ by doing your work faithfully and with excellence. The plumber serves Christ when he/she fixes leaky pipes; the stockbroker serves Christ when giving investment advice; the waitress serves Christ when serving food; the missionary serves Christ on the mission field; the

---

11. Ecclesiastes also proclaims the vanity of work, due to the impact of sin. Work is a mixed blessing, involving both satisfaction and pain (Eccl 2:17–23).

health care professional serves Christ in the hospital, doctor's office or dental chair; and the software engineer serves Christ at the computer terminal. Paul said that in whatever you do for your work, you are serving Christ. No one serves Christ more or less in one job or another.

Your work can well be part of your ministry in the world. In fact, the word "ministry" is most often translated "service." To have a ministry simply means to be in service to God. The term "ministry" comes from the Greek word *diakonia* which is translated "service," and our word "deacon" is derived from that term. In the New Testament, some of the first people who were described as having a *diakonia* (in Acts 6) were the ones who freed up the apostles to preach, teach, and pray. Do you know what their *ministry* was? Waiting on tables for the widows in the community. It doesn't sound very "spiritual," but it was, and it was an important part of the ministry of the early church. If you're in business, your work may serve as an altar: a part of your service to God, or your ministry. It is not your entire ministry, since you're also called to serve God in the church, in your neighborhood, and around the world. But ministry does not stand in contrast to business. Business is ministry, part of the work of God in the world. All of us are in *full-time* ministry, if we are followers of Christ, and we entered full-time service/ministry at the time we came to faith. We all serve God full-time, whether it's in the world, in the church, or on the mission field. These are simply different arenas of service, all of which have significant value to God.

This is what Tom Chappell discovered during his Sabbatical from his business. He founded the company, *Tom's of Maine*, a personal care products company. He was quite successful, but as a Christian, he had a nagging sense that there ought to be more that he could do with his life. So he took a year off from his business and decided to do something very different. He enrolled as a student at Harvard Divinity School in an attempt to "find his calling." At the end of the year of study, he came away convinced that business was his calling and he went back to his business with a fresh perspective and a new desire to pursue his business to "work at it with all your heart, as working for the Lord, not men, since . . . it is the Lord Christ you are serving" (Col 3:23). He realized that running his company was a sacred task, for which God had gifted him and was using him to make a difference in the world.[12]

---

12. See Chappell, *Soul of a Business*.

Application to Work in a Virtual Age

The "virtualization" of work would seem to have some obvious benefits, such as unprecedented flexibility for employees and indies to order their lives and balance work and other priorities, primarily family. Further, it provides increased freedom of mobility and geographic freedom, as it matters less where contractors live if they can connect virtually to their employers and clients. In addition, it lowers costs for employers and can raise productivity if managed properly.

This restructuring of work increasingly turns employees/contractors into a "workforce of one." People are increasingly working more on their own and the virtual teams that are formed comprise a different sort of community than the traditional workplace. The daily interaction with co-workers is of a different sort, and the sense of identity and belongingness is different. Workplace relationships are more tenuous and temporary, and the sense of belongingness may come more from the organizations that network these contractors, somewhat akin to guilds. For many workers, they realize that they must forego meaningful community in the workspace, and find it elsewhere. Some would suggest that this is a more stable alternative, but it seems clear that the sense of identity and community that were traditionally drawn from the workplace are more fragile today. Work can become less a source of a person's identity and more a means of simply earning a living, possessing a merely instrumental value. It seems to me that one of the risks of work in this changing environment is this very possibility in which the intrinsic value of our work is lost, thus reducing work to its instrumental value only.

Others have been more critical of aspects of the virtual world of work. For example, in his 2003 book entitled *The New Ruthless Economy*, Simon Head argued that the increasing virtualization of the workplace was, in part, responsible for income stagnation of workers, even as productivity was increasing. Head further argues that the increased technological monitoring of all of workplace life, what he calls the "industrialization of white collar work," created a virtual assembly line in many workplaces providing a digital way of applying the turn of the 20th century "scientific management" practices to many workplaces. He cites specifically the examples of call centers and medical practices, and how many service industries have utilized technology to reengineer themselves.[13] The result in the domain of

---

13. See Head, *New Ruthless Economy*, 80–99 and 117–52.

health services has been that even the practice of medicine has been made into a type of work that is focused on repetitive tasks. This trend toward depersonalizing the workplace has troubling aspects to it and merits continual scrutiny as work continues to adapt to the virtual age.

Regardless of challenges and benefits of the virtualization of work, theologically it's important to hold on to the intrinsic value of all legitimate work as part of one's service to Christ.

Bibliography

Chappell, Tom. *The Soul of a Business: Managing for Profit and the Common Good*. New York: Bantam, 1993.

Colson, Charles W., and Harold Fickett. *The Good Life: Seeking Purpose, Meaning and Truth in Your Life*. Carol Stream, IL: Tyndale, 2005.

Grudem, Wayne. *Business for the Glory of God: The Bible's Teaching on the Moral Goodness of Business*. Wheaton, IL: Crossway, 2003.

Head, Simon. *The New Ruthless Economy: Work and Power in the Digital Age*. New York: Oxford University Press, 2005.

Meilander, Gilbert, ed. *Working: Its Meaning and Limits*. Notre Dame: University of Notre Dame Press, 2000.

Sayers, Dorothy. *Creed or Chaos?* Manchester: Sophia, 1974.

Stevens, Paul R. *Doing God's Business: Meaning and Motivation for the Marketplace*. Grand Rapids: Eerdmans, 2006.

———. *The Other Six Days*. Grand Rapids: Eerdmans, 2000.

Volf, Miroslav. *Work in the Spirit: Toward a Theology of Work*. New York: Oxford University Press, 1991.

7

Mark's Jesus and the Internet

Exegetical Reflections on Authority, Identity, and Community

JEN GILBERTSON

Introduction

While working on my PhD at the University of St Andrews, I was privileged to live in the coastal medieval town of St. Andrews. As a farm girl from the landlocked prairies of Canada, the excitement of living next to the North Sea never waned for me so I aimed daily during my Scottish life to "see the sea." A quick walk through the cathedral ruins and I was at East Sands, walking the beach or the pier, gazing intently at the waves of the North Sea. Over the years, I became familiar with this small stretch of the sea. I knew how the waves would crash or swirl against the pier. I knew where and when to look for the sea glass and pottery that the waves deposited on the sand, and I wondered why razor clam shells are strewn across West Sands, but not East. I learned about the tides and got a sense of how the currents flowed. If I went too many days in the office without some time at the coast, I would start to feel a bit trapped. One quick walk along East Sands would put me back to rights.

Yet, for all the time I spent at East Sands, I know very little about the North Sea: its creatures, its shipping lanes, its ecology, its physics, its coastlines on other nations, or even its history. All I can offer is a perspective from my limited vantage point.

My relationship with East Sands is analogous to my relationship with the internet. I use it every single day for communication, research, and entertainment, and I feel unsettled whenever I do not have access to it. Yet despite my daily dependence on the internet, as I researched for this article, I was quickly overwhelmed by not only my naiveté but also the diversity, quality, and quantity of topics concerning the internet and human society. As I read articles which touched on everything from coding to religion to sociology to mental health to media theory, I found myself intrigued but completely overwhelmed. How can I, a biblical scholar whose research has focused on the Gospel of Mark, offer an intelligent, informed, and helpful addition to the emerging and established discussions about the internet?

As I researched, I noticed that in discussions of the internet and religion certain areas of concern emerge repeatedly. As Anna Neumaier comments, "a specific canon seems to have been established with regard to the possible fields of research on religion and the internet. Current research questions focus mainly on the topics of authority, community, identity, and sometimes ritual or authenticity."[1] These topics are, of course, not new, but longstanding areas of human concern. Moreover, many are themes which run through the Bible, and thus, as a biblical scholar, I am equipped to address them.

Therefore, from my vantage point as a Markan scholar, what I offer in this article is a discussion of three currents in internet research—authority, identity, and community— which also run through Mark's presentation of Jesus and his ministry. My aim is to illustrate how biblical exegesis can inform Christian thinking and practice in the twenty-first century context in which the internet has become an integral facet of the everyday.

Method

Below, I examine in turn each of my three themes (authority, identity, and community) through a three-part discussion. First, I discuss aspects of each theme as they are presented in research on the internet and religion. In this section, I draw on the insights of established researchers, relying primarily on the respective thematic chapters in the 2012 volume *Digital Religion: Understanding Religious Practice in New Media Worlds*, edited by Heidi A. Campbell, as my points of entry into the discussion of internet

---

1. Neumaier, "Because Faith Is a Personal Matter," 442. For examples of research conducted along these lines, see her fn. 5.

and religion.² My purpose in this step is to introduce the broad emphases that are prevalent in these discussions and researchers' observations about Christian internet practices and mindsets.

Second, I trace how each theme is presented in the depiction of Jesus and his ministry in the Gospel of Mark. Through a narrative reading of Mark, I sketch how such features as characterization, plot, imagery, and repetition develop each theme.

Third, I offer a reflection on how the Markan development of each theme intersects with or challenges the prevalent tendencies and patterns identified by research on the internet and religion. My purpose here is not to critique research but rather to foster Christian thinking with a biblical imagination. If Christians are "people of the book," how can the Gospel of Mark shape Christian thought and praxis in a world where the internet is now a facet of everyday reality? What questions arise when our internet culture is observed through the lens of Mark's Gospel?

Authority

The Theme of Authority in Research

The topic of authority attracts persistent attention in discussions of religion and the internet. On the internet, religious authority can be manifested in different forms, depending on the context. Pauline Hope Cheong notes that it "can be vested or constructed, constituted from various perspectives referring to a range of thinking on divinely related control and influence, to exact obedience, judge, govern, and make consequential pronouncements."³ Within the broad notion of religious authority, Heidi Campbell differentiates four layers: hierarchy, structure, ideology and text.⁴

In her overview of the topic of religious authority in internet studies, Cheong observes two predominant logics in operation. First, she notes that "the dominant logic, inspired by initial studies of internet research, is that religious authority is eroded by online religious activities."⁵ With

---

2. In Campbell, *Digital Religion*, see Cheong, "Authority," 72–87; Lövheim, "Identity," 41–56; and Campbell, "Community," 57–71.

3. Cheong, "Authority," in Campbell, *Digital Religion*, 74.

4. See Campbell, "Who's Got the Power?," 1043–62; Campbell, "Religious Authority," 251–76. I am aware that in this article, I am appealing to the authority of the *text* of Mark as Christian Scripture.

5. Cheong, "Authority," in Campbell, *Digital Religion*, 74.

the proliferation of information and choice on the internet, traditional authorities are challenged or displaced. Instead of having to rely on traditional leaders, nonprofessionals acquire greater access to information, including "potentially oppositional information" that may weaken the credibility of the traditional religious leaders and allow "schismatic leaders to emerge."[6] The structure of authority is also altered with the creation of new authoritative figures such as webmasters.[7] In sum, "religious interpretation, texts, ecclesiastical structures, and the importance of positions like webmasters and forum moderators (all framed as components of religious authority) are changed by online communication and the capabilities of the internet to expand resource access, facilitate new ritual practices, and support new positions of power."[8]

In contrast to this dominant perspective, Cheong notes a second logic, one of continuity in which online practices relate to religious authority through "connectedness, succession, and negotiation."[9] According to this logic, local authorities may exercise control over online practices through surveillance or censorship, or online activity may serve to affirm the local authority.[10] The role of clergy changes as well, with ministry expansion into social media and a shifting of roles from "commanders and sage to guides and mediators of knowledge" in both online and offline contexts.[11]

In both logics, the internet alters how religious authority is perceived and received, even in offline contexts. Indeed, "the internet facilitates both the weakening and strengthening of religious authority, offering possibilities for conflict, yet also for understanding and accommodation."[12]

The Theme of Authority in Mark

Authority is also an important issue in the Gospel of Mark, the one at the root of Jesus's conflict with his chief opponents, the scribes.[13] The scribes are the most prominent Jewish group in Mark. They are mentioned more

6. Cheong, "Authority," in Campbell, *Digital Religion*, 76.
7. Cheong, "Authority," in Campbell, *Digital Religion*, 78.
8. Cheong, "Authority," in Campbell, *Digital Religion*, 78.
9. Cheong, "Authority," in Campbell, *Digital Religion*, 78.
10. Cheong, "Authority," in Campbell, *Digital Religion*, 79–80.
11. Cheong, "Authority," in Campbell, *Digital Religion*, 80–81.
12. Cheong, "Authority," in Campbell, *Digital Religion*, 82.
13. Cf. Schams, *Jewish Scribes*, 150; Lührmann, "Pharisäer und Schriftgelehrte," 185.

than anyone else (their name, γραμματεύς, occurs 21 times in contrast to 12 mentions of the Pharisees and a single reference to the Sadducees), and they are portrayed "in contrast or in conflict with Jesus" more than anyone else (eighteen occasions compared with nine for the Pharisees).[14] The scribes are also Jesus's first and last human opponents (1:22; 15:31), opposing Jesus both in Galilee and in the temple and ultimately participating in his trial. The scribes thus provide the frame for Jesus's conflict with the Jewish leadership.

The consistent point of contention between Jesus and his most consistent opponents is *authority*. The Greek word for authority, ἐξουσία, first appears in Mark in the account of Jesus's first mighty deed, the exorcism in the Capernaum synagogue (1:22–28). Jesus is teaching in the synagogue on the Sabbath, and Mark 1:22 sets up the contrast between Jesus and the scribes by describing the people's reaction to Jesus: "They were astounded at his teaching, for he taught them as one having *authority*, and not as the scribes" (emphasis added).[15] Jesus then casts an unclean spirit out of a man, and the crowd's reaction is narrated again: "They were all amazed, and they kept on asking one another, 'What is this? A new teaching—with *authority*! He commands even the unclean spirits and they obey him" (1:27; emphasis added).

Several aspects of this passage are pertinent to our discussion of authority. First, Jesus possesses the authority the scribes lack. This is a paradigmatic contrast that, as we shall see below, recurs in Jesus's interactions with the scribes. Second, the crowd recognizes his authority. Third, this is an authority in word and deed. Jesus is teaching (word) and the way his authority is manifest is through liberating a man possessed by an unclean spirit (deed). His exercise of authority is therefore redemptive: it brings freedom from the bondage of possession.

Jesus's authority is at issue again in 2:1–12, the healing of the paralytic. When Jesus pronounces the paralytic's sins forgiven, the scribes consider Jesus's words as blasphemy for he is presuming to do something only God can do (2:5–7). Jesus responds by prompting the paralytic to arise "so that you [the scribes] may know that the Son of Man has authority on earth to forgive sins" (2:10). Once again, Jesus's authority is established through his words and deeds, and this time he frees the man from his sin and his paralysis.

---

14. Pickup, "Matthew's and Mark's Pharisees," 73.
15. All Scripture citations are taken from the New Revised Standard Version.

The next two uses of ἐξουσία further underscore Jesus's authority for not only does he possess authority, he is also the one who bestows authority to his disciples (3:15; 6:7; cf. 13:34). Thus, Mark portrays Galilean fisherman as authoritative while the scribes are not. Note again where this authority is directed: the disciples are appointed "to have authority to cast out demons" (3:15) and they are sent out with "authority over the unclean spirits" (6:7). As an extension of Jesus's ministry, the disciples also exercise his liberating authority.

Jesus's conflict with the scribes over authority culminates in Jerusalem following his action in the temple (11:15–19). Now in the company of the chief priests and the elders, the scribes question Jesus about the source of his authority (11:27–33). Jesus's response is a question: is John's baptism from heaven or from humans? (11:31), and the leaders refuse to answer and feign ignorance (11:33–34). Jesus next condemns them by telling the parable of the tenants against them (12:1–12). This final confrontation about authority highlights that Jesus's authority is divine. He is on God's side, and his unauthoritative opponents are not.

In sum, authority in Mark is God-given. Jesus is the one who teaches with authority and the one who bestows authority, especially the authority to cast out demons. Thus, authority involves word and deed, and brings about freedom and redemption.

Reflections on Authority

The Markan portrait of Jesus's authority should give pause to those who follow the first logic identified by Cheong and fear the weakening of traditional authority because of online activities. In Mark, the ones who were traditionally the authoritative ones and are threatened by Jesus's exercise of authority are the scribes. They are the ones who question Jesus's authority and who refuse to recognize it as divine. This is not to say that everyone who is concerned with maintaining authority online can be equated with Jesus's enemies, the Markan scribes, but rather it is to say that such concerns are fodder for contemplation. In Mark's Gospel, divine authority is distributed in surprising ways. Indeed, such ordinary people as Galilean fishermen were bestowed with God's authority! This narrative detail suggests that traditional Christian leaders need humility for discussing and exercising authority online because divine authority might not look as one would expect. Also, recognition and popularity cannot serve as verification of authority. Both can be short-term and fickle responses. The crowds may have recognized Jesus's authority (1:22, 27), but by the end of Mark the crowds demand his death (15:13–14).

Moreover, the portrait of Jesus's authority challenges many conceptions of what it means to exercise authority. We noted above that Jesus's authority in teaching is revealed through his exorcisms and healings. Jesus's authority in word and deed brought about redemption and restoration. In exercising or promoting authority online, does one's deeds line up with their actions? Does the use of authority bring healing and forgiveness? Is it an authority motivated to serve (10:45)? Is it a liberating authority that welcomes people into the kingdom of God?

Identity

The Theme of Identity in Research

In her article on "Identity," Mia Lövheim notes that a central concern in studies of identity and the internet is the "relations between the offline context in which individuals live their everyday life and the ways in which they use digital media," and religion finds its place in this discussion as a "core dimension" of identity.[16] As internet use rapidly increased, the focus of research shifted from discussions of disembodiment and identity expression "to how the internet is embedded in everyday life."[17] It is recognized that the ubiquity of the internet no longer allows for a sharp online/offline distinction. Areas of research include identity formation through self-representation and performance online, changes in how authentic identity is understood, and the consequences of constant connected presence.[18]

The research on identity, religion, and the internet can be divided into three waves. The first, largely speculative wave focused on the plurality of religious options online with the potential for individuals to "pick-and-mix their religious identities," and on how the disembodied nature of online communication could permit an individual fluid and multiple religious identities.[19] The second wave, in contrast to the first, brought in critical empirical studies and established the connection between online and offline

---

16. Lövheim, "Identity," in Campbell, *Digital Religion*, 41.
17. Lövheim, "Identity," in Campbell, *Digital Religion*, 44.
18. Lövheim, "Identity," in Campbell, *Digital Religion*, 44–45.
19. Lövheim, "Identity," in Campbell, *Digital Religion*, 45–46.

religiosity. For example, most people engaging in religious activity online were still active in offline community, and online interaction usually occurs "within already established offline social networks."[20] This "integration of digital media into everyday life and existing social networks, and the convergence of media forms also meant the emergence of new individual uses of the internet for forming and representing religious identities."[21] The third wave then explores "religious identities online as integrated into everyday life," picking up on such themes as how individuals participate in religious practices and narratives as producers, how "religious individuals using digital media take part in the reshaping of technology to fit their values and lifestyle," and "how digital media enable individuals to integrate religious aspects of their identity into other spheres of everyday life and to mediate between traditional and/or culturally specific values, identities and norms, and those promoted by a neoliberal consumer culture."[22]

Religious identity online should be studied as a part of religious identity in general in contemporary culture, in which "religious identities are formed around the individual autobiography rather than geographical space or a particular religious affiliation." Because digital media provides "a new form of social infrastructure for the individual's religion" through the network, Lövheim concludes, "religious identity in modern society is still a social thing, deeply anchored in the social situations and relations individuals want and need to stay connected to in order to find meaning and act in everyday life."[23]

The Theme of Identity in Mark

In Mark, Jesus's strongest statements about identity are found in the context of discipleship. After the first passion and resurrection prediction (8:27–30) and Peter's rebuke of Jesus because his mind is "not on divine things but on human things," Jesus explicates the cost of discipleship in a passage that emphasizes one's life or soul (ψυχή).

> If any want to become my followers, let them deny themselves (ἑαυτόν) and take up their cross and follow me. For those who

---

20. Lövheim, "Identity," in Campbell, *Digital Religion*, 46.
21. Lövheim, "Identity," in Campbell, *Digital Religion*, 48.
22. Lövheim, "Identity," in Campbell, *Digital Religion*, 49.
23. Lövheim, "Identity," in Campbell, *Digital Religion*, 52.

> want to save their life (τὴν ψυχήν) will lose it, and those who lose their life (τὴν ψυχήν) *for my sake*, and *for the sake of the gospel*, will save it. For what will it profit them to gain the whole world and forfeit their life (τὴν ψυχήν)? Indeed, what can they give in return for their life (τῆς ψυχῆς)?[24]

In this teaching, Jesus portrays self-denial as a key feature of discipleship. Rather than self-motivation, the disciple follows Jesus, losing his ψυχή for the sake of Jesus and the gospel (cf. 10:29–30). This strong statement expresses two recurrent themes in Mark: following Jesus and self-sacrifice. These two attributes are key features of the identity of a disciple in Mark and are developed elsewhere in Mark's story, as we shall see below.

The repeated call in Jesus's ministry is "Follow me" (1:17; 2:14; 10:21; 8:33).[25] Thus, Jesus places himself at the center as he proclaims the kingdom of God. The centrality of Jesus is at the fore when he appoints twelve to be his disciples. Two purposes are given: "to be with him" and "to be sent" in order to proclaim the gospel and to have authority over the unclean spirits (3:14–15). The important thing to note for the purposes of this study is that a primary aspect of apostleship is *being* with Jesus.

Following Jesus and self-sacrifice are often intertwined in Jesus's teaching on discipleship as they are on the way to Jerusalem. In response to the disciples' argument about who is the greatest among them, Jesus first responds with an adage about self-sacrificial discipleship: "Whoever wants to be first must be last of all and servant of all" (9:35). Then, his words after hugging a child connect servanthood with following him: "Whoever welcomes one such child in my name welcomes me, and whoever welcomes me welcomes not me but the one who sent me" (9:37). Thus, 9:33–37 resonates with the concerns of 8:34–37.

A similar teaching to the disciples comes after James and John request exalted positions (10:35–40) and the other disciples take umbrage (10:41). Jesus corrects them, stating that they are not to be power-hungry like the Gentile rulers. Instead, "whoever wishes to be great among you must be your servant, and whoever wishes to be first among you must be slave of all. For the Son of Man came not to be served but to serve, and

---

24. Mark 8:34–37, emphasis added.

25. When Jesus rebukes Peter in 8:33 by saying, "Get behind me, Satan!" (ὕπαγε ὀπίσω μου), the language evokes Peter's initial call in 1:17 (δεῦτε ὀπίσω μου). Jesus then explains the true nature of following him (8:34). This indicates that 8:33 should be understood as "a rebuke and a recall to adopt the correct posture of a true disciple" (Whitaker, "Rebuke or Recall?," 673).

to give his life a ransom for many" (10:43–45). Once again, Jesus stresses servanthood and sets himself as the model of self-giving service which they are to follow. This is in essence the same message he gives the rich man whom he counsels to give up his wealth in order to help the poor and then follow Jesus (10:21).

In sum, Mark 8:34–37 offers Jesus's strongest statements on the self, characterizing the life of the disciple as one of following Jesus and of self-denial for Jesus's sake. Disciples are to be Jesus-centered and others-focused, two characteristics illustrated and affirmed elsewhere in Mark's story of Jesus.

Reflections on Identity

The way that identity is formed in contemporary society, in which the internet is embedded in everyday life, focuses on the autobiography. The self is at the center, making individual choices about self-representation and how to integrate facets of life.

Like contemporary identity, the identity of a disciple of Jesus is not defined by geography. Yet, apart from that similarity, the identity of the disciple (as delineated by Mark's Jesus) is starkly different from contemporary understandings of identity. For disciples of Jesus, it is *Jesus himself*—not one's personal autobiography—that takes center stage. The disciple is defined by following Jesus. Instead of self-representation, there is a self-denial, motivated by Jesus and the gospel, which is manifest in service. The disciple's identity is found not in herself but in relation to Jesus.

The gap between these two forms of identity—that of a disciple and the one current in online/offline society—necessitates intentionality on the part of the disciple because social media and contemporary culture foster a self-centered approach to identity formation. Intentionality and awareness is required to counteract the identity trends identified in the research. Therefore, some key questions to consider are: How can Christians engage in a culture pervaded by the internet in such a way that exemplifies servanthood? What does social media look like when the motivation is not self-gratification but is others-focused? What does it mean to follow Jesus as a self-denying servant in an online context?

Community

The Theme of Community in Research

Heidi A. Campbell's overview of community in studies of religion and the internet highlights how the "internet's ability to facilitate and mediate social relations has shifted many people's notions of friendship, relationship, and community in an age of networked, digital communities."[26] Whether authentic "community" is possible online is debated. Yet, the fact remains that people *are* connecting online, and that "while the space of interaction may have changed, the basic act of social exchange has not."[27] Campbell characterizes the study of religious community online in three waves. The first was descriptive and "helped identify the variety of expressions of religious community emerging online and reflect on how online practices could create an online version of an online faith tradition."[28] The second offered a critical analysis, defining the relationship of online and offline community. This wave established that, by and large, "online religious community is not a substitute, but rather a supplement to extend offline relationships and communication in unique and novel ways."[29] The third wave marks a more theoretical and interpretive turn, locating the study of online community within the study of life in "an information-dominated culture."[30] For example, research illustrates that people are involved in online community "in order to meet specific relational needs," but, because online community does not fulfill the need for embodied, face-to-face contact, they remain involved in online religious activity.[31]

In this overview, Campbell stresses that online community involvement can shape members' conception of what offline community entails. The dominant metaphor is the network, which now describes online and offline social connections: each person has a "personalized network of connections."[32] Campbell explains, "Rather than operating as tightly bounded social structures, they function as loose social networks with

---

26. Campbell, "Community," in Campbell, *Digital Religion*, 57.
27. Campbell, "Community," in Campbell, *Digital Religion*, 59.
28. Campbell, "Community," in Campbell, *Digital Religion*, 61.
29. Campbell, "Community," in Campbell, *Digital Religion*, 62–63.
30. Campbell, "Community," in Campbell, *Digital Religion*, 63.
31. Campbell, "Community," in Campbell, *Digital Religion*, 63.
32. Campbell, "Community," in Campbell, *Digital Religion*, 64.

varying levels of religious affiliation and commitment."[33] Community is no longer based on geographic proximity. Rather, "the logic of the network is replacing notions of place-based community, shaping how religious community is perceived as well as how it is understood to function in the twenty-first century."[34]

The Theme of Community in Mark

The dominant image which governs how community is understood in the Gospel of Mark is the kingdom of God. The kingdom of God is a central theme in Jesus's ministry and teaching. His programmatic opening sermon encapsulates the good news: "The time is fulfilled, and the kingdom of God has come near; repent, and believe in the good news" (1:15).[35] Repeatedly, his teaching emphasizes the kingdom of God (9:1, 47; 10:14–15, 23–35; 12:34; 14:25). The kingdom figures most prominently in his parables (4:11, 26, 30), so much so that commentators argue that even where the terminology of "kingdom of God" is absent, the concept is not. Therefore, all the parables are about the kingdom.[36] As we have seen in our survey of identity in Mark, Jesus's ministry in announcing the kingdom of God calls the disciples to follow Jesus and to deny themselves.

Throughout Mark, as Jesus teaches and heals, he transforms communities. For example, he eats with sinners and tax collectors, an action which elicits the scrutiny of the scribes of the Pharisees (2:15–16). He responds, "Those who are well have no need of a physician, but those who are sick; I have come to call not the righteous but sinners." In this case, Jesus is associating with people who are generally seen as undesirable, including them in fellowship. His explanation defines his purpose: coming to people who have need. Throughout the Gospel, Jesus repeatedly meets people's needs and brings them back into community: the cleansing of the leper (1:40–45), the healing of the Gerasene demoniac (5:1–20), the raising of the dead girl and the healing of the woman with the hemorrhage (5:21–43). His compassion (6:34; 8:2) compels him to meet the hunger needs of the crowds who

---

33. Campbell, "Community," in Campbell, *Digital Religion*, 64.
34. Campbell, "Community," in Campbell, *Digital Religion*, 68.
35. Cf. Malbon, "Markan Narrative Christology," 187.
36. Dodd, *Parables of the Kingdom*, 28; cf. Snodgrass, *Stories with Intent*, 2: "The parables of Jesus presuppose the kingdom they seek to disclose."

flock to the wilderness to hear him (6:30–44; 8:1–10). Thus, throughout Mark, Jesus draws a community around himself and meets their needs.

Moreover, Jesus redefines family, a central human community. With his own family waiting outside, Jesus looks at "those who sat around him" and proclaims, "Here are my mother and my brothers! Whoever does the will of God is my brother and sister and mother" (3:34–35). The logic of family is now centered on the kingdom of God, and Jesus is the locus around whom this community forms. Following Jesus is of greater importance than family obligation, as illustrated in the disciples leaving everything "for [Jesus's] sake and for the sake of the good news" (10:28–30). The family of God takes priority over the human family.

Additionally, Mark shows a weakening of geographical ties. Jesus's ministry fails in his hometown of Nazareth (6:1–6). He is "amazed at their unbelief" (6:6). As the narrative progresses, Jesus crosses ethnic and geographic boundaries when he heals the daughter of a Syrophoenician woman (7:24–30).

In sum, community in Mark is best understood through the lens of the kingdom of God. In Jesus's ministry, people's needs are met as he draws them into fellowship. The family is redefined as those who do God's will.

Community in Reflection

The dominant image from the internet—the network—is so pervasive that it is altering expectations of offline community. The network consists of loose social connections with varied levels of commitment in which people engage to have their needs met.

Once again, the Gospel of Mark presents a very different picture. Instead, the governing image is the kingdom of God, in which Jesus invites people into fellowship as he meets their needs. His actions are motivated by compassion, and the commitment he requires from his disciples is total. This presents a challenge to the twenty-first century church as it disciples in an online context. How can the image of God's reign inform our thinking and counteract some of the deficiencies inherent in the notion of the network? That is, what does it mean to approach online activity with a view to meeting the needs of others instead of constantly seeking for oneself? What does compassion look like in an online setting? How is commitment to Jesus and the gospel fostered in a world of multiple loose commitments and connections? How can the ministry of Jesus's disciples today transform communities in online and offline environments?

Like the network, the community around Jesus is not defined by geography or familial bonds; unlike the network, however, the family of God centered around Jesus is defined by obedience to God's will. Jesus is the center and not the self or one's own interests. Thus, the community depicted in the Gospel of Mark presents a challenge to the image of community as a network.

Conclusion

As the internet increasingly becomes a central part of everyday life, our traditional notions of authority, identity, and community are challenged. The narrative of the Gospel of Mark shows Jesus and his ministry challenging the traditional notions of his day. Indeed, the Markan portrait of Jesus can still challenge our culture today. From my vantage point as a biblical scholar on the coast of the internet, I contend that Gospel of Mark presents a different view of authority, identity, and community, one which prompts us to live in a way that challenges the new status quo emerging in the online/offline reality of the twenty-first century.

Bibliography

Campbell, Heidi A., "Religious Authority and the Blogosphere." *Journal of Computer-Mediated Communication* 15 (2010) 251–76.

———. "Who's Got the Power? Religious Authority and the Internet." *Journal of Computer-Mediated Communication* 12 (2007) 1043–62.

———, ed. *Digital Religion: Understanding Religious Practice in New Media Worlds.* New York: Routledge, 2012.

Dodd, C. H. *The Parables of the Kingdom.* London: Nisbet, 1935.

Lührmann, D. "Pharisäer und Schriftgelehrte im Markusevangelium." *Zeitschrift für die neutestamentliche Wissenschaft und die Kunde der Älteren Kirche* 78 (1987) 169–85.

Malbon, Elizabeth Struthers. "Markan Narrative Christology and the Kingdom of God." In *Literary Encounters with the Reign of God*, edited by Sharon H. Ringe and H. C. Paul Kim, 177–682. New York: T. & T. Clark, 2004.

Neumaier, Anna. "'Because Faith Is a Personal Matter!' Aspects of Public and Private in Religious Internet Use." *Journal of Religion in Europe* 9 (2016) 441–62.

Pickup, Martin. "Matthew's and Mark's Pharisees." In *In Quest of the Historical Pharisees*, edited by Jacob Neusner and Bruce D. Chilton, 67–112. Waco: Baylor University Press, 2007.

Schams, Christine. *Jewish Scribes in the Second-Temple Period.* JSOTSup 201. Sheffield: Sheffield Academic Press, 1998.
Snodgrass, Klyne. *Stories with Intent: A Comprehensive Guide to the Parables of Jesus.* Grand Rapids: Eerdmans, 2008.
Whitaker, Robyn. "Rebuke or Recall? Rethinking the Role of Peter in Mark's Gospel." *Catholic Biblical Quarterly* 75 (2013) 666–82.

8

The Solomonic Temple

Technology and Theology

WALTER KIM

Introduction

We move through the world as embodied beings. The spaces that we occupy provide more than mere shelter. They orient us within a context of meaning. Right now, I am sitting in a magnificent library with a vast and airy interior space, and surrounding me are rows and rows of books tucked within rich, dark shelves that line the walls. Ideas envelop me. Massive marble columns rise to buttress a ceiling with ornate plasterwork and stained glass skylights, as if the weight and beauty of humanity's collective thoughts required such support. My laptop—itself a product of design and technology—rests upon a solid wooden table, which is needlessly hefty to support the simple task of researching and writing. Yet, such design is not arbitrary. The room invites the mind to explore.

Although he was not an architect, Winston Churchill understood the impact of crafted space upon human psyche and relationships. In October 1943, he addressed the House of Commons, which was considering plans to rebuild its Parliamentary Chamber: "On the night of 10th May, 1941, with one of the last bombs of the last serious raid, our House of Commons was destroyed by the violence of the enemy, and we have now to consider whether we should build it up again, and how, and when. *We shape our buildings and afterwards our buildings shape us.*"[1] Churchill argued that

---

1. Churchill, "House of Commons Debate."

the shape of the Chamber not only reflected the convictions of British parliamentary democracy but also determined the conduct of democracy. The alignment of the chairs and the allotment of space facilitated vigorous debate, so essential to the free exchange of ideas, the respect for the conscience of individuals, and the responsibilities of those individuals to the collective body politic.

In her work *Alone Together: Why We Expect More from Technology and Less from Each Other*, Sherry Turkle, Professor of the Social Studies of Science and Technology at MIT, extrapolates from Churchill's observation to suggest that "we make our technologies, and they, in turn, shape us."[2] She explores the promise of the internet to foster new and richer bonds of human connection, and while those possibilities exist, her research also reveals some profound perils. Technology such as the internet is not merely functional, but "poses itself as the architect of our intimacies."[3] The internet is not an inert conduit for communication, but actually influences behavior and modes of thinking.

Architecture is likewise a technological endeavor. Indeed, from the first efforts to build a home with tools and trees, it is the ancient and ubiquitous means of humans to exert control over the environment and to apply technical skill. The great American architect Frank Lloyd Wright boldly asserted that "architecture is the scientific art of making structure express ideas."[4] As a phenomenon of applied technology and philosophy, architecture provides a rich arena for exploration. The architectural design of the Solomonic Temple illustrates the multi-faceted interaction between technology and theology. Under God's direction, Solomon shaped a building that continues to shape us today.

Temple as Theological Construct and Technological Construction

While the intersection between technology and theology is a complex challenge today, it is not unprecedented. Even as we hurtle forward toward new horizons of technology, we can discover ancient wisdom from the Temple, which pervades Scripture as a central theological construct. The Book of Exodus begins with fourteen chapters about Israel's deliverance

---

2. Turkle, *Alone Together*, 19.
3. Turkle, *Alone Together*, 1.
4. Gutheim, *Frank Lloyd Wright on Architecture*, 141.

from Egypt—the central redemptive event in the Old Testament—and ends with thirteen chapters of detail about the construction of the ancient Tabernacle; Leviticus is a revelation to Moses at the Tabernacle complex and deals substantially with the Temple cultus. Deuteronomy contains the guiding directive "to seek the place the Lord your God will choose from among all your tribes to put his Name there for his dwelling" (Deut 12:5). The prophets further envisioned the Temple as the eschatological center of the cosmos (Isa 2:2–4; Ezek 47; Zech 14). So fundamental was the Temple to Israel's identity that the prophet Jeremiah rebuked the people for their self-deception regarding the Temple's mere existence as divine approbation (Jer 7:4).

The centrality of the Temple continues into the New Testament. In the Gospel of John, the Tabernacle/Temple becomes a rubric for understanding the incarnation, with the language of dwelling and glory alluding to the descent of divine glory at the dedication of the Tabernacle, God's dwelling place (John 1:14; cf. Exod 40:34–38). Jesus himself uses the Temple in a typological fashion to describe his soteriological mission, when he says, "Destroy this temple and in three days I will raise it up again" (John 2:19). In turn, the destruction of Christ's physical temple eventuated in the concept of God's people as the new Temple (Eph 2:21; 1 Pet 2:5).

However, the Temple's development into a prevalent and variegated theological construct should not obscure its original existence as an actual building. God's people shaped the Temple, and afterwards the Temple shaped them. The basis and force of its theological meaning arose from the physicality, cultural understanding, and social prominence of such monumental structures in antiquity. These buildings were so vital and central to cultural self-definition that the best human technology was employed in their construction. Solomon certainly did so in the hiring of Hiram from Tyre, a leading Phoenician city-state (1 Kgs 5:6), and the use of the cedars from Lebanon.

Because the ancient world was fundamentally religious, temples represented "physical manifestations of the coming together of the creative and intellectual lives of the communities that built and used them."[5] Regarding one of the most recognized temples surviving from antiquity, renowned architecture critic Sarah Goldhagen notes how "the complex interplay of embodied math and embodied physics creates a sense of rightness about

---

5. Mierse, *Temples and Sanctuaries*, 228.

the Parthenon's composition."[6] Likewise, the Solomonic Temple was a technological artifact of exquisite design that made theology concrete. It was a reified theological construct.

Scripture not only acknowledges the technological aspects of the Temple but actually accentuates them. Since sacred structures served a central function in the ancient Near East, it is not surprising that glowing accounts about their construction exist as royal propaganda. However, the biblical account of the Temple's construction (1 Kgs 6) reads differently. Unlike Mesopotamian descriptions of temples and temple-building, "the descriptions of buildings found in Kings . . . are striking in the exact details given, and especially the fact that dimensions are provided. . . . The information provided by the biblical descriptions seems to be intent on enabling the reader actually to visualize the building or object described."[7] It was not simply the existence of the Temple as God's house that was important, but the specific architecture. The extensive narrative displays a fascination with the precise mathematical dimensions of the various rooms and their spatial orientation to one another. The descriptions of the doorways to the nave, i.e., the main hall, and to the inner sanctuary contain technical language that makes a precise understanding of the mechanical engineering somewhat provisional at this historical distance (1 Kgs 6:31–35).[8] Nevertheless, the interest in the architectural design is patent.

Relationship between Theology and Technology at the Temple

The powerful associations between physical objects and metaphorical connotations provide a rubric for exploring ancient Israel's Temple as both a theological and a physical construct. This interplay was as textured as its architecture. The Temple adopted universal motifs expressive of the human experience as an embodied creature, and adapted facets of symbolic architecture shared with pagan temples. Yet, the Temple also repudiated prevailing aspects of ancient sacred buildings, in order to promote distinct theological commitments. In between the poles of adoption and repudiation, the Temple displayed innovations to demonstrate that Israel was on the vanguard of using technology to express theological truth. The exploration

6. Goldhagen, *Welcome to Your World*, 231.
7. Hurowitz, *I Have Built You an Exalted House*, 245–46.
8. For discussion see Cogan, *1 Kings*.

of these ancient responses—adoption, adaptation, repudiation, and innovation—presents a rubric of biblical theology for present considerations about the intersection between theology and technology.

Adoption of Universal Symbolism

Because of our embodied existence, we interact with the world in particular ways and appear to have a set of universal symbolic associations with physical objects. Psychologists report in the journal *Science* that haptic interactions with even incidental objects subconsciously yet profoundly shape our interpersonal interactions.[9] Employers who reviewed résumés placed on a heavy clipboard judge those candidates to be more substantive than applications presented on light clipboards. The former were viewed as weightier in both senses of the word. Similarly, a negotiator seated in a soft chair was less likely to drive a hard bargain than one seated on a hard chair. Our interactions within inhabited spaces produce meaning, often in ways that are deeply subconscious, and for this reason, even more powerful.

Since physical attributes shape conceptual perception, certain structural motifs in the Temple evoked inherent cognitive associations. Societies throughout the ancient world often built religious structures on hilltops, as paradigmatically represented by the Acropolis of Athens. Height communicates transcendence. Even today in Athens, perched high above the city, the Parthenon dominates the vista and demands attention. A ground-level observer must look up toward this sacred structure, and in so doing, the line between the heavens and the earth becomes blurred, since the sky becomes the only background to the temple. This experience of transcendence exists as part of the visual language of ancient religious structures. The recurring command in the Old Testament to destroy the "high places" (e.g., Num 33:52; Deut 12:2) and the repeated construction of those "high places" (e.g., 1 Kgs 12:31; 2 Kgs 21:3) exhibit the instinctual connection between height, transcendence, and the holy.

The location of Solomon's Temple similarly employed this universal visual language of transcendence. Although modern Jerusalem is a large city, it was not so during the time of the United Monarchy of ancient Israel. Solomon inherited a capital from his father David that was merely 15 or 16 acres. The building of the royal temple precinct on the hilltop in Jerusalem

---

9. Ackerman, Nocera, and Bargh, "Incidental Haptic Sensations."

tripled the acreage of the city from 15 to about 50 acres.[10] Such an expansion of the urban landscape and placement of the Temple on a height above the city "accorded the House of YHWH the prominence and the sense of awe and inspiration worthy of the dwelling of the national deity."[11] The Temple towered over the city. As a point of orientation physically and spiritually, the Temple became a theological affirmation of Yahweh's kingship.

The notion of transcendence conveyed by the location on the Temple Mount found a corresponding expression within the internal design of the structure. The Temple's interior dimensions were sixty cubits long, thirty cubits high, and twenty cubits wide (1 Kgs 6:2), which translates to 90 x 45 x 30 feet.[12] This space comprised three areas: vestibule, nave, and inner sanctuary (i.e., Most Holy Place). The nave, or main hall, was 60 ft long x 45 ft high x 30 ft wide (1 Kgs 6:17). As with modern cathedrals, the cavernous space contained a high ceiling with respect to the width of the room, which was exceptional among any known Canaanite or Phoenician temple.[13] This verticality directed the eye upward to engender the sense of transcendence and connection to heaven. This grand space produced other visual and auditory effects. The sheer magnitude of the room inculcated a sense of minuteness, that is, an experience of "losing oneself" in an expansive space. Furthermore, in her analysis of the celebrated Amiens Cathedral in France, Goldhagen notes:

> Cathedrals create highly unusual sonic landscapes. In an interior as large as Amiens Cathedral, sound lingers . . . because in such spaces, sound waves reverberate for an unusually long time, from six to ten seconds. The result is what acousticians call *ubiquitous sound*, whereby the long reverberation of sound emissions makes it seem as though sounds come from everywhere and nowhere.[14]

The Temple's construction created an interior space that reinforced a transcendent sense of otherness, an experience of liminal time and space. In

---

10. Tarler and Cahill, "David, City Of," 65.

11. Cogan, *1 Kings*, 251.

12. Assuming a standard conversion of 18 inches at the time of the Solomonic period. These dimensions do not account for the thickness of the exterior stone walls nor interior dividing walls, which would have substantially added to the imposing impression of the building. The remains of the Ain Dara Temple suggest walls of nearly 3 meters, and given the larger dimensions of Solomon's Temple, it is reasonable to expect walls of similar scale.

13. Mazar, *Archaeology of the Land*, 376.

14. Goldhagen, *Welcome to Your World*, 127.

other words, the Temple understood the impact of architecture to shape human experience and employed principles of engineering and design to produce specific results.

Whereas the proportion of height (45') vs. width (30') emphasized a vertical axis, the relationship of length (90') vs. width (30') fostered a natural movement through space. The Temple's spatial orientation employed the universal visual language of verticality as transcendence and induced directionality via a horizontal corridor. This directionality of movement through an elongated axis is a common visual motif. It appears in large scale urban planning, as is the case in a well-known section of Paris which underwent massive reforms in the nineteenth century to eliminate slums through major demolition and master-planned building projects. An aerial view of this city aptly displays the manner in which the broad, straight Avenue des Champs-Élysées draws people through the city to the famed Arc de Triomphe. Indeed, this monument honoring French soldiers and victories stands at the center of twelve avenues that radiate out as straight spokes. This design exerts a centripetal force toward the city center as an expression of cultural identity and celebration.

In addition to invoking this universal principle of horizontal orientation, the Temple applied an architectural design that corresponded to its cultural context. Long-room temples occurred throughout contemporaneous Syria-Palestine. This basic form had "a rectangular space in which the longitudinal axis is emphasized, usually at the terminal points, by means of entrances and built items. The long-room format stresses a steady progression through space in a fixed direction."[15] More specifically, the tripartite division of vestibule, nave, and inner sanctuary appeared around the time of Solomon at Ain Dara (approximately forty miles from Aleppo) and at Tell Tayinat (near ancient Alalakh).[16] These exemplars suggest that the tripartite building had its architectural origins among the Phoenicians of northern Syria, which fits with the expected influence of Hiram of Tyre (1 Kgs 5).[17]

The creation of an inner sanctuary was not particularly novel, since "privileging a space by burying it within layers of surrounding spaces is well known in Mesopotamian sacred architecture . . . and in New Kingdom

---

15. Mierse, *Temples and Sanctuaries*, 159–60.

16. For fuller discussion, see Mazar, *Archaeology of the Land*, 377, and King and Stager, *Life in Biblical Israel*, 334–38.

17. Cogan, *1 Kings*, 252.

Egyptian temple architecture."[18] The horizontal axis naturally moved from its entrance through each successive space, while simultaneously each partition "with their three gradations seeks with increasing degrees of holiness to protect the figure of God from any profanation."[19] The parallel biblical nomenclature of "Most Holy Place" to depict the inner sanctuary firmly establishes this basic idea (e.g., 1 Kgs 6:16; 7:50; 8:6).

Adaptation of Cultural Designs

The adoption of universal visual language (height for transcendence, the natural instincts of movement through horizontal axes) affirms the common grace reflected in architectural design. Theologically sanctioned adoption assessed the coherence between technological phenomena and human proclivities that God has established. Moreover, this embodied common grace invited creative adaptation by the Israelites. This impulse of adoption and adaptation of universal visual language is not a capitulation of theological concerns to contemporary trends, but rather an assertion that common grace exists.

The biblical account is not content with the intimation of the horizontal axis to communicate divine holiness. Although the contemporaneous temple at Ain Dara had a tripartite division, its separation between the nave and the inner sanctuary was indicated merely by making the latter into a raised platform with no intervening wall.[20] Unlike the remains at Ain Dara, the Bible draws attention to the Temple's clear differentiation of the three spaces, with doorways as transitional structures to control access. In requiring passage through an actual doorway, each entry provided a moment of birth into the reality of a new space. The architectural additions accentuated the inaccessibility and otherness of the divine.

The author's descriptions far exceed what is necessary to make the theological point: "For the entrance to the inner sanctuary he made doors of olivewood; the lintel and the doorposts were five-sided. . . . So also he made for the entrance to the nave doorposts of olivewood, in the form of a square, and two doors of cypress wood. The two leaves of the one door were folding, and the two leaves of the other door were folding" (1 Kgs 6:31, 34–35). The types of wood—olive and cypress—used to make the

18. Mierse, *Temples and Sanctuaries*, 175.
19. Albertz, *History of Israelite Religion*, 131.
20. King and Stager, *Life in Biblical Israel*, 334–35.

doors indicated the relative sanctity of the respective spaces, with the more valuable olivewood used for the doors to the inner sanctuary. They also demonstrated the technical expertise in using olivewood, which is much harder than cypress, in the nave doorposts. Even though the mechanism of the doorjambs is notoriously difficult to translate and its precise meaning is no longer understood, its presence in the account displays a concern for both the technical and theological aspects of the architecture.

While the biblical account demonstrates the adoption of visual language that is both universal and culturally specific, the Temple's construction of defined, enclosed spaces revealed an architectural variation from more open tripartite areas of the temple at Ain Dara. Theological concerns apparently compelled an architectural design that sought to buttress the otherness of Yahweh via closed entrances.

Repudiation of Visual Language

The willingness to adapt visual language found more pronounced expression in the repudiation of some prominent features of ancient Near Eastern sacred architecture. The use of garden imagery in the interior design exemplifies this negotiation of adaptation and of repudiation. Many of the Temple's interior features symbolized Yahweh's presence in a sacred garden. This visual language recurred throughout the ancient Near East. The *Investiture of Zimri-Lim*, a large mural discovered at the Royal Palace in the ancient Syrian city of Mari, depicts the king receiving royal paraphernalia from the goddess Ishtar. The broader scene contains two sacred trees with cherubim and flowers, some of them opening. The Temple also incorporated these visual motifs in its design. Not only did Solomon construct two cherubim statues for the inner sanctuary, but he also "carved all the walls of the house round about with carved figures of cherubim and palm trees and open flowers, in the inner and outer rooms" (1 Kgs 6:29). Also within the Temple were carvings "in the form of gourds and open flowers" (1 Kgs 6:18). This iconography evoked the royal garden in which the sacred trees, mythic creatures and luxuriant flora all depict a scenario of cosmic order and abundance. Through architecture and artistry, the Temple became a place from which the waters of life transformed the nations and created order (cf. Ezek 47). Thus, this Solomonic building project presented Jerusalem as "a miniature cosmion, the source of 'living waters' that flow forth from Zion."[21] Overlooking the city, the Temple stood as a reminder of Yahweh's presence on earth, his commitment to humanity, and his eschatological purposes for the world.

Despite the generous borrowing of pervasive cultural motifs, these visual cues point more specifically to Genesis. Numerous features of the Temple's design are reminiscent of the biblical creation account: the luxuriant flora of Eden and in the Temple; the huge bronze "sea" which served the dual function of lustrations and of idealizing Yahweh's control over the cosmic waters of chaos (1 Kgs 7:23–24; cf. Gen 1:2); the two pillars with "lily"-like capitals appearing as stylized palm trees and perhaps alluding to the two sacred trees in the Garden (1 Kgs 7:21–22); and the cherubim who guarded both the Temple's inner sanctuary (1 Kgs 6:23) and the entrance to the Garden of Eden, which faced eastward, as did the Temple (Gen 3:24; cf. Num 3:38; Ezek 47:1). Hurowitz concludes that these features in Genesis "must be interpreted as an attempt to describe Creation in terms of building . . . the Creation as an act of building, and the Creator as a wise, knowledgeable and discerning architect."[22] Scripture depicts humanity's initial interaction with the world through the rubric of a temple, and humanity's initial vocation as priests at the Temple that God built. In other words, the central theological point that begins the Bible comes through a technological metaphor.

Yet, while the Temple adopted some features of universal and cultural meaning embedded within the architectural technology, it starkly repudiated other aspects associated with the visual language of ancient monumental building. As opposed to the *Investiture of Zimri-Lim*, which prominently featured a transactional encounter between the king and the goddess Ishtar, no such visual depiction occurred in the Temple: "When the Temple wall reliefs are compared to Mesopotamian examples, the most striking feature is the absence of the deity and the king from the Solomonic depictions."[23] The idol of a deity normally resided in the inner sanctuary of sacred buildings. Instead, the Temple's inner sanctuary was guarded by two massive cherubim and contained the ark of the covenant as the symbol of God's kingship and covenantal relationship. Yahweh's royal presence was

21 Stager, "Jerusalem and the Garden of Eden," 183.

22. Hurowitz, *I Have Built You an Exalted House*, 242. The temple at 'Ain Dara prominently features two large columns, very similar to the biblical Joachin and Boaz. Before the threshold are two colossal imprints of the deity's feet heading into the temple.

23. Bloch-Smith, "'Who Is the King of Glory?'" 26.

undoubtedly understood to be represented, as suggested by the formulaic epithet "the ark of the covenant of the Lord Almighty, who is enthroned between the cherubim" (1 Sam 4:4; cf. Pss 80:1; 99:1; Isa 37:16). Nevertheless, the architectural design studiously affirmed the aniconism of Israelite theology. The absence of a divine image captured in architectural terms the theological commitments expressed in Solomon's dedicatory prayer that, on the one hand, "I have indeed built you an exalted house, a place for you to dwell in forever" (1 Kgs 8:13), but on the other hand, "will God indeed dwell on the earth? Behold, heaven and the highest heaven cannot contain you; how much less this house that I have built!" (1 Kgs 8:27).

Innovation

The Temple was not merely passive or reactive in its architecture; it was also constructive. Israelite architectural innovations employed fresh visual language to reify powerful theological commitments. The two massive freestanding pillars that stood at the entrance represented several novel developments (1 Kgs 7:15–22). The capital atop the bronze pillars included complex decorations of latticework and stylized pomegranates and culminated in lily-work design at the apex. These capitals appeared at major administrative buildings during the Solomonic period.[24] This sort of design—pillar with a flowering capital—predated very similar architecture in Greece. The proto-Ionic capitals used on Solomonic royal buildings appear to be an Israelite innovation that was exported to Greece.[25] Moreover, the engineering was as innovative as the artistry: "Freestanding nonstructural columns as reported for the temples of Solomon and Heracles (Melqart) were certainly a new form in Iron Age II. . . . They required a high degree of specialized technical skill to manufacture."[26] This artistic innovation and technical expertise also applied to the massive freestanding cherubim in the inner sanctuary, which "represent something new. In North Syria, interior sculpture seems to have been limited to relief work, while fully independent sculptures were used for entrances and exterior decoration."[27]

As noted above, the Bible's interest in the Temple's dimensions differed from other ancient Near Eastern descriptions of sacred buildings. This

24. Mazar, *Archaeology of the Land*, 383.
25. Meyers, "Kinship and Kingship," 251.
26. Mierse, *Temples and Sanctuaries*, 207.
27. Mierse, *Temples and Sanctuaries*, 215.

fascination extended more particularly to the manner and implications of the dimensions. Among the remains in Syria-Palestine, the Temple displayed a remarkable regard for mathematical proportionality, with the interior dimensions of 20 x 30 x 60 cubits reflecting an arithmatic progression (2:3:6). Furthermore, the Temple's long-room plan created a natural sense of movement along a horizontal axis through this space. The design clearly eventuated in the inner sanctuary, as the crucial conceptual feature.

The significance of the inner sanctuary was conveyed not only by its position buried deep within the structure or by its containment of the ark of the covenant, but also by the mathematical dimension as a perfect cube: 30 x 30 x 30 feet.[28] What does this communicate? A cube represents perfection, and so may signify the perfection of God's rule. Yet, from a design perspective that takes into consideration embodied human perception, the cubic space would have produced a startling effect. While the elongated space from entrance through the nave produced a natural sense of directionality and movement, the dimensions of the inner sanctuary would offer neither. Perfectly dimensioned rooms provide no axial orientation.

The experience inside a cube is one of stasis, a lack of movement, and the geometry is a statement of the invisible order behind all things. The Temple's inner sanctuary was built according to this innovative design principle of cubic space, which suspended the imaginative worshiper in a moment of holy stasis. The space served as the *axis mundi* between the heavenly realm and the earthly realm. Indeed, this Temple design was so remarkable that Renaissance "architects attempted to re-create the perfection of this lost archetype from which all the other orders were thought to be derived."[29]

This design strategy lives on in the architecture of Inigo Jones for the Queen's Estate in Greenwich, England, built in the seventeenth century. The layout directs visitors toward cubic royal reception halls at the back of the building in order to intimate the origin and center of power in the British Empire.[30] The mathematical innovation of the Temple design became the blueprint for the future.

---

28. Given the difference in the height between the nave (45') and the inner sanctuary (30'), the cubic dimensions of this space may signify a raised shrine with approaching stairs (as at Ain Dara), a lowered ceiling (cf. Egyptians structures with slanted roofs), or unused attic space between the shrine's ceiling and the temple's exterior roof. See discussion in Cogan, *1 Kings*, 243.

29. Wittkower, "Principles of Pallidio's Architecture," 82.

30. "Proportion was itself a matter of visual correspondence, of parts that 'agree,'

Final Reflections

When Sherry Turkle of MIT began to explore the phenomenon of seeking to make connection through the internet, the technology was in its infancy and full of promise. Would this be a boon for human connection? After years of research, she came to some very unsettling conclusions. Of course, technology has the promise to help human connection. However, by the very design of a phone and attending technologies, communication prioritizes control and convenience. If an unwelcome text appears, then the phone can simply disappear into a pocket. However, unpleasant company at a dinner table cannot be so readily silenced. By making control and convenience a function of communication, we in fact diminish our ability to truly connect. Turkle suggests a sober realism about the promise and perils of technology with respect to human relationships:

> What I call *realtechnik* suggests that we step back and reassess when we hear triumphantist or apocalyptic narratives about how to live with technology. *Realtechnik* is skeptical about linear progress. It encourages humility, a state of mind in which we are most open to facing problems and reconsidering decisions. It helps us acknowledge costs and recognizes the things we hold inviolate.[31]

Ultimately, the issue is wisdom, the ability to ask what and why and how technology "expands our capacities and possibilities or exploits our vulnerabilities."[32]

Theology can tend to be reactive in nature, seeking to apply Scripture to the exigencies of cultural transformations that move at a rapid pace. The speed of technological advancement seems at times to outstrip theological reflection, which by its very nature is deliberative and therefore requires time to encompass contemporary issues. It is, however, also the case that theological positions can steep in a cultural environment, either by incorporating or rejecting worldviews without sufficient reflection. Upheavals generated by technology can provoke healthy theological contemplation. We are certainly at such a moment. But such crucibles have also existed in the past, not only with the paradigm shifts of the Copernican revolution or of Darwinian evolution, but also in the biblical past. Our exploration of

---

'answer,' or are 'even' with one another through shared dimensions or the alignment of wall surfaces." Higgott, "Varying with Reason," 72.

31. Turkle, *Alone Together*, 294.

32. Turkle, *Alone Together*, xxii.

the Temple seeks wisdom from the responses of God's people under God's guidance to the promises and perils of architecture as a universal and cultural expression of technology.

The textured responses reflect a broadly incarnational approach to theology. While the Incarnation of grace and truth in the flesh and blood of Christ was *sui generis*, the Temple reified theology via meaning created by technological products and processes. Wisdom is needed to discern what to adopt, adapt, repudiate, or supersede through innovation. The adoption and adaptation of architectural design and engineering evince a positive regard for the creative possibilities of common grace in the dialectic between technology and theology. However, the interactions are not always so congenial and must occasionally be rejected. As noted at the beginning of the chapter, Frank Lloyd Wright defined architecture as "the scientific art of making structure express ideas." But his remarks go further: "Architecture is the scientific art of making structure express ideas. Architecture is the triumph of human imagination over materials, methods, and men to put man into possession of his own earth. Architecture is man's great sense of himself embodied in a world of his own making. It may rise as high in quality only as its source because great art is great life."[33] His exuberance for architecture is understandable, given his extraordinary accomplishments. However, they also point to a challenging dynamic between technology and theology. The endeavors of technology entail both the divine gift of creation and the possibility of self-exaltation. When the visual language of accepted architecture threatened theological commitments, the Temple displayed a more severe repudiation of those elements.

The adoption of universal symbolism demonstrates that the technology of the day, as communally exercised by the intellectual and creative endeavor in architecture, may be used for God's purposes and even be a means for mediating God's creative and royal presence in the world. Some culturally-specific designs may need to be adapted, and some must actually be repudiated. The Temple exemplifies the varied relationships between technology and theology, culminating with innovation that supersedes culture. The use of free-standing sculptures and the mathematical dimensions of the Temple were extraordinary inventions. As Meyer observes:

> This leaves Israel, with its reported construction of an extraordinary temple-palace complex in Jerusalem, as a trendsetter in the material world of its day. Ancient Israel is best known in

---

33. Gutheim, *Frank Lloyd Wright on Architecture*, 141.

postbiblical religious tradition for its spiritual and literary contributions, for its wisdom documents and prophetic calls for justice. But for one brief period in the millennium or so of its history it may have taken the lead in artistic creativity.[34]

For ancient Israel, technological advance did not produce theological retreat.

Recent developments have altered the ways in which humans interact with one another and with the physical world. The challenges are complex, and defy easy explanations, but that does not mean we need to be unmoored or unreflective about the ways in which technology impact us and how we can shape technology to impact others. The artistic innovation of the Solomonic Temple should inspire us to creativity. Humans are technological and theological creatures. To deal with one without the other is to deny our existence as beings created in the image of God, who function as architects of technology and meaning, because God himself proved to be the architect and temple-builder *par excellence*.

Bibliography

Ackerman, Joshua M., Christopher C. Nocera, and John A. Bargh. "Incidental Haptic Sensations Influence Social Judgments and Decisions." *Science* 328 (2010) 1712–15.

Albertz, Rainer. *A History of Israelite Religion in the Old Testament Period.* Vol. 1, *From the Beginnings to the End of the Monarchy.* 1st American ed. The Old Testament Library. Louisville: Westminster John Knox Press, 1994.

Bloch-Smith, Elizabeth. "'Who Is the King of Glory?' Solomon's Temple and Its Symbolism." In *Scripture and Other Artifacts: Essays on the Bible and Archaeology in Honor of Philip J. King,* edited by Michael D. Coogan, J. Cheryl Exum, and Lawrence Stager, 18–31. Louisville: Westminster John Knox Press, 1994.

Churchill, Winston. "House of Commons Debate." 28 October 1943, vol. 393 cc403–73. http://hansard.millbanksystems.com/commons/1943/oct/28/house-of-commons-rebuilding.

Cogan, Mordechai. *1 Kings: A New Translation with Introduction and Commentary.* Anchor Bible 10. New York: Doubleday, 2001.

Goldhagen, Sarah Williams. *Welcome to Your World.* New York: Harper, 2017.

Gutheim, Frederick, ed. *Frank Lloyd Wright on Architecture: Selected Writings (1894–1940).* New York: Grosset's Universal Library, 1941.

Higgott, Gordon. "Varying with Reason: Inigo Jones's Theory of Design." *Architectural History* 35 (1992) 51–77.

Hurowitz, Victor. *I Have Built You an Exalted House: Temple Building in the Bible in Light of Mesopotamian and North-West Semitic Writings.* Journal for the Study of the Old

---

34. Meyers, *Kinship and Kingship*, 256.

Testament Supplement Series. Edited by David J. A. Clines and Philip R. Davies. Sheffield: JSOT Press, 1992.

King, Philip J., and Lawrence E. Stager. *Life in Biblical Israel*. 1st ed. Library of Ancient Israel. Louisville: Westminster John Knox Press, 2001.

Mazar, Amihai. *Archaeology of the Land of the Bible 10,000–586 B.C.E.* The Anchor Bible Reference Library. New York: Doubleday, 1992.

Meyers, Carol L. "Kinship and Kingship: The Early Monarchy." In *The Oxford History of the Biblical World*, edited by Michael D. Coogan, 221–71. Oxford: Oxford University Press, 1998.

Mierse, William E. *Temples and Sanctuaries from the Early Iron Age Levant: Recovery After Collapse*. History, Archaeology, and Culture of the Levant. Edited by Jeffrey A. Blakely and K. Lawson Younger. Winona Lake, IN: Eisenbrauns, 2012.

Stager, Lawrence. "Jerusalem and the Garden of Eden." *Eretz Israel* 26 (1998) 83–88.

Tarler, David, and Jane M. Cahill. "David, City Of." In vol 2 of *The Anchor Bible Dictionary*, edited by David Noel Freedman, 52–67. New York: Doubleday, 1992.

Turkle, Sherry. *Alone Together: Why We Expect More from Technology and Less from Each Other*. Revised and expanded ed. New York: Basic Books, 2017.

Wittkower, Rudolf. "Principles of Pallidio's Architecture." *Journal of the Warburg and Courtauld Institutes* 8 (1945) 68–106.

9

The Internet Gaze

Eric Stoddart

"Turn that TV off! You'll get square eyes," was a threat used by parents to overly avid young viewers in the 1950s and 1960s. Forty-odd years later we learned that The Doctor had had to come to the rescue of Londoners watching the broadcast of the coronation of Queen Elizabeth the Second in 1953. An alien entity, "The Wire," was sucking out viewers' minds as they gazed intently at new mass-produced TV sets.[1] The writer of that episode of *Dr Who* was surely recalling the dire warnings from his childhood. Such concerns are probably not new. Our ancestors must have been enthralled watching projections of cut-out figures moving on a screen in Paris for the first time in 1798. Their 21st-century descendants collide with street furniture because their attention is fixed on the screen now in the hand.

For the first few years of its public release people gazed *at* the internet. It was not long before the internet gazed back. Once reliant on a telephone line, the internet was set free with the arrival of Wi-Fi and 4G data. Even then, the internet was confined to a screen. Now the connectivity of smart objects means the internet reaches into our fridge, controls our sound system, and receives reports from our hairbrush.[2]

Our desire for news, shopping options, entertainment, relationships, and self-worth propels us to scroll our screens. At the same time, what we see shapes our desires. Our searching and our personal data compose precious trails by which the internet sirens identify us and lure us in their

---

1. "The Idiot's Lantern," *Dr. Who*, episode 7.2, directed by Euros Lyn, written by Mark Gatiss, BBC, May 27, 2006.

2. Kleinman, "CES 2017."

direction with their enchanting songs. This chapter aims to problematize the everyday internet gaze as one that is best understood through the frames of surveillance and commodification. Such an approach will open up questions of exploitation in the wider context of the marketization of life. We will discover that the internet gaze is one of desire and that this is the key for a fruitful theological critique. The Gospel will furnish us with the means for a grace-full gaze that means Christians do not need to eschew the internet but rather discover a renewed critical gaze.

The Quotidian Gaze

Gazing into the internet is an everyday practice, generally intentional but for a range of quite different purposes. We swipe across the screen to find out what our friends have been up to and to be sure we do not miss an invitation to socialize. With a few clicks we share our reaction to yet another picture of a kitten. A similar action expresses an opinion on a recent holiday destination, public transport trip, or class teacher at college. In just a few minutes we pay a utility bill, download a movie, check the traffic on our route to work, and, depending on our moral standpoint, set up a random sexual encounter for lunchtime. In the afternoon, we check that our biometric data has uploaded and we arrange a virtual cycle trip to exercise on a Pacific island while pedalling strenuously in a kitchen 5,000 miles away.[3] A quick flick through news outlets reassures us that the right people are protesting about the right things and that democracy continues to limp its way into the future. Two more clicks and some typing lets a preacher in a far-off country know that we are offended at recent activities in his church about which we have been informed by similarly affronted non-attending correspondents. Once we have eaten the meal we have just photographed and shared on Facebook, and recovered from our virtual cycle ride, we catch up with TV-on-demand because we are two episodes behind a friend. Pulling up the bed covers we fire off a few urgent emails for work before trying to get to sleep.

---

3. Zwift is just one of a range of virtual cycling apps (zwift.com).

The Surveillance Gaze

In the days of web 1.0, webmasters had information limited largely to the traffic to their site. The public gazed *at* the internet. With the advent of interactivity (web 2.0) the game changed. A visit to a website normally involves accepting a cookie (a small piece of code) that surrenders some user-data. Registering to access a site, or using an existing service such as Facebook or Google as an alternative authentication method, provides corporations, government agencies, or web managers in general with copious and rich personal information. This is the internet gaze as a panoptic gaze; the few, in the shadows, watching the many.[4] The many, in this case, acquiescing to the gaze that is impersonal (an automated process) but highly personal in terms of the data scraped from people's digital footprint.

Social media permit a different gaze. The many, the internet audience, are watching (and judging) the few. This synoptic gaze is directed towards those who are sometimes willing performers (two minutes of fame on YouTube) but also those who are either captured unawares or unwillingly.[5] There is also a lateral gaze in which peers known to one another exchange information and images as they develop a relationship.[6]

With the offering, retrieving, and analyzing of personal information, with a view to influencing behavior, we find ourselves firmly in the territory of surveillance. As Thomas Mathieson has claimed: "surveillance is the cardinal point of the internet."[7] People's capacity to exert a critical gaze can seem very limited. Just as we filter our friends, we make choices over the news or political sites we regularly visit. However, much of the filtering can be done on our behalf, without much awareness on our part. Algorithms (some with, and some without human editorial intervention) select what is added to our social media timeline. Satirical new sites, obviously comedic, have been joined by insidious deliberate "fake news" sites. The attempt of the latter is to manipulate public opinion, cast doubt on the veracity of any news site, and advance a political agenda through what is really propaganda.[8]

---

4. See, for example, Lyon, *Theorizing Surveillance*.
5. Mathieson, "Viewer Society," 215–34.
6. Trottier, *Social Media as Surveillance*.
7 Mathieson, "Preface," xviii.
8. Facebook's vice-president of product management announced further refinements to their algorithms on January 25, 2017. See Cathcart, "Continuing Our Updates."

The Anxious Gaze

We gaze wistfully out to sea thinking of absent friends. We gaze anxiously from on-board ship day after day in the hope of spotting land. We gaze adoringly into the eyes of our lover, but lasciviously towards a figure across the restaurant. We gaze absentmindedly at an online newspaper then intently when trying to find again the article that momentarily flitted past our sight. While we usually take gazing to be a steady look, its intensity, purposefulness and motivation can take many forms. French philosopher Michel Foucault turned our attention to the disciplinary gaze—illustrated by the watchtower of a panopticon prison, but extended to include the uncertainty of being monitored by any authority.[9] We, he argues, internalize the possibility of the gaze and modify our behaviour accordingly.

For Jean Paul Sartre, being looked at induces anxiety.[10] We no longer belong to ourselves but we are the project of the other who is gazing at us. This results in us becoming objects of our own contemplation. We are not in control of how our appearance is evaluated by the gazer and, in that sense, we now belong ("are slaves") to the one who is looking at us.[11] This means that Sartre's "gaze" is fundamentally anti-social.[12] Particular mechanisms are not necessary for the gaze to be anxiety-inducing (although some, such as a watchtower illustrate and exacerbate) because this is how human relations simply are. Maurice Merleau-Ponty, however, contends that, contra Sartre, the gaze in its anxiety-inducing is grounded in practices and relations.[13]

Merleau-Ponty rejects any notion of mind/body dualism; sentience is a property of the body, not a consciousness sensing through a body.[14] Perception is not thought but inter-subjectivity in which we open *onto* one another and on to the same world. While inter-subjectivity may turn to objectifying one another—as we deploy language and social practices—it is

---

9. Foucault, *Discipline and Punish*.

10. Sartre, *Being and Nothingness*, 252–302. For this discussion of Foucault, Sartre, and Merleau-Ponty I am indebted to Nick Crossley, "Politics of the Gaze," 399–419. For a detailed discussion of Merleau-Ponty on the gaze, see also Yngvesson, "To See the World."

11. Sartre, *Being and Nothingness*, 267.

12. Crossley, "Politics," 408.

13. Merleau-Ponty, *Visible and the Invisible*.

14. "The perceptual presence of the world is . . . our experience, prior to every opinion, of inhabiting the world by our body, of inhabiting the truth by our whole selves," Merleau-Ponty, *Visible and the Invisible*, 28.

not inherently so. The disciplinary effect of the gaze occurs when we come to feel (through their actions in given situations) that one party is observing us while being correspondingly closed to us.[15]

It can take some effort and technical knowledge to be able to gaze anonymously into the internet. Human rights activists, in danger of arrest or harassment by the state can cloak their internet activity and communications (The future of encryption is, however, unclear given that some governments demand back-door access on grounds of "national security"). Trolls, abusers, and black-market agents deploy similar tactics to conceal their identity and activities.

The Commodified Gaze

Arguably the most dominant gaze is that of the consumer, and that directed at potential consumers. It is a surveillance gaze—watching that is legitimated and stimulated within a neoliberal economic culture. While we might think we are only watching a vendor's site, she is gazing back at us—not normally through the lens of our inbuilt webcam—but at our data-double.[16] The gaze we are considering includes interaction with people, albeit heavily mediated by digital technologies, but also—and significantly—with material objects of desire (commodities) and intangible assets (knowledge). However, the internet is a system within and by which people, objects, and knowledge are all commodified. The internet gaze is a commodified gaze.

It was around 1994 that I recall noticing for the first time a roadside billboard on which a well-known retailer now included a URL. This elementary step of online advertising came as no surprise given the novelty of the new medium and the availability of "ultrafast" 14.4k modems. A platform that enabled students in one specific US college to exchange information and photographs was developed quite quickly into the almost ubiquitous Facebook™. Weaving advertising seamlessly into our social networks has been a rich vein to be mined for generating profit. Christian Fuchs argues that "sharing," the stimulus for social networking, is really a euphemism for hard commercial transactions:

15. Crossley, "Politics," 408.

16. Soltani and Lee, "Research Shows." "Data-doubles," generated from the "disassembling and reassembling" of our digital traces that become "virtual/information profiles that circulate in various computers and contexts of practical application," Haggerty and Ericson, "New Politics of Surveillance and Visibility," 4.

Its privacy policy is the living proof that Facebook is primarily about profit-generation by advertising. "The world will be better if you share more?" But a better world for whom is the real question? "Sharing" on Facebook in economic terms means primarily that Facebook "shares" information with advertising clients. And "sharing" is only the euphemism for selling and commodifying data.[17]

Generally speaking, people are blasé about the commodification of their social networks. Monetizing the internet of course does not stop there. Gathering, editing, printing, and disseminating news has almost always been a commercial activity. Newspapers carry advertisements both as an income stream and way of locating the publication in a particular stratum of society. In other words, newspapers and their advertisers operate in a mutual reputational relationship. Online media differs from traditional print for a number of reasons but not least because advertisements can be responsive to particular categories of reader. Regional variations notwithstanding, readers of *The Washington Post* in print are confronted with the same advertisements. Thanks to cookies this is anything but the case for online readers.

Small-town shopkeepers, knowing their customers and the power of reputation, might discreetly offer special deals to some but not everyone. Sophisticated algorithms now allow online retailers to target desirable customers; customers who have been segmented into categories through the statistical analysis of not only previous purchases, but the personal information surrendered through loyalty cards, more general browsing behaviour, correlated with geo-demographic data.[18] Customer categorization through data management goes well beyond online shopping. Internet connectivity, now highly mobile, makes it possible for insurance companies to offer reduced rates to car owners who will agree to a monitoring device in the vehicle. A family with a youngster who has just passed the driving test could well find submitting their travel data to be a desired, perhaps even necessary, compromise of privacy. Some joggers will view capturing and uploading their exercise activities as part of a fun motivational method. However, being required to surrender such data by one's employer is a different matter. Reducing health insurance costs ostensibly in the guise of encouraging employee well-being is a murky pit of overlapping interests.

---

17. Fuchs, "Critique of the Political Economy," 36.
18. Pridmore, "Collaborative Surveillance," 107–21.

In all these respects, and many more, the gaze of the internet is commodified and commodifying of our personal data. That our involvement is voluntary does not exclude it being exploitative.

The Exploited and Exploitative Gaze

Tiziana Terranova argues that "the consumption of culture is translated into productive activities"; something about which the consumers are quite well aware but while these activities are "pleasurably embraced" they are "at the same time often shamelessly exploited."[19] Mark Andrejevic presses this further to identify a vicious, rather than virtuous spiral of consumer activity that has a sting in the tail:

> There is more at stake in such forms of surveillance than profit: specifically the prospect that consumers will be put to work marketing to themselves, and, through this extra work, generate a customized product for which they are required to pay a premium.[20]

This is like you, at your own expense, decorating the flat you are renting and then finding the landlord raises your rent because it is now a nicer property. Andrejevic agrees this is far from the sweat-shop conditions which we might normally frame as exploitation; online users *choose* to be online. Nevertheless, he points out, talking about consumer exploitation opens up critical discussion of the commodification of social, even domestic, relationships; "to anticipate potential consequences of the migration of forms of sociability and communication onto a commercially supported platform."[21] Andrejevic's example of the commercial structure of US broadcasting then influencing what is broadcast is a compelling warning.

What is at stake is the "colonization of social life by commerce and marketing."[22] The online equivalent of the (rapidly-diminishing) public library is Google which is saturated with advertisements. This occurs in parallel with what Adam Arvidsson calls the "branding of life."[23] What happened in England to once Common Land, later enclosed by legislation

19. Terranova, "Free Labor," 37.
20. Andrejevic, "Exploitation," 73.
21. Andrejevic, "Exploitation," 74.
22. Andrejevic, "Exploitation," 82.
23. Arvidsson, "Brands," 251. Cf. Arvidsson, "Creative Class or Administrative Class?," 8–23.

and legal property rights that gave these new "owners" opportunities for exploitation, is an interesting parallel to the enclosure of the digital commons. On the one hand, we have ready-access to information and repositories of knowledge that are arguably part of our common heritage. On the other hand, the monetizing of the internet, of which the branding of life is integral, flings a fence up. It is not so simple as the presence or absence of pay-wall. In fact, the absence of a pay-wall may make it more difficult to be aware of where the cost is being borne—and it might be, in a circuitous route, our willingness to quantify our selves. Here, argues Andrejevic, is alienation in Marxist terms: "our own activity appears as something turned back against us."[24]

It is blindingly obvious that markets exist to competitively meet the desires of consumers. Producers therefore have an interest in not only identifying desires but shaping desires. Car manufacturer Toyota not only wants me to choose their vehicle over one offered by the Ford Motor Company. Toyota wants me to buy the most enhanced car I can afford, albeit on credit. My desire for a car may actually reflect a need for transport that cannot be made by public infrastructure. I do, however, need to be informed about luxury gadgets which I don't yet know I have a "need." The freedom of markets to compete for my attention is part and parcel of everyday life. So much so that we scarcely notice that we are exhorted to "feel special and anxious" (anxious lest we miss out).[25]

It appears that almost everything is for sale. Michael Sandel offers copious examples including paying people to take place in a queue for limited sports or opera tickets. More insidiously is the market sizing that is veiled under the guise of rewards systems. Ought children be financially recompensed for reading? Such a system might increase reading but might also teach children "to regard reading as a chore rather than a source of intrinsic satisfaction."[26] In any such motivational attempts, says Sandel, we failed to see that "markets don't only allocate goods; they also express and promote certain attitudes toward the goods being exchanged."[27] Wendy Brown concludes that democracy is under threat from something that is more than simply the freedom of markets. Rather, the "model of markets" is becoming the single way in which people view the world, including social

---

24. Andrejevic, "Exploitation," 85.
25. Turow, "Cracking the Consumer Code," 296.
26. Sandel, *What Money Can't Buy*, 9.
27. Sandel, *What Money Can't Buy*, 9.

relationships, civic participation, and we could perhaps add religion. For Brown this process "configures human beings exhaustively as market actors, always, only, and everywhere as *homo oeconomicus*."[28] Rather than find political answers (in the sense of the public or common good), solutions can only be framed in terms of market conduct.[29]

This is not to deny the presence of public-spirited action that is co-ordinated, and perhaps energized through the internet. Rather Sandel's and Brown's warnings are that such activities are counter to an immensely powerful mode of constructing reality. The internet molds our desires and at the same time reinforces the message to us that markets are the only way to conceive of life in all its fullness. Quantifying the self in a perpetual task of measurement, surrendering data, being categorized, encouraged to compete with ourselves and others turns care for oneself into a market-based task. Systemic injustices as well as mental or physical health limitations are somewhat airbrushed out of this market paradigm:

> This [self-tracking] user is privileged, autonomous, willing and able to conform to the dictates associated with the notion of a self-responsible actor. The contradictions, apparent irrationalities and ambivalences that are part of most people's life experience are elided, as are the vagaries of fate and the social determinants of living conditions.[30]

The surveillance gaze at, and of, the internet, taps into our anxieties regarding being evaluated by others or missing out on what might be on offer as a way of enhancing our status. The internet gaze is, therefore, fundamentally a gaze of desire but the everydayness and mundanity of this gaze in a milieu of marketization of life dulls our critical consideration of how our desires are being shaped. Timothy Gorringe's theological work on the education of desire is, therefore, highly apposite.

The Desiring Gaze

Our desires, argues Gorringe, are being trained within a worldview so familiar to us that we scarcely notice it to be idolatry.[31] Although Jesus desired

---

28. Brown, *Undoing the Demos*, 31.
29. Brown, *Undoing the Demos*, 39.
30. Lupton, *Quantified Self*, 140.
31. Gorringe, *Education*, 82.

to eat Passover and Paul desired to see friends, the New Testament is overwhelmingly negative about desire.[32] It is the "desire for other things" that chokes the sown word (Mark 4).[33] That parable, with its agricultural backdrop, remains relevant, although a networked society might more easily recognize information congestion and internet distractions as inhibitors of the flourishing of the word. The tenth commandment (against coveting), says Gorringe, is "about failing to respect limits . . . to recognise that enough is enough."[34] This is more than just single or even repeated grasping at what belongs to another. The apostle Paul articulates the addictive element.[35] The desire comes to consume or possess us; to be abandoned to the power of our own desires is a form of the outworking of God's wrath (Rom 1:24).

Gorringe follows Aquinas in recognizing that we are drawn toward an object we find attractive. We seek union with that which we desire. This allows Gorringe to make the distinction between false and true desire as one between egoism and outward-reaching relationship.[36] We might talk here of the difference between a miser and a philanthropist. Healthy desire is expansive, mutually recognizing in others the gaze as in Merleau-Ponty rather than Sartre. It is the difference between desiring to eat the Passover with friends, and coveting those same friends to bolster a poor self-image. False desire clings, true desire holds in an open hand—with the concomitant possibility of loss. Philip Sheldrake, in his definition of desire, sees its "sense of incompleteness" as "the condition of our openness to possibility, to future and to the 'always more,' the infinite."[37]

Gorringe articulates the importance of the education of desire, because unless we choose our educator, she is chosen for us.[38] In other words, our desires are being shaped, whether we think so or not, and it is incumbent upon us to select from amongst all who are vying to mold our desires. Sheldrake talks of "befriending our desires" in much the same sense, "rather than simply responding to needs we are implying the desires involve a positive and active reaching out to something or someone."[39]

---

32. Gorringe, *Education*, 85.
33. Gorringe, *Education*, 86.
34. Gorringe, *Education*, 86.
35. Gorringe, *Education*, 86.
36. Gorringe, *Education*, 89.
37. Sheldrake, *Befriending*, 93.
38. Gorringe, *Education*, 91.
39. Sheldrake, *Befriending*, 4.

Capitalist desire, says Gorringe, is an "education to refuse limits. . . . It does not draw out, but seeks to confine and limit us."[40] This might seem counterintuitive given the notion of "worldwide" web and it's supposed opening of the world to us. However, it opens the world to seduce and stimulate desire to be a better consumer. In this sense of life being commodified and marketized, might it not be likened to the devil showing Jesus the kingdoms of the earth and offering them to him in return for worship? The rhetoric of the internet is connectedness and opportunity but it comes at a price, namely being willing to be shaped in its image. Gorringe pinpoints this largely overlooked tactic of the market; it "infantilize[s] us in order to survive."[41] He understands the market as a mode of thinking; a means to have us functioning on the pleasure rather than reality principle.

Our desires, so the logic goes, want to be met but of course are insatiable. Although Gorringe identifies a lure towards instant gratification, I am not so sure that that is quite what is always on offer by the internet gaze. Rather we are presented with the possibility of gratification and the means by which we can compare ourselves with others. We are promised that the marketers on the internet are keeping an eye out for us so that we do not fall behind and that we get the opportunities which our social status warrants. The commodified, surveillance gaze of desire is therefore our security blanket that we are not going to miss out on any opportunity for gratification. In this sense also, it is infantilizing.

The Mimetic Gaze

This draw to an infantile condition is not to be mistaken with the innocent and harmlessness of infancy. Jung Mo Sung interprets marketized desire as, in Girardian terms, mimetic, with its integral violent scapegoating. It is mimetic desire "because the majority—imitating the elite's desire for consumption—also desire to consume the novelties of progress that this same progress proceeds by increasing the production of these goods for the masses."[42] The key to mimetic desire is not desire for the object itself but because another, whom we wish to emulate (and surpass), desires it.[43] Rivalry ensues between those desiring an object because the object is

40. Gorringe, *Education*, 92.
41. Gorringe, *Education*, 93.
42. Sung, *Desire, Market and Religion*, 36.
43. Girard, "Triangular Desire," 33–44.

scarce. Equilibrium is re-established by both contenders turning upon a scape-goat (a vulnerable third party) who is blamed for the limitation of the objects and upon whom the violence of mimetic desire is poured. The contribution of the Gospel is not, argues Sung, to demonize mercantile relations but to confront and unmask the sacralizing of the market.[44] The sacrificing of human lives (in spirals of rivalry and if not direct violence then social exclusion) in the name of accumulation is anathema to the vision of the New Testament. Translated into the context of marketization this means that "the economy must exist for the life of all people rather than people existing for economic laws based in the objective of accumulation of wealth."[45] Sung focuses the question down to the difference between an economy aimed at wealth accumulation or one organised for overcoming poverty. This is not simply a structural question because behind it lies a gaze that opens onto the world: "For the pain of injustice and of hunger and the joy of encounter among persons who mutually recognize each other in grace transcend any language."[46]

The Grace-Full Gaze

I have argued that the internet gaze is a commodified surveillance gaze involving a degree of exploitation, and grounded in mimetic desire. What then are the implications and to whom, and in what ways, are these significant?

The first thing we can say is that the internet gaze is never neutral. It is a way of looking that is profoundly entangled with the logic of markets. This logic has leaked from the economic domain, as Sandel and Brown have argued, and now contaminates, although not yet wholly compromising social health. As when encountering bacteria our bodies have a considerable measure of natural defenses, to talk metaphorically, so too are we able to fight the infection of the branding of life or our mutation into nothing but *homo oeconomicus*. The internet gaze is a route of such infection but, to switch metaphors, involves us encouraging the lascivious approaches of marketers. Alternatively, to take up the claim that false desire is addictive, we might say that the internet gaze feeds the habits of users and rewards suppliers—in a vicious spiral of co-dependency. To gaze into the

---

44. Sung, *Desire, Market and Religion*, 71.
45. Sung, *Desire, Market and Religion*, 72.
46. Sung, *Desire, Market and Religion*, 154.

internet—and to be gazed back at— is to collude with the spectrum of good through bad within the network.

I am not suggesting that Christians need to eschew computer-mediated engagement. It is the sacralizing, totalizing of the internet gaze that the Gospel unmasks. In his classic critique of surveillance, George Orwell makes a point that is often missed when readers' focus is on the view-screens and monitoring of citizens' behavior. The central theme of *1984* is new-speak, the re-writing of history (and of more contemporary events) to fit the Party's narrative.[47] Language is desiccated; "unnecessary" words are excised so that people are unable to conceive of resistance to the Party. The diminution of language is the primary reason for surveillance. The intention is that surveillance will become unnecessary because citizens will no longer be able to imagine the idea of resistance. Enriching our language about the surveillance gaze of the internet, and here its close association with the totalizing of us as *homo oeconomicus*, is the path of subversion.[48] Problematizing the internet gaze, appreciating its complications, requires not only vocabulary but the Gospel.

Grace that opens us to God, to one another, and to ourselves exposes the infantilizing gaze of the internet that positions us in the pleasure rather than the reality principle. Grace breaks the cycle of mimetic desire because we are free to not find our value in what others desire. As, if not more, important is the breaking of the cycle of mimetic violence that the death of Christ has instantiated. His death, as a political scape-goat upon whom the wrath of the frustrated desires of the Romans and Jewish leaders was poured, unmasks this process.[49] Scape-goating as a means of managing relationships between those desiring scarce resources is exposed and rejected. The (internet) gaze in order to consume can be radically re-framed as a gaze for caring. The gaze can be one of wonderment, of worship and of openness, and connection to others. Such a gaze contains the antibodies to the metaphorical bacteria that infect with commodification and the marketization of (internet) life.

In the Eucharist, whatever might be our tradition, we look at the bread and the wine variously symbolizing, memorializing, or sacramentalizing

---

47. Orwell, *Nineteen Eighty-Four*.

48. Orwell expounded his ideas of language in "Politics and the English Language," 252–65. Rowan Williams offers an insightful advancing of this argument in "War, Words and Reason."

49. Girard, *I See Satan Fall Like Lightning*, 138. See also, Girard, *Things Hidden*.

Christ's life, death, and continued presence in the Holy Spirit. This is a gaze that consumes and by which we are consumed—but not a gaze that commodifies. The church has the opportunity to teach how to gaze differently. Equally, she has the challenge to avoid reinforcing the wrong sort of gaze into, and from, the internet presence for which the church is responsible. Any commodification of Christianity imperils the Gospel. In public theology, the Gospel offers a critical standpoint from which the surveillance, marketized gaze of the internet can be challenged.

There is no Doctor with a sonic screwdriver to save us once we are sucked into the internet. The Savior, however, teaches us to gaze knowingly, openly, and gracefully.

Bibliography

Andrejevic, Mark. "Exploitation in the Data Mine." In *Internet and Surveillance: The Challenges of Web 2.0 and Social Media*, edited by Christian Fuchs et al., 71–88. New York: Routledge, 2012.

Arvidsson, Adam. "Brands: A Critical Perspective." *Journal of Consumer Culture* 5 (2005) 235–58.

———. "Creative Class or Administrative Class? On Advertising and the 'Underground.'" *Ephemera: Theory & Politics in Organization* 7 (2007) 8–23.

Brown, Wendy. *Undoing the Demos: Neoliberalism's Stealth Revolution*. New York: Zone Books, 2015.

Cathcart, Will. "Continuing Our Updates to Trending." Facebook, January 25, 2017. http://newsroom.fb.com/news/2017/01/continuing-our-updates-to-trending/.

Crossley, Nick. "The Politics of the Gaze: Between Foucault and Merleau-Ponty." *Human Studies* 16 (1993) 399–419.

Foucault, Michel. *Discipline and Punish: The Birth of the Prison*. London: Penguin Books, 1977.

Fuchs, Christian. "Critique of the Political Economy of Web 2.0 Surveillance." In *Internet and Surveillance: The Challenges of Web 2.0 and Social Media*, edited by Christian Fuchs et al., 31–70. New York: Routledge, 2012.

Girard, René. *I See Satan Fall Like Lightning*. Leominster: Gracewing, 2001.

———. "Politics and the English Language," *Horizon* 13 (1946) 252–65.

———. *Things Hidden Since the Foundation of the World*. Stanford: Stanford University Press, 1987.

———. "Triangular Desire." In *The Girard Reader*, edited by James G. Williams. New York: Crossroad, 1966.

Gorringe, Timothy. *The Education of Desire: Towards a Theology of the Senses*. London: SCM, 2001.

Haggerty, Kevin D., and Richard V. Ericson. "The New Politics of Surveillance and Visibility." In *The New Politics of Surveillance and Visibility*, edited by Kevin D. Haggerty and Richard V. Ericson, 3–34. Toronto: University of Toronto Press, 2006.

Kleinman, Zoe. "CES 2017: Smart Hairbrush Listens for Breaking Hair." BBC, January 4, 2017. http://www.bbc.co.uk/news/technology-38503932.

Lupton, Deborah. *The Quantified Self: A Sociology of Self-Tracking*. Cambridge: Polity, 2016.

Lyon, David, ed. *Theorizing Surveillance: The Panopticon and Beyond*. Cullompton: Willan, 2006.

Mathieson, Thomas. "Preface." In *Internet and Surveillance: The Challenges of Web 2.0 and Social Media*, edited by Christian Fuchs et al., xv-xx. New York: Routledge, 2012.

———. "The Viewer Society: Michel Foucault's 'Panopticon' Revisited." *Theoretical Criminology* 1 (1997) 215–34.

Merleau-Ponty, Maurice. *The Visible and the Invisible*. Evanston: Northwestern University Press, 1968.

Orwell, George. *Nineteen Eighty-Four*. London: The Folio Society, 2001 [1949].

Pridmore, Jason. "Collaborative Surveillance: Configuring Contemporary Marketing Practice." In *The Surveillance-Industrial Complex: The Political Economy of Surveillance*, edited by Laureen Snider and Kirstie Ball, 107–21. London: Routledge, 2013.

Sandel, Michael J. *What Money Can't Buy: The Moral Limits of Markets*. London: Penguin, 2013 [2012].

Sartre, Jean-Paul. *Being and Nothingness*. London: Routledge, 1969.

Sheldrake, Philip. *Befriending Our Desires*. London: Darton, Longman and Todd, 1994.

Soltani, Ashkan, and Timothy B. Lee. "Research Shows How MacBook Webcams can Spy On Their Users Without Warning." *Washington Post*, December 18, 2013. https://www.washingtonpost.com/news/the-switch/wp/2013/12/18/research-shows-how-macbook-webcams-can-spy-on-their-users-without-warning/?utm_term=.20a82b5eb3e3.

Sung, Jung Mo. *Desire, Market and Religion*. London: SCM Press, 2007.

Terranova, Tiziana. "Free Labor: Producing Culture for the Digital Economy." *Social Text* 18 (2000) 33–57.

Trottier, Daniel. *Social Media as Surveillance*. Aldershot: Ashgate, 2015.

Turow, Joseph. "Cracking the Consumer Code: Advertisers, Anxiety, and Surveillance in the Digital Age." In *The New Politics of Surveillance and Visibility*, edited by Kevin D. Haggerty and Richard V. Ericson, 279–307. Toronto: University of Toronto Press, 2006.

Yngvesson, Susanne Wigorts. "To See the World as It Appears: The Look, the Camera and the Flesh." In *Living in Surveillance Societies: The State of Surveillance*, edited by William R. Webster et al., 314–23. CreateSpace, 2013.

Williams, Rowan. "War, Words and Reason: Orwell and Thomas Merton on the Crises of Language—The Orwell Lecture 2015." The Orwell Foundation, December 17, 2015. https://www.orwellfoundation.com/the-orwell-foundation/news-events/the-orwell-lecture/2015-dr-rowan-williams/.

10

Virtual Counterfeit of the Infinite

Emmanuel Levinas and the Temptation of Temptation

DONALD WALLENFANG

Introduction

There is no question that the internet is one of the most—if not the most—significant advances in technology and mass communications of our era. It has been remarked that what the printing press was for the fifteenth and sixteenth centuries, the internet is for us today. Virtually everything has changed and just about every matter of business networking around the world depends in some way on use of the internet. But what is the meaning of the internet for the individual person concerning the most intimate recesses of the self? This is the question with which we will be concerned here.

The phenomenality of the internet presents to its user a plethora of possibilities. There is an inherent promiscuity of the self in relation to the possibilities that transpire through internet activity. In a virtual world, everything seems to be positioned always at arm's reach in such a way that reinforces the sense of engaging the world yet all the while remaining disengaged from it. In a virtual world, I can behold the world while it cannot behold me—or at least an authentic, in-the-flesh presence of me. I remain hidden like Gyges within the free play of the virtual world. My identity is concealed not only from the masquerade of the virtual world, but from myself as well. Subconsciously, I become a stranger to myself even as I exist as an invisible stranger to the anonymous "online community." My name becomes Anonymity in a world called Ambiguity.[1] The more I can conceal my identity, the more savvy I am as a web user. Even through live video applications, my countenance is reduced to a collection of incandescent pixels that can be detached consciously from my corporeal self. Within the intensified ambiguity of the virtual worlds of social media, one can flirt with virtual personas without immediate consequence or notice. It becomes possible to spend time with people online and acquire much knowledge about them without even having a conversation. Curiosity begins to control the cursor as one becomes transfixed on a multiplicity of virtual encounters through the singularity of an incognito medium. Far removed virtual encounters quickly merge into participatory channels of private conversation within a secret and confidential space of meeting. From texting, to email, to Facebook and beyond, virtual worlds undergo a metamorphosis into veritable worlds of speech and flesh. As human beings, we are not content with virtual relationships but instead demand that they come to life in flesh and bone. The hide-and-seek game of virtual ambiguity can last only for so long, and then it will be transmogrified inevitably into a pseudo-real world which can never be separated from the virtual façade from which it originated. It is likely that one will attempt once again to retreat to the virtual world which suspends all commitments and trials for the elusive pleasures of digital fantasy—a preference of pixels over persons and upright relationships.

For the remainder of the text, I will be puzzling over the phenomenality of the internet and, especially, on the experience of using search engines. I will argue that a tremendous ethical dilemma confronts the individual person upon turning on a computer and facing a blank search engine box with a blinking cursor. I name this allegedly innocent position "the temptation of temptation." In order to unpack what is meant by the temptation of temptation, I will rely almost exclusively on the 1964 Talmudic reading of Emmanuel Levinas (1906–95) entitled, "The Temptation of Temptation." Levinas's lecture has much to say given the question of internet ethics today.

The line of my argument will be as follows: (1) I will briefly elucidate the primary meanings of Levinas's 1964 lecture, "The Temptation of

---

1. One need think only of the growing phenomenon of cyberbullying to understand the terrifying lure of acting without responsibility for the other through the shifting vicissitudes of online communication tethered to anonymity. See, for example, Guzzo et al., "Bullying Victimization"; Pelfrey and Weber, "Talking Smack"; and Rafferty and Vander Ven, "'I Hate Everything About You."

Temptation"; (2) I will apply these meanings to the contemporary phenomenon of internet search engines and its ethical freight; and (3) I will propose a virtuous approach to internet usage in light of Levinas's insights and the Judeo-Christian tradition. Let us turn now to the first part of the argument and examine the intellectual contributions of Levinas's text, "The Temptation of Temptation."

Tempted by Temptation

In her 2002 book, *Emmanuel Levinas: The Problem of Ethical Metaphysics*, Edith Wyschogrod articulates well what Levinas means by "the temptation of temptation" and its relevance for people today:

> According to Levinas, the difficulty of Western man is rooted in his need to experience everything that can be experienced, to taste all the possibilities that life affords. This is the temptation of temptations. The paradigms of Western man are Ulysses, whose life is filled with novel and perilous adventure, and Don Juan, for whom a multiplicity of seductions provides a heightened sense of existence. It is of great moment to engage one's passions in life and to live dangerously. Innocence seems infantile and merely provisional, awaiting transformation by life itself.[2]

"Leave no stone unturned"—this is the essence of twenty-first century wisdom, especially within a popular liberal paradigm of unbridled individualism and relativism. Wyschogrod's summary of Levinas's brilliant insight called, "the temptation of temptation," is made with precision. The heightened sense of existence is the prize won for ceding all constraints of law, conscience, religion, authority (other than the self), and any predetermined conception of the Good whatsoever. Life is lived to the fullest inasmuch as it is filled with new and unpredictable experiences, endless prospects of enjoyment, and sensational excursions on the brink of peril and misfortune. Ulysses and Don Juan are paragons of the good life because of their promiscuous pursuit of the varied flavors of life. Innocence and childlike naïveté are to be awakened and vacated for the sake of becoming a seasoned adult, who assumes the privilege of connoisseur in relation to the plethora of stimulating experiences life has to offer. There is an acronym in circulation today, "YOLO," which stands for, "You Only Live Once." Many young people swear allegiance to this life philosophy before any other tradition of

2. Wyschogrod, *Emmanuel Levinas*, 208.

faith or standard of rationality. Actions are justified in the name of pillaging virgin experience. Many would prefer to regret what they have done rather than regret what they have not done. Enter the temptation of temptation.

For Levinas, the temptation of temptation refers precisely to the temptation of knowledge in which "what tempts the one tempted by temptation is not pleasure but the ambiguity of a situation in which pleasure is still possible but in respect to which the Ego keeps its liberty, has not yet given up its security, has kept its distance. . . . What is tempting is to be simultaneously outside everything and participating in everything."[3] In other words, the temptation of temptation occurs in the dark interstices of ambiguity between the object of temptation and the tempted, between marginal culpability and accusation, between anonymity and personal identity. In the experience of being tempted by temptation, the ego is disengaged just enough to render itself incognito before the light of conscience. Being tempted by temptation escorts the ego to the threshold of the threshold of sin all the while suspending an explicitly sinful act, advancing as far as possible before the buffer of actual temptation. Living in the temptation of temptation is to enjoy the anonymous autonomy before all that is possible, knowable, and pleasurable. The temptation of temptation exalts free will as divine since the very notion of free will indicates self-determination rather than being determined from without. The temptation of temptation brackets and sets aside all that would impinge upon the sovereignty of the will.

Levinas argues that "Westerners, opposed to a limited and overly well defined existence, want to taste everything themselves, want to travel the universe. But there is no universe without the circles of Hell!"[4] Levinas insists on the sober reality that everything is not good and therefore we should conduct our search for knowledge with careful discretion. Who desires to roam about the circles of Hell? Yet it is the temptation of temptation which wants to keep the circles of Hell within its ambiguous range of possibilities. Levinas says that "the temptation of temptation is philosophy, in contrast to a wisdom which knows everything without experiencing it."[5] The philosopher feeds on the ongoing temptation of temptation, arrested in the pretense to omniscience without admitting limit or restriction. The covenantal sage, in contrast, is he who binds

---

3. Levinas, "Temptation of Temptation," 33–34.
4. Levinas, "Temptation of Temptation," 33.
5. Levinas, "Temptation of Temptation," 34.

himself to divine wisdom through filial trust.⁶ Unlike the symbolic eating of the tree of the knowledge of good and evil, the wise one is the man who trusts God's command and renounces the possibility of transgressing this life-giving command.⁷ The truly wise one knows what is good and evil by trusting in divine testimony rather than demanding to determine this knowledge on his own apart from God. Levinas writes that "overcoming the temptation of temptation would then mean going within oneself further than one's self."⁸ Toward whom does one go further than oneself if not the other?⁹ To overcome the temptation of temptation requires going further than complacent and solipsistic self-sufficiency by committing oneself at all times to responsibility for the other.

Levinas defines the freedom which transcends the self in its movement toward the other as "a freedom of responsibilities."¹⁰ Freedom is revealed as a paradox, for it is not realized by shedding responsibility for the other but by embracing it. Levinas develops his freedom of responsibilities by reflecting on the Talmudic excerpt of the Tractate *Shabbath*. Within this

---

6. See ibid., 49: "We think, like our text, that consciousness and seeking, taken as their own preconditions, are, like naivete, the temptation of temptation, a tortuous path leading to ruin. The *bogdim* are the unfaithful, breaking a fundamental covenant. To them are opposed the *yesharim*, the upright."

7. See John Paul II, *Veritatis splendor*, 35, in speaking of the divine prohibition to eat from the tree of the knowledge of good and evil: "With this imagery, Revelation teaches that *the power to decide what is good and what is evil does not belong to man, but to God alone*. The man is certainly free, inasmuch as he can understand and accept God's commands. And he possesses an extremely far-reaching freedom, since he can eat 'of every tree of the garden.' But his freedom is not unlimited: it must halt before the 'tree of the knowledge of good and evil,' for it is called to accept the moral law given by God. In fact, human freedom finds its authentic and complete fulfillment precisely in the acceptance of that law. God, who alone is good, knows perfectly what is good for man, and by virtue of his very love proposes this good to man in the commandments."

8. Levinas, "Temptation of Temptation," 34.

9. See Levinas, "Temptation of Temptation," 48: "An innocence without naivete, an uprightness without stupidity, an absolute uprightness which is also absolute self-criticism, read in the eyes of the one who is the goal of my uprightness and whose look calls me into question. It is a movement toward the other which does not come back to its point of origin the way diversion comes back, incapable as it is of transcendence—a movement beyond anxiety and stronger than death." Cf. Pascal Bruckner's idea of innocence as "the disease of individualism" in Bruckner, *Temptation of Innocence*, e.g., 8–9: "I call *innocence* the disease of individualism; it consists in trying to escape the consequences of our own acts, attempting to enjoy the advantages of liberty without suffering any of the disadvantages."

10. Levinas, "Temptation of Temptation," 37.

text, Israel is depicted as the people who commit themselves to doing before hearing in the context of the giving of the Law on Mount Sinai.[11] Before hearing the words of the Torah, the Israelites bind themselves to it by virtue of its divine origin. Their unwavering trust in divine Goodness is the beginning of the Law's fulfillment in their daily lives. Because they completely trust the Lawgiver, they obey the divine command even before hearing it. In other words, they do not insist first on hearing the prescriptions and then considering for themselves whether or not they are amenable to them. That, after all, was the essence of the original sin. Instead of pretending to pass judgment on the divine Judge, the Israelites willfully submit to divine legislation before its articulation. This amounts to an inversion of the original sin and a refusal of the temptation of temptation. Disobedience begins with the temptation of temptation. It begins with the audacity of the finite to pass judgment on the Infinite. It begins with the demand to measure and scrutinize the Law of God according to arbitrary standards of human calibration. Disobedience stems from a subjectivity, which considers itself as the ultimate authority. Obedience to Torah, in contrast, expresses "the structure of a subjectivity clinging to the absolute."[12] Obedience recognizes the anteriority of Torah before logic, the anteriority of freedom before free will, the anteriority of God before humanity.[13]

---

11. See Levinas, "Temptation of Temptation," 42–43: "One accepts the Torah before one knows it. . . . It is a perfectly adult effort . . . acting before understanding. . . . The excellent choice that makes doing go before hearing does not prevent a fall. It arms not against temptation but against the temptation of temptation. . . . This undoubtedly indicates that the doing which is at stake here is not simply *praxis* as opposed to theory but a way of *actualizing without beginning with the possible*, of knowing without examining, of placing oneself beyond violence without this being the privilege of a free choice. A pact with good would exist, preceding the alternative of good and evil." This passage marks the striking metaphysical character of Levinas's thought within his overarching method of phenomenology.

12. Levinas, "Temptation of Temptation," 48. Cf. Levinas, "Temptation of Temptation," 38: "That the mind needs training suggests the very mystery of violence's anteriority to freedom, suggests the possibility of an adherence prior to free examination and prior to temptation."

13. See Levinas, "Temptation of Temptation," 37, 40: "The teaching, which the Torah is, cannot come to the human being as a result of a choice. That which must be received in order to make freedom of choice possible cannot have been chosen, unless after the fact. . . . Wouldn't Revelation be precisely a reminder of this consent prior to freedom and non-freedom? . . . To receive the gift of Torah—a Law—is to fulfil it before consciously accepting it. . . . Without being less pure than the freedom that would arise from freedom (in the non-engagement of the one who is tempted and who tries his luck), the freedom taught by the Jewish text starts in a non-freedom which, far from being slavery or

Levinas speaks of this obedience to Torah as uprightness that, as "an original fidelity to an indissoluble alliance, a belonging with, consists in confirming this alliance and not in engaging oneself headfirst for the sake of engaging oneself."[14] The alliance is between Torah and the human subject. A covenant relationship obtains between God and humanity through the mediation and signification of Torah and its ethical imperatives. Fidelity to Torah takes precedence over self-discovery because Torah contains "a lucidity without tentativeness," "a history whose conclusion precedes its development," "a 'practice' prior to voluntary adherence," an ethical order prior to the world.[15] Does any knowledge rival that proclaimed in the Torah? What could compare to the unrelenting ethical summons to responsibility before my neighbor? What other knowledge contains its future history in its past declaration? What other knowledge prescribes a way to live anchored in the infinite because it proceeds from "a past more ancient than any present"?[16] The alliance between Torah and the self is the very alliance between the self and the other. Torah is materialized within

---

childhood, is a beyond-freedom." Cf. Levinas, *Otherwise Than Being*, 10: "The freedom of another could never begin in my freedom, that is, abide in the same present, be contemporary, be representable to me. The responsibility for the other can not have begun in my commitment, in my decision. The unlimited responsibility in which I find myself comes from the hither side of my freedom, from a 'prior to every memory,' an 'ulterior to every accomplishment,' from the non-present par excellence, the non-original, the anarchical, prior to or beyond essence."

14. Levinas, "Temptation of Temptation," 49.

15. Levinas, "Temptation of Temptation," 40, 45, 48. Cf. Levinas, "Temptation of Temptation," 36, 41: "It may be, however, that the notion of action, instead of indicating *praxis* as opposed to contemplation, a move in the dark, leads us to an order in which the opposition of engagement and disengagement is no longer decisive and which precedes, even conditions, these notions. . . . The meaning of being, the meaning of creation, is to realize the Torah. The world is here so that the ethical order has the possibility of being fulfilled."

16. Levinas, *Otherwise Than Being*, 24. Unlike Levinas's admonition to consider Torah as primal and ultimate knowledge, we often insist on knowledge prior to and apart from living. See Levinas, "The Temptation of Temptation," 34: "To join evil to good, to venture into the ambiguous corners of being without sinking into evil and to remain beyond good and evil in order to accomplish this, is to know. One must experience everything through one's own self but experience it without having experienced it yet, before engaging oneself in the world. For experiencing itself is already committing oneself, choosing, living, limiting oneself. To know is to experience without experiencing, before living. We want to know before we do. But we want only a knowledge completely tested through our own evidence. We do not want to undertake anything without knowing everything, and nothing can become known to us unless we have gone and seen for ourselves, regardless of the misadventures of the exploration. We want to live dangerously, but in security, in the world of truths."

the fabric of human relationships where it takes on flesh through uprightness and responsibility. No additional knowledge informs Torah or adds to its primordial message.

Especially in a digital age, "the European is certain at least of his retreat as subject into his extraterritorial subjectivity, certain of his separation with respect to any other, and thus assured of a kind of irresponsibility toward the All."[17] The notion of a private life, removed and withdrawn from a public network of transparent relationships, is symptomatic of the postmodern era. To pretend to exercise an imagination entirely absent of consequences and effect on others is the grand illusion of our epoch. Today, one believes that he can live in windows of time absent of all responsibility toward the other and removed from everyone. The frequent experience of solitude relieved of all solicitude has become the premier way of life. News feeds do not so much provoke concern for the other as serve as a form of entertainment at which to gawk, balk, and mindlessly forget in the casual movement to yet another personal enjoyment. It is a sinister privilege to sit on the hind side of a screen and watch the world suffer, all the while neglecting the charge to come to its assistance. The temptation of temptation insulates the choice of the self to act or not to act—or at least to act not yet. Action and the sense of responsibility for the other are suspended by the primacy of free will and its self-interested ranking of more urgent matters. However, Levinas avers that the freedom afforded by Torah is rooted in the ultimatum of *eyn berera*, or "no choice": "the Torah or death"—a dilemma pressed on the human subject from without.[18] It is not Torah that is determined by humanity, but humanity which is determined by Torah. Will we humanize or destroy one another? This is the question which confronts everyone at all times, and me before all others. Responsibility does not begin, first of all, with free will. Rather, the call to responsibility precedes free will, is the *raison d'être* of free will, and compels free will to actualize its latent potential to become truly free.

---

17. Levinas, "Temptation of Temptation," 36.

18. Levinas, "Temptation of Temptation," 37. Cf. Levinas, "Temptation of Temptation," 49: "The Torah is an order to which the ego adheres, without having had to enter it, an order beyond being and choice. The ego's exit from being occurs before the ego-which-decides. . . . It happens through the weight exerted on one point of being by the rest of its substance. This weight is called responsibility. Responsibility for a creature—a being of which the ego was not the author—which establishes the ego. To be a self is to be responsible beyond what one has oneself done. *Temimut* [i.e., 'uprightness'] consists in substituting oneself for others."

In the ethical paradigm of Levinas, being itself is relegated to an ancillary position in relation to Torah: "Being receives a challenge from the Torah, which jeopardizes its pretension of keeping itself above or beyond good and evil. In challenging the absurd 'that's the way it is' claimed by the Power of the powerful, the man of the Torah transforms being into human history. Meaningful movement jolts the Real."[19] This is to say that Torah serves as a guide for the humanization of being. In giving lasting meaning to being through their ethical activity, human persons attest to the ancient primacy of the Good over Being.[20] In other words, being is because it is good to be. Through ethical relationships we likewise testify against all nihilistic worldviews, which leave no room for holiness or redemption. Being is stale or even suffocating without its transformation into meaningful acts of love and service by us rational creatures. Torah subverts the propensity toward a self-insulating power, which only ever ends in self-consuming attrition, and instead relocates power as the prophetic inspiration of responsibility. I am ordered by the other through the interiority of my guilty conscience, which holds me responsible for how the other fares. The suffocation of being, the inescapable experience of being riveted to oneself in existence, and the banality of pleasure are all overcome through the affirmative response to the call of the other to the point of abandonment. To become human is to become responsible for the other without remainder. Giving up all, including the totality of one's very self, results in the freedom of the other and, paradoxically, in the freedom of the self. By foregoing the temptation of temptation through responsibility for the other, freedom is won for all.

Googling Temptation

So what does Google have to do with the temptation of temptation? Everything.[21] Now that we have explained what Levinas means by "the temp-

---

19. Levinas, "Temptation of Temptation," 39.

20. See Levinas, *Totality and Infinity*, 103: "The Place of the Good above every essence is the most profound teaching, the definitive teaching, not of theology, but of philosophy."

21. For more on the formative role of search engines on personal identity, see Sanz and Stančík, "Your Search." In addition, for more on the issue of Google's competition with other search engines to control the internet search engine marketplace, see Hazan, "Stop Being Evil." It must be noted that the notion of a pure, unbiased search engine has been long since extinct. Every search engine injects bias—often ideologically charged from the Left—in both its search window presentation and tendered search results. One

tation of temptation," let us apply these ideas to the problem of internet ethics. First, we must define the contours of this problem by describing the phenomenon of performing a web search. A search engine draws us into the phenomenality of the temptation of temptation. There is nothing inherently evil about a blank box and a blinking cursor. However, I already enter the temptation of temptation when I take my place comfortably behind a screen which opens to the world in all of its ambiguity with no one else looking back at me or looking over my shoulder. I am at the helm of this ship of unlimited possibility for good or for ill. Therefore I enter a zone of perception in which my free will is virtually unlimited. Even though there may be factors in my mind which would restrict some of these possibilities, the point is that all of the possibilities remain. Confronted by the blank search engine box, I am not yet being tempted with any image or idea in particular. The blank box is innocent, but I already have commenced the temptation of temptation. All knowledge and virtual experience is set before me in its wonder and mystery. The looming question leveled by the temptation of temptation is "What should I type in this box?"

I hover over the distinction between good and evil as long as I remain within the temptation of temptation. I pretend to be above the difference between good and evil as long as I suspend the question. Returning to the symbolic tree of the knowledge of good and evil, before partaking of the forbidden fruit, I hearken to the voice of the tempter and consider the possibility of the possibility of possibility, etc. Levinas says as much when he writes,

> The temptation of temptation is thus the temptation of knowledge. The repetition once begun no longer comes to a stop. It is infinite. The temptation of temptation is also the temptation of temptation of temptation, etc. The temptation of temptation is philosophy, in contrast to a wisdom which knows everything without experiencing it.[22]

Knowledge, as a concept, is identical neither to good nor evil. Knowledge is good insofar as what is known is good. Knowledge could be bad if its object is deficient of goodness in some way or if it distracts in some way from doing what is good. The term knowledge bears a rather neutral connotation or, if anything other than neutral, a positive meaning. It may be readily

---

needs only to reflect on the persons and events highlighted on almost a daily basis on Google (and other search engines) to recognize the overwhelming display of bias.

22. Levinas, "Temptation of Temptation," 34.

agreeable that to know is good. So, how can the temptation of knowledge constitute this menacing temptation of temptation? The reason is that the temptation of knowledge mimics the infinite while not being identical to it. Knowledge is an imposture of the infinite since it displays an infinite character that only recoils back into itself upon every additional thing known. By knowing more and more, I am neither closer nor further away from the infinite. Even worse, is Qoheleth correct when he says, "For in much wisdom there is much sorrow; whoever increases knowledge increases grief"?[23] How can Levinas assure us of "a wisdom which knows everything without experiencing it"?

This wisdom is characterized by love and responsibility. Overcoming the pretensions of knowledge, love's aim is to act always in accord with the good. Knowledge's aim is to keep a distance from the good so as not to be swayed by anything other than the pure act of knowing and the subsequent purity of free will. For knowledge, the distinction between good and evil is arbitrary inasmuch as the neutrality of knowledge is indifferent to moral distinctions in its proclivity for "raw data and facts." The phenomenality of Google pretends to signify neutrality and, by virtue of its originally blank contents, strikes consciousness with an aura of technological indifference. Just as a computer is indifferent to good and evil, so is the phenomenon of a web search engine. In extending our noetic consciousness through the neutral composition of digital technology, we take on virtual avatars of robotic and androgynous personas that soar above the distinction between good and evil in the name of knowledge. Even more nefarious, when knowledge is blended with curiosity, there is no end to post-innocent, post-ignominious, and impenitent virtual exploration. The temptation of temptation commences and sustains this virtual world which hovers above good and evil. The temptation of temptation opens onto a happy place where all is permissible and nothing is taboo.[24] It is reinforced all the more by ideological strongholds—whether liberal or conservative—which, too, claim to be beyond good and evil. For liberal ideology, Google symbolizes emancipation from censorship and a beacon of the freedom of choice. For conservative ideology, Google is a hub of consumerism and the endless foray into

---

23. Eccl 1:18 (NABRE).

24. See Jennifer Geddes's essay, "Attending to Suffering," in Brooks and Toth, *Mourning After*, 77–78, where she writes, "Because 'temptation makes nothing irreparable,' it also makes nothing forbidden and everything safely permissible. Mistakes can be erased, risks taken safely, and, hence, nothing is really at stake."

the free marketplace of knowledge, enjoyment, and novelty. Extremes meet in the temptation of temptation.

Torah and Virtual Reality

Now that the temptation of temptation has been described both in its concept and as applied to the internet, let us next examine how the temptation of temptation can be overcome. Lurking behind the temptation of temptation is the temptation to evil.[25] A fine line runs between the temptation of temptation and the temptation to evil. Once one passes into the field of the temptation of temptation, one is found at the door of the temptation to evil. Yet Levinas claims a way out: "overcoming the temptation of evil by avoiding the temptation of temptation."[26] So, how is the temptation of temptation to be avoided both in a general sense and as applied to online ethics? In a word: Torah. Binding one's self to the eternal law of God is the only way to circumvent the temptation of temptation. We are dealing with a covenant relationship which risks everything for the one thing. All alternatives are renounced for the sake of the singular path of living according to the divine will. Forming a personal covenant with Torah forces one to forsake choice for the sake of responsibility. Free will admits a vocation that precedes it and realizes that responding affirmatively to this vocation is the only way to freedom. Indeed, this is the vocation to the freedom for excellence by renunciation of the freedom of indifference. It is the freedom of responsibility for the other to which Torah is an indicator. As evinced in C. S. Lewis's book, *The Great Divorce*, to live as children in the kingdom of God requires the complete renunciation of the possibility of temptation in any form whatsoever. The temptation of temptation proves to be inimical to the kingdom of God.

Binding oneself to Torah paradoxically limits the self to many perceivable finite goods, pleasures and enjoyments but at the same time opens the self to the infinite. The finitude of knowledge gives way to the infinity of love. A veritable death to self-assertion and vanity is required to pass over into the terrain of love and responsibility. When Torah rules one's life, every thought, word and action is scrutinized by the exigencies

---

25. See Gen 4:6–7: "The LORD said to Cain, 'Why are you angry, and why has your countenance fallen? If you do well, will you not be accepted? And if you do not do well, sin is lurking at the door; its desire is for you, but you must master it'" (RSV).

26. Levinas, "Temptation of Temptation," 41.

of responsibility. It is not that knowledge is resisted at every turn. Rather, knowledge is viewed as beneficial if it serves the greater good of being responsible for the other. Entering into a covenant with Torah does not only forfeit every temptation to evil, even more importantly, it forfeits the temptation to temptation. The very venue in which one hearkens to the possibility of being tempted is obliterated, never to return. One may respond to such a proposal with the concern that free will is also desolated in the face of Torah. If the temptation of temptation is included in the concept of free will, then that is correct: free will is undone before the demands of Torah, and that is the point.[27] For Levinas, Torah is not revealed primarily in a text and in the self's fidelity to a text. Torah speaks through the face of the other and in the heart of the self. Just as I can never take leave of the call of the other in the name of some autonomous free will, neither can I dodge the prescriptions of Torah as proclaimed through the relational proximity between the other and me. The phenomenological shape of the human being is the asymmetrical relation between self and other. The face of the other speaks to me in its radical vulnerability and nakedness: "Do not kill me." My affirmative response to the call of the other takes form in the prophetic words that well up within me: "Here I am!" In a freedom of responsibility which forsakes the temptation of temptation, the self lays down its rights to autonomy and non-disturbance. The self is liberated from itself through forgetfulness of self and awakening to the needs of the other. Freedom of the self from itself is wrought by the incessant disruption of the self by the other.[28]

The point at which the internet is viewed exclusively as a powerful tool through which to serve the other through love is when the temptation of temptation is eradicated. The point at which the accumulation of the miserable pleasures of the flesh gives way to the sober vocation of responsibility for the other is when the temptation of temptation is despoiled. The point at which the profligacy of "free time" is invested instead in the

---

27. See, for example, the moving *Suscipe* prayer of Ignatius of Loyola in his *Spiritual Exercises*: "Take, Lord, and receive all my liberty, my memory, my understanding, and all my will—all that I have and possess. You, O Lord, have given all that to me. I now give it back to you, O Lord. All of it is yours. Dispose of it according to your will. Give me your love and your grace, for that is enough for me" (Ignatius of Loyola, *Ignatius of Loyola*, 177).

28. See Levinas, *Otherwise Than Being*, 180: "Freedom is animation itself, breath, the breathing of outside air, where inwardness frees itself from itself, and is exposed to all the winds."

mission to come to the assistance of the other through prayer and sacrifice is when the temptation of temptation is forgotten. The Gordian knot of original sin is untied by the ethical eloquence of Torah and its transmutation into flesh.[29] Flesh does not take place within a virtual world. It is not composed of a panoply of pixels. True human flesh is that which extends itself in space and time for the sake of the other. Flesh comes alive and achieves its *raison d'être* when it goes outside of itself because the other has invaded its innermost recesses. This phenomenon is what Levinas calls inspiration and it is a prerequisite for following the prescriptions of Torah.[30] By adhering to Torah with perfect fidelity, one rejects the temptation of temptation manifest in the phenomenality of the internet, refusing to be frozen to stone as one who gazes transfixed on the face of Medusa. After all, serpents of paralyzing possibility do not promote the flourishing of humanity. The just one who lives according to Torah acts as the hero Perseus by beheading Medusa, only to use her head as a weapon for good. In other words, the one who resolves to live in responsibility for the other anathematizes the temptation of temptation and instead uses its dissipate energies for serving the needs of the other.

As applied to internet usage, the adherent of Torah approaches the internet exclusively as a tool to serve the vocation of responsibility for the

---

29. See Levinas, *Otherwise Than Being*, 105, 109, and 195 (n. 12): "In the exposure to wounds and outrages, in the feeling proper to responsibility, the oneself is provoked as irreplaceable, as devoted to others, without being able to resign, and thus as incarnated in order to offer itself, to suffer and to give. . . . The body which makes giving possible makes one *other* without alienating. For this other is the heart, and the goodness, of the same, the inspiration or the very psyche in the soul. . . . The body is neither an obstacle opposed to the soul, nor a tomb that imprisons it, but that by which the self is susceptibly itself. Incarnation is extreme passivity; to be exposed to sickness, suffering, death, is to be exposed to compassion, and, as a self, to the gift that costs. The oneself is on this side of the zero of inertia and nothingness, in deficit of being, in itself and not in being, without a place to lay its head, in the no-grounds, and thus without conditions. As such it will be shown to be the bearer of the world, bearing it, suffering it, blocking rest and lacking a fatherland. It is the correlate of a persecution, a substitution for the other."

30. See Levinas, *Otherwise Than Being*, 181–82, 191 n. 3: "In human breathing, in its everyday equality, perhaps we have to already hear the breathlessness of an inspiration that paralyzes essence, that transpierces it with an inspiration by the other, an inspiration that is already expiration, that 'rends the soul'! It is the longest breath there is, spirit. Is man not the living being capable of the longest breath in inspiration, without a stopping point, and in expiration, without return? To transcend oneself, to leave one's home to the point of leaving oneself, is to substitute oneself for another. . . . The soul is the other in me. The psyche, the-one-for-the-other, can be a possession and a psychosis; the soul is already a seed of folly."

other. There is no other purpose. Entertainment, leisure, selfish enjoyment, and curiosity are all set aside in the name of the other. The self forgets itself under the weight of responsibility it senses in relation to the other. One does not stare aimlessly into the blank gaze of Google (read: Medusa) but performs a web search only when a definite purpose is in mind that will serve to build up the other. To be ever mindful of the other is to dismiss the temptation of temptation in every thought, word and deed. Encounter with the infinite short-circuits in its quest through the accumulation of knowledge. The internet, posing as a virtual counterfeit of the infinite, indeed may provide the self with countless stimulating pleasures for self-centered mind and flesh. However, the pleasures provided by the internet never seem to keep their promises of authentic and lasting liberation of the self from itself, wallowing in the cold static of being.[31] Through the phenomenality of the internet search engine, the temptation of temptation acts as a virtual quicksand that enslaves free will to its alleged sovereignty, indecision, indifference, and autonomous autonomy.[32] Only the intrusive

---

31. See Levinas, *On Escape*, 62: "Pleasure is a process; it is the process of departing from being [*processus de sortie de l'être*]. Its affective nature is not only the expression or the sign of this getting-out; it is the getting out itself. Pleasure is affectivity, precisely because it does not take on the forms of being, but rather attempts to break these up. Yet it is a deceptive escape. For it is an escape that fails. If, like a process that is far from closing up on itself, pleasure appears in a constant surpassing of oneself, it breaks just at the moment where it seems to get out absolutely. It develops with an increase in promises, which become richer the closer it comes to its paroxysm, but these promises are never kept."

32. See Ricoeur, *Freedom and Nature*, 445–47, 463: "The initial act of freedom for the classical thinker is suspicion: it is a doubt, and that doubt is an act of withdrawal: the 'I think' withdraws from the snare of the body and the world. It is exalted in defying the malevolent demon. In the same way freedom, according to the existential thinker, trembles since it is the crisis of being, it is anguished by the wide spaces it creates through possibility, it is anguished by the negation which it introduces into the fullness of antecedent being. Starting with its own infinity, it is the permanent possibility of disproportion, it experiences itself as its own temptation, the temptation to exalt itself infinitely, just as it experiences the world and its body as temptation, the temptation to sink into and lose oneself in the object. . . . I suffer from being one finite and partial perspective of the world and of values. I am condemned to be the 'exception': this and nothing else, this not that. . . . I suffer from being condemned to a choice which consecrates and intensifies my particularity and destroys all the possibles through which I am in contact with the totality of human experience. . . . Ah! If only I could grasp and embrace everything!—and how cruel it is to choose and exclude. That is how life moves: from amputation to amputation; and on the road from the possible to the actual lie only ruined hopes and atrophied powers. How much latent humanity I must reject in order to be someone! . . . Freedom responds to the *no* of condition with the *no* of refusal. . . . In effect *what* we refuse, is always, in the last analysis, the limitation of character, the shadows of the unconscious,

call of the other can rupture the entropic force of self-aggrandizement and the apathetic virus of pleasure for pleasure's sake. By diagnosing the phenomenon of Google as the temptation of temptation, we are able to call it out and overcome its suffocating effect on humanity, turning Medusa's severed head into a weapon of virtue.

Conclusion

In this essay, the meaning of the temptation of temptation and its application to the phenomenality of the internet has been described. Also, a strategy for overcoming the temptation of temptation in regard to internet usage has been suggested. The crucial error that the temptation of temptation is necessary for human freedom was exposed and the integral relationship between freedom and Torah was, in turn, substantiated. At this point, several questions arise concerning the practical implementation of Torah in one's personal and communal life in order to overcome the temptation of temptation: Are communal contexts necessary through which to reinforce a collective covenantal relationship with Torah? What specific internet activities are consonant with overcoming the temptation of temptation and which are not? Are people who use social media especially prone to succumbing to the temptation of temptation? What offline activities can counteract the immediate experience of the temptation of temptation engendered by web search engines? How is one to remain in a covenant relationship with Torah? How is one to remain resolute in living in responsibility for the other? These and similar questions lead us from the abstract sensibility of the temptation of temptation and its ongoing threat to the concrete application of surmounting it through faithful adherence to Torah.

One final question I want to entertain, however, is this: What is the role of testimony in mediating the summons to overcome the temptation of temptation? More specifically, how does my responsibility for the

---

and the contingency of life. I cannot tolerate being only that partial consciousness limited by all its obscurity and discovering its brute existence. Thus we know the initial content of the refusal: the most remarkable trait of this triple refusal is that it does not present itself at first as a refusal but conceals itself in an affirmation of sovereignty whose implicit negativity it is important to bring to light. The disguised form of refusal is the haughty affirmation of consciousness as absolute, that is, as creative or as self-producing. It is the very sorrow of negation of all experienced parts which stimulates the passion of freedom to engender itself as sovereign, to posit itself as being of itself. Briefly, exaggeration is the privileged form of refusal."

other—especially my responsibility for those younger than I—play out in terms of the personal witness I give to the other concerning internet use? As a father of six young children, this question is especially relevant and close to home. But whether or not one recognizes oneself to be a parent, I would argue that all adults play the role of mother or father in relation to children. No adult is exempt from being responsible for children and providing significant witness to them. This asymmetrical relationship, based on difference in age and development, is governed by the call of the adult to be responsible for the child in all things. All that we do testifies to those younger than ourselves and every thought, word and act is inscribed on the testaments of our own lives and those of others. In addition to the term "law," Torah may also be translated as "instruction" or "teaching." Torah has an inherent pedagogical character and it is extended through the ethical activity of adults in relation to children.[33] My own life becomes an incarnate Torah before the face of every child.

This fact underscores all the more the living identity of Torah. It is certainly not a dead letter on a page, but the witness of its adherents who live in constant fidelity to responsibility for the other. The parental attributes of the divine are enacted through human parental relationships laced with unambiguous testimony. Every human life radiates a message within the matrix of responsibility and, for adults, our living testimonies become the legislative fabric of the child's world. If this relational fact is recognized each and every time we turn on a computer or mobile device, how would it shape our online activity? If every click of a button or tap on an interactive screen is ordered toward the good of the child who I teach and lead, what difference would that make for how I spend my time navigating the World Wide Web? Put more bluntly, is one willing to forego responsibility for the

---

33. See Levinas, *Totality and Infinity*, 171, 180: "The calling in question of the I, coextensive with the manifestation of the Other in the face, we call language. The height from which language comes we designate with the term teaching. . . . This voice coming from another shore teaches transcendence itself. Teaching signifies the whole infinity of exteriority. And the whole infinity of exteriority is not first produced, to then teach: teaching is its very production. The first teaching teaches this very height, tantamount to its exteriority, the ethical. . . . The contradiction between the free interiority and the exteriority that should limit it is reconciled in the man open to teaching. Teaching is a discourse in which the master can bring to the student what the student does not yet know. It does not operate as maieutics, but continues the placing in me of the idea of infinity. The idea of infinity implies a soul capable of containing more than it can draw from itself. It designates an interior being that is capable of a relation with the exterior, and does not take its own interiority for the totality of being."

child in exchange for the dissipation and eventual frozenness of the temptation of temptation? It is in this real-life scenario of the adult's relation to the child that Levinas's description of the temptation of temptation comes alive in all of its vigor. To say yes to the temptation of temptation is simultaneously to say no to the child as one willfully omits one's duty to live in utmost responsibility for the child in everything.

In sum, Torah is spoken through testimony within the ethical web of human relationships. Overcoming the temptation of temptation is sustained through the efficacy of testimonies in fidelity to Torah, forming a harmonious communal mission aimed at serving the other in love, especially the most vulnerable persons whose cry for help is most acute. According to the ultimate demands of Torah, the internet is used either to build the other up or to tear the other down, whether by direct assault or negligent omission. My life vocation already has been determined and its clarion call echoes within the chambers of my heart wherein the other speaks an urgent word, commanding me to come to her assistance. The call of the other issues from my own lips in the form of my affirmative response: "Here I am!" At this definitive utterance, the temptation of temptation is dissolved and a passable (passible) way is opened through which both self and other are forever liberated from the bondage of irresponsibility. Solitude gives way to solicitude and Google meets grace in the primary form of abstention.

Bibliography

Aronowicz, Annette. "Introducing 'The Temptation of Temptation': Levinas and Europe." *The Journal of Scriptural Reasoning* 11.2 (2012). http://jsr.shanti.virginia.edu/back-issues/volume-11-no-2-december-2012-levinas-and-philosophy/introducing-the-temptation-of-temptation-levinas-and-europe/.

Beals, Corey. *Levinas and the Wisdom of Love: The Question of Invisibility.* Waco: Baylor University Press, 2007.

Brooks, Neil, and Josh Toth, eds. *The Mourning After: Attending the Wake of Postmodernism.* New York: Rodopi, 2007.

Bruckner, Pascal. *The Temptation of Innocence: Living in the Age of Entitlement.* New York: Algora Publishing, 2000.

Guzzo, Giovanni, et al. "Bullying Victimization, Post-Traumatic Symptoms, and the Mediating Role of Alexithymia." *Child Indicators Research* 7.1 (2014) 141–53.

Hazan, Joshua G. "Stop Being Evil: A Proposal for Unbiased Google Search." *Michigan Law Review* 111.5 (2013) 789–20.

Ignatius of Loyola. *Ignatius of Loyola: The Spiritual Exercises and Selected Works.* Edited by George E. Ganss. New York: Paulist Press, 1991.

John Paul II. *Veritatis splendor*. 1993.
Kaplan, Lawrence. "Israel under the Mountain: Emmanuel Levinas on Freedom and Constraint in the Revalation of the Torah." *Modern Judaism* 18.1 (1998) 35–46.
Levinas, Emmanuel. *Nine Talmudic Readings*. Translated by Annette Aronowicz. Bloomington: Indiana University Press, 1990.
———. *Of God Who Comes to Mind*. Translated by Bettina Bergo. Stanford: Stanford University Press, 1998.
———. *On Escape*. Translated by Bettina Bergo. Stanford: Stanford University Press, 2003.
———. *Otherwise Than Being or Beyond Essence*. Translated by Alphonso Lingis. Pittsburgh: Duquesne University Press, 1981.
———. *Totality and Infinity: An Essay on Exteriority*. Translated by Alphonso Lingis. Pittsburgh: Duquesne University Press, 1969.
Marion, Jean-Luc. *Being Given: Toward a Phenomenology of Givenness*. Translated by Jeffrey L. Kosky. Stanford: Stanford University Press, 2002.
———. *The Erotic Phenomenon*. Translated by Stephen E. Lewis. Chicago: The University of Chicago Press, 2007.
Pelfrey, William V., and Nicole Weber. "Talking Smack and the Telephone Game: Conceptualizing Cyberbullying with Middle and High School Youth." *Journal of Youth Studies* 17.3 (2014) 397–414.
Pinckaers, Servais. *Morality: The Catholic View*. Translated by Michael Sherwin. South Bend: St. Augustine's Press, 2001.
———. *The Sources of Christian Ethics*. Translated by Mary Thomas Noble. Washington, DC: Catholic University of America Press, 1995.
Rafferty, Rebecca, and Thomas Vander Ven. "'I Hate Everything About You': A Qualitative Examination of Cyberbullying and On-Line Aggression in a College Sample." *Deviant Behavior* 35.5 (2014) 364–77.
Ricoeur, Paul. *Freedom and Nature*. Translated by Erazim V. Kohák. Evanston: Northwestern University Press, 1966.
Sanz, Esteve, and Juraj Stančík. "Your Search—'Ontological Security'—Matched 111,000 Documents: An Empirical Substantiation of the Cultural Dimension of Online Research." *New Media and Society* 16.2 (2014) 252–70.
Tracy, David. *Plurality and Ambiguity: Hermeneutics, Religion, Hope*. Chicago: The University of Chicago Press, 1987.
Wyschogrod, Edith. *Emmanuel Levinas: The Problem of Ethical Metaphysics*. New York: Fordham University Press, 2002.

11

The Church and Electronic Media—Foundational Issues

Our Addiction to Efficiency and the Myth of Neutrality[1]

MARK D. BAKER

It is imperative that we reflect with care on the use of specific applications of electronic media in the church. It is also imperative, however, that we do not simply use the same framework and mindset of electronic media itself as we do this discernment. In this paper I address two common misperceptions at the foundational or framework level and offer corrections to them.

First Thesis

In order to discern well appropriate use of electronic media we must recognize that efficiency is only one characteristic of many to use when evaluating what is best. Efficiency is not synonymous with best; yet for many people in the world today "most efficient" and "best" have become synonymous. For instance, for someone to state that one alternative is more efficient than another is often taken to be equivalent to stating that it is the preferable alternative. To be told a more efficient model is available tugs at people to get it—to have the best.

---

1. This essay was originally delivered in a plenary presentation at the Ecclesia and Ethics II Online Conference: "Gospel Community and Virtual Existence—A Conference Exploring the Ethics and Theology of the internet from a Biblical and Ecclesial Perspective," March 8, 2014.

A definition of "best" is: to do something in the most advantageous, suitable, or desirable way. To do something in the most efficient way means to do it in a way that uses the least amount of time, money, energy, space, etc. Efficiency is calculated; it can be measured by numbers. Sometimes the most efficient alternative is the best, but not always. For instance, we have a front-loading washing machine in our house. It is more efficient than a top loading washer. It washes clothes cleaner using less water, less electricity, and less soap. It also is easier on clothes and spins them dryer. It would seem this front-loading washer is both better and more efficient than a top-loading washer. I think we did the best thing in buying this washer. In Honduras, however, I would say that buying this efficient washer would not be the best thing to do. When we lived in Honduras, Norma did our laundry. She washed it by hand on a cement washboard. She used a lot of water, but no electricity. She got the clothes as clean or cleaner than a washing machine, but it took her hours to do so and it was very rough on the clothes. They wore out faster. In some ways she is as good as a front-loading washing machine and in others much worse. It is, however, definitely not the most efficient way to clean clothes. But in a land where unemployment is extremely high, we thought having our friend Norma wash our clothes was a much better way of getting them clean than buying a washing machine. Not because it is more efficient, but because it gave Norma a job and allowed us to share meals with her on washing days.

Efficient is also not the same as effective. To be effective is to achieve a desired result or purpose. You can be effective without being efficient, and at times efficiency might hinder effectiveness. The following example from Shane Hipps's book, *The Hidden Power of Electronic Culture*, demonstrates that efficient communication is not always effective. He recounts how early in his career in an ad agency he mirrored what others did "shooting off e-mails to the relevant parties in other departments detailing . . .requests and noting deadlines." People in the company considered E-mail a lifesaver; stating it was so much more efficient. Yet Hipps found that people in other departments often did not meet deadlines. He would physically have to track down the people and negotiate a solution to the problem at hand. Often when he did, they would dig in their heels and not cooperate. He decided to try an experiment. He reports:

> For two weeks I decided only to make my project requests in person. I would sit down in other people's offices; inevitably, we would carry on inefficient conversations about non-work-related

matters and eventually discuss my project needs. It was often difficult to find people, and I spent a lot of time walking around the building, looking for my colleagues. It felt like a lot more work to do it this way, and initially, it took longer—but I found there to be a number of benefits.

As deadlines approached, people from other departments actually came to find me to deliver my requests in person, and I encountered none of the typical resistance. I also discovered they worked on my projects before they worked on my colleagues' e-mail requests, even those requests with tighter deadlines. Our face-to-face meetings built a relationship in a way e-mail could not. These relationships made all the difference in making both of our jobs more enjoyable. It was somewhat inefficient at first, and I was in contact with them less frequently, but our face-to-face connections were more meaningful and effective in the long run.

A few years later I learned my personal experiment had been done on a larger scale by professors at Stanford Business School. They focused on business negotiations made face to face, over the telephone, and via e-mail. Not surprisingly, they found that negotiations performed exclusively over e-mail broke down far more often than face-to-face or even telephone negotiations.[2]

What are some examples from your life where the most efficient approach and the best approach are not necessarily the same? Some are probably simple, I prefer "old fashioned" oatmeal that takes five minutes to cook over the more efficient one-minute or instant varieties. Others are of more significance. We would not necessarily agree on all of them—you may think the more efficient oatmeal actually is the best. I ask the question not in order to make a list of things where best and most efficient do not match, rather to invite reflection on what other characteristics we use to determine what is the best option. In addition to efficiency we might also consider aesthetics, and also ask whether it is fair, just, or truthful? Will it enhance our relationships with others and creation; how will it affect our health, our soul? We must include these and other values as we discern the appropriate use of electronic media.

To include other values is not to erase efficiency from the list. Note: in my thesis I did not reject efficiency as a value, rather I said that we must recognize that efficiency is only one characteristic of many. This is, perhaps, a moderate thesis, but in a context in which efficiency often trumps all it is not necessarily an easy one to live out. Kosuke Koyama,

---

2. Hipps, *Hidden Power of Electronic Culture*, 113–14.

among others, would tell us we must resist efficiency as the default best option because at the heart of Christianity is not efficiency but the cross. Koyama would add meaning-making to the above list of values. He writes that efficiency suffocates meaning. Yet, "the most extreme example of the triumph of meaning over the idolatry of efficiency is the crucifixion of Christ. There Christ demonstrates the depth of his sincerity in the most painful and 'inefficient' way."[3]

Second Thesis

People commonly refer to electronic media, the internet, cell phones, tablets, etc. as morally-neutral tools. They state that it is the use of them that is either good or bad. In response I have a two-part thesis. *First, no tool or medium is neutral; it influences both the content it carries and the user of the tool. Second, to treat the medium as passive is a grave mistake because it leads to ignoring the medium itself and only evaluating whether the intended purpose for using it is good or bad.* I want to add a clarification on language. Although it is accurate to say that tools are not neutral, it may be more helpful to use the terms "passive" and "active." To argue that no medium is neutral is not to advocate for then evaluating which ones are good and which ones are bad, but to maintain that they are not passive.

The medium affects the content communicated through that medium. Part of this phenomenon has to do with reception. An audio book with the same exact content is received differently than one that is read. A movie telling the same story can move a person through using images and music in a way a book cannot. The medium, however, is not just about reception; it also shapes and changes the content itself. A book must include words to identify who is talking. The movie does not have to; it will show us. A book takes us inside a character's head in ways a movie cannot. Movies will edit out many details—time is limited and the medium requires movement, action. We can think of more extreme examples. Think of tools like PowerPoint or Twitter; you can only put so much information on one screen or so many characters in one tweet. These mediums limit, shape, and influence their content.

Clearly, as communicators of the gospel and theological truths we must discern how the mediums we use act upon the content communicated through them. Just as important, if not more important, is to

---

3. Koyama, "Crucified Christ Challenges Human Power," 150–51.

recognize that as we actively use tools they also act upon us, change us. As John Culkin states, "We shape our tools and thereafter our tools shape us."[4] John Dyer, in his book *From Garden to the City* has excellent chapters on this theme of the presumed neutrality of mediums. He wisely starts with an example far from the internet—the shovel. If you use a shovel to dig holes all day what will happen? There will be holes in ground, but also you will have blisters and sore muscles. If you continue using it what will happen? You will build muscles and develop callouses. We use the shovel and the shovel changes us.

Electronic media is active in a variety of ways. I will share just a few examples. Think about the changes that occur in a room if we turn on the television—it is active, not neutral. Regardless of the content—good or bad—the device itself influences our lives. Arthur Boers, in his book, *Living in Focus*, reports what a friend told him about his experience of exercising at the YMCA over many years.

> When he started, he noted the camaraderie of fellow exercisers. They would laugh and chat. . . . Over time, he got to know some of them a little and they would pick up the line of conversation from when they had last seen each other. Then one year, televisions were installed. Conversation diminished, as people uniformly focused on the screens. There were occasional comments on or laughter about what was shown, but there was a lot less visiting than previously. Some years after that, people began exercising with their own MP3 players and now everyone was cut off from each other.[5]

We shape our tools and then our tools shape us. A colleague, a chemistry professor, observed how the switch to online homework has brought changes beyond efficiency and the opportunity for the students to receive immediate feedback. The computer program only checks the answer, not how the student got the answer. He said, "In science how you get the answer, how you think is what is key—we are training students to do science. The medium, however, leads students to focus on answers as being important and I no longer see or interact with the work they do to get an answer."

A final example displays all three of the points I have made. The medium is not only active at the level of how content is received, the medium is active in shaping and changing content because of the limits and demands of the tool, and the medium is active in changing the user. On April

---

4. Quoted in Dyer, *From the Garden to the City*, 36.
5. Boers, *Living into Focus*, 127.

26, 2010 there was an article in the *New York Times* by Elisabeth Bumiller titled, "We Have Met the Enemy and He is PowerPoint." Gen. James N. Mattis is quoted in the article as saying "PowerPoint makes us stupid." Brig. Gen. H. R. McMaster observed, "[PowerPoint is] dangerous because it can create the illusion of understanding and the illusion of control. . . Some problems in the world are not bullet-izable." He critiques the use of rigid lists of bullet points (in, say, a presentation on a conflict's causes) that take no account of interconnected political, economic, and ethnic forces. "If you divorce war from all of that, it becomes a targeting exercise."[6] The frequent use of PowerPoint slides has changed what many officers do in their daily work. Some junior officers are now called PowerPoint Rangers because of how much time they put into preparing slides. The article acknowledges there are some excellent uses of PowerPoint. My point is not that this tool is totally negative. Rather, the point is that it is active. We shape our tools and then our tools shape us.

Therefore since the tools and applications related to the internet and electronic media are active our biggest error is to be passive in evaluation of the tool by only actively evaluating the purpose for using the tool. John Dyer, the Executive Director of Communications and Educational Technology for Dallas Theological Seminary, captures the contrast between passivity and active discernment in these lines in *Christianity Today*. He wrote,

> When it comes to technology in the church, I believe that the technology that has the most promise in the church is not the latest thing that comes off the assembly line. Rather, it is the technology—any technology—that church leaders openly discuss with other leaders and their congregations. Conversely, the technology that is most perilous for a church is the one that leaders immediately adopt without thinking through and addressing how it will subtly reshape our spiritual lives.[7]

In relation to the first thesis, I advocated for doing more than asking what is the most efficient when seeking the best option. In relation to the second thesis, I join Dyer in advocating for not only evaluating the purpose of a technological tool, but also asking questions about how the use of a tool changes us and shapes content. We must ask what does this tool displace? What will be gained? What will be lost? Perhaps even more important is to not just ask these questions before adopting a tool, but to stop and ask the

---

6. Bumiller, "We Have Met the Enemy."
7. Abare, Kellner, and Dyer, "Best and Worst New Tech," 63.

same questions after it is in use. Insodoing we can address unforeseen ways the medium has shaped and changed us.

We get a hint of this sort of active reflection on medium options in 2 Cor 1:23—2:4 as Paul discusses his choice to write a letter rather than go to Corinth. There are, however, very few examples of this explicit reflection on medium choice in the Bible. Yet, even though we do not have access to the evaluative discernment process we still can profit from observing the medium choices in the Bible. For instance we can reflect on why Jesus commonly used parables as a medium of discourse, or why he chose not to write documents.

We will briefly explore just one example, what missiologist Lamin Sanneh has called the translation principle.[8] At the heart of Christianity is a very significant decision about medium. Christianity is a unique missionary religion in that it is not language based. It is always translated; it uses all languages. This was true from the beginning. Sanneh reminds us that the Gospels themselves "are translated and interpreted versions of the teaching and preaching of Jesus."[9] And it is not just that they are in Greek rather than Aramaic; it is the Greek of the market rather than literary Greek. As C.S. Lewis wrote, "The same divine humility which decreed that God should become a baby at a peasant-woman's breast, and later an arrested field-preacher in the hands of Roman police, decreed also that He should be preached in a vulgar, prosaic and unliterary language."[10] Sanneh, himself a convert from Islam, notes the marked contrast with Islam which rejected translation. In Islam, the word of God became a book, and Islam is bound up in words and symbols. In Christianity, the word of God became flesh wearing a crown of thorns. I will highlight a few ways that Sanneh's work on the translation principle relates to our theme.

First, it underscores the thesis that the medium is not neutral. Sanneh points to many impacts that flow from translation of the Bible, impacts far beyond what many translators imagine. For instance an early modern missionary may have translated for the simple goal of being better able to communicate the gospel. But Sanneh argues that "Christianity is a form of indigenous empowerment by virtue of vernacular translation."[11] And this cultural empowerment happened in spite of some of the missionaries'

---

8. Sanneh, *Translating the Message*.
9. Sanneh, *Summoned from the Margin*, 222.
10. C. S. Lewis, quoted in Sanneh, *Summoned from the Margin*, 222–23.
11. Sanneh, *Summoned from the Margin*, 217.

latent or intentional imperialism. Mediums are active and powerful. And as I have already stated, we shape them, but they also shape us. For instance, new insights arise from translating the Bible into other languages. Theological change flows both ways in the missionary endeavor.

Second, the translation principle points to God's dynamic activity in the world. God does not choose one right language for all times and places. In a related way, we can say that God has not chosen one correct medium for all times and places. We are free to adopt new mediums. We appropriately explore using new tools of electronic media in God's mission today. Saying there is no right language points to the reality that all languages have both merits and demerits as bearers of the gospel. Just as we do well to acknowledge and work to address weaknesses in a particular language, we should do the same in relation to particular applications of the internet.

Third, Sanneh correctly relates the translation principle to the incarnation itself. In both we see God making medium decisions. God chose to use humble mediums that prioritize connection and presence over control of information. We must keep this model and these priorities in mind as we evaluate the use of electronic media in our Christian communities today.

Conclusion

God became flesh and dwelt amongst us. Presence matters. Incarnation, Emmanuel, God with us, is at the heart of Christianity. Let us include presence as one of the characteristics we use along with others, including efficiency, as we evaluate what are the best tools for discipleship and mission today. As we discern and evaluate the active roles of various media, let us ask how they might increase or decrease presence. That may sound like an indirect critique of most all the tools of electronic media. It is true that the digital age teaches us that presence does not matter. Electronic media often separates us from those we are with even as it connects us with those who are distant. (Think of the image of a group of people sitting at a table in a coffee shop all engaged —not with each other—but with their phones or tablets). To highlight the importance of presence is not, however, meant as blanket rejection of all mediated communication. Rather, in the spirit of this paper it is a call to deliberate, careful, and profound reflection. There are not simple or universal answers in relation to the questions of presence and the internet. For instance, those researching the question of whether Facebook increases connection or increases loneliness point out many variables. If Facebook users have strong networks of friends outside of Facebook and use it to build on those relationships, and to coordinate face-to-face social gatherings, then Facebook can increase connection. But as the proportion of online interaction to face-to-face interaction increases, the more people use Facebook the lonelier they become. Researchers would add that it also depends how you are using Facebook.[12] I mention this one example just to underscore the importance of careful, deliberate, and in-depth discernment. As we consider particular uses of specific mediums may the Spirit guide us in reflecting on the broad foundational issues explored in this chapter. Through that reflection, may we be better enabled to facilitate profound connection and act as agents of God's presence in a world of alienation and absence.

Bibliography

Abare, Brad, Mark Kellner, and John Dyer. "The Best and Worst New Tech: Which New Technologies Hold the Most Promise—and the Most Peril—For Use in Church Ministries?" *Christianity Today*, November 2009.

Boers, Arthur P. *Living into Focus Choosing What Matters in an Age of Distractions*. Grand Rapids, Brazos, 2012.

Bumiller, Elisabeth. "We Have Met the Enemy and He is PowerPoint." *New York Times*, April 27, 2010. https://www.nytimes.com/2010/04/27/world/27powerpoint.html.

Dyer, John. *From the Garden to the City: The Redeeming and Corrupting Power of Technology*. Grand Rapids: Kregel, 2011.

Hipps, Shane. *The Hidden Power of Electronic Culture: How Media Shapes Faith, the Gospel, and Church*. Grand Rapids: Zondervan, 2006.

Koyama, Kosuke. "The Crucified Christ Challenges Human Power." In *Asian Faces of Jesus*, edited by R. S. Sugirtharajah, 149–62. Maryknoll, NY: Orbis, 1993.

Marche, Stephen. "Is Facebook Making Us Lonely?" *Atlantic Monthly* 309 (May 2012) 60–69.

Sanneh, Lamin O. *Summoned from the Margin: Homecoming of an African*. Grand Rapids, Eerdmans, 2012.

———. *Translating the Message: The Missionary Impact on Culture*. American Society of Missiology Series 13. Maryknollm NY: Orbis, 1989.

12. Marche, "Is Facebook Making Us Lonely?," 60–69.

12

Crafting or Bearing the Present

Reflections on the Character of Christian Community

CLARK ELLISTON

Introduction

Online video gaming constitutes a multi-*billion* dollar industry, generating over $6 billion annually in China alone. In the United States, over twenty million people regularly participate in online games. The most popular incarnation of such games are massively multiplayer online games, or MMOs. MMOs join together thousands of players scattered across the world in a true virtual world where normal categories of reality do not apply. Most people do not, for example, wage war against goblins or ride griffons to work. One of the most successful MMOs, *World of Warcraft*, at its height boasted over 12 million monthly subscribers. As of 2012, 20 million users had active accounts on MMOs.[1]

In addition to being widely popular, MMOs are often intensely involving. The average "gamer" spends twenty hours a week playing online video games.[2] Quite frequently this time is devoted to one particular game, rather than a spread of different games. This intensity of participation raises

---

1. Yee, *Proteus Paradox*, 3. This number, however, only references online role-playing games. Games like *Halo* or *Call of Duty* boast even bigger numbers in their multiplayer formats.

2. Yee, *Proteus Paradox*, 26. The average American, by comparison, spends over thirty-three hours per week watching television. See Anonymous, "How Americans Are Spending."

the question: why are such MMOs so *interesting*? Richard Bartle famously classified players as belonging to one of four groups: achievers, explorers, killers, or socializers.[3] Achievers seek to accomplish the various goals within the game as quickly as possible. Explorers test the boundaries of the virtual worlds, attempting to "go" everywhere or investigate out of the way locations. Once the world has been explored the challenge is over. Killers attempt to dominate other players within the world. Their interest is primarily competitive. Socializers join the game to belong to a group; they seek out other players to ask questions and provide assistance. Although these are fluid categories, most players fit into one category more than the others. This last category in particular contributes to sustained involvement in MMOs. There is a prominent *social* and even *communal* motivation for participating in online video games.[4]

MMOs find success beyond typical or traditional video games because they draw upon a human desire for community. Modern internet technologies, like online games, undoubtedly increase the communicative possibilities of human beings. Yet, what *kind* of communities are formed by internet technologies? To address this admittedly complex question, we will first consider technological community in the form of MMOs.[5] This will be balanced by brief considerations of three thinkers who are less than positive about the communal possibilities of internet technologies: Albert Borgmann, Martin Heidegger, and Marshall McLuhan. Having briefly considered their concerns, we will then focus on the church-community in the context of Dietrich Bonhoeffer's theology. The

---

3 See Bartle's website for greater detail: http://www.mud.co.uk/richard/hcds.htm

4. Sustained involvement, rather than casual involvement, indicates a commitment to the game or, more appropriately, the individuals within the game. Most gamers quit playing particular a game when they have "beaten it," or when the ultimate challenge of the game has been overcome. In MMOs, however, many people stay on after having accomplished the primary mission of game. They do so because of the uniquely social component of MMOs.

5. MMOs may seem to be a less intuitive example of technological community than something like Facebook. However, while Facebook ostensibly connects people, it has a strongly informative and individualistic focus; one accesses one's account to either update or be updated. In contrast, MMO players are united by a common purpose or goal that exceeds either the provision or the reception of information. This commonality of purpose can *generate* new relationships rather than *mediate* preexisting relationships. Furthermore, online games constitute an enormously lucrative future market. There is reason to believe that MMOs will be every bit as pervasive as Facebook in the near future. This potential for growth, combined with the innate "buy-in" of having a common purpose, makes MMOs more theologically interesting.

church-community for Bonhoeffer participates in Christ's life by bearing the burdens of its members. Finally, we will tentatively assess potential issues for internet communities by considering three guiding questions. This constellation of questions should then help us consider, if only partially, how contemporary churches engage internet technologies for the sake of community. With regard to the extreme end of this engagement, or completely online churches, we will argue that they lack a fundamental feature of Christian communal identity: they cannot be incarnate with or bear the burden of their neighbors.

On Modern Internet Technologies

In the span of approximately two decades in the United States, access to the internet has gone from being a novelty and luxury for a technological minority to being a perceived necessity for the general populace. The internet has streamlined numerous aspects of modern life including commerce, information gathering, and perhaps most critically, communication. What Amazon and Google have done for the consumer and the information gatherer respectively, companies like Skype and Apple have done for the communicator. Skype, as a premiere example of voice-over-internet protocol software, allows the user to communicate over the internet without traditional phone service for a nominal fee. For those overseas, Skype has revolutionized the nature of communication. Instead of enormous charges for phone time, Skype allows for instant and economically viable communication. Apple's contributions are even more substantial. The iPhone has revolutionized personal communication devices. Not only does the iPhone still set the standard for mobile phone technology, it also contributed to the swift demise of both independent personal planning devices and independent handheld gaming systems.[6] In short, the iPhone represents the current pinnacle of communication as a device which unites a host of internet applications. Ironically, however, the iPhone has also indirectly contributed to the unique isolation of the technological world. Social scientist and psychologist Sherry Turkle recounts an instance where this isolation is all too clear:

---

6. This is not to say that handheld gaming systems are no longer popular (which they are), but that the iPhone provides so much entertainment as to render most personal gaming systems superfluous.

> I needed a new nanny. When I interview nannies, I like to go to where they live, so that I can see them in their environment, not just mine. So I made an appointment to interview Ronnie, who had applied for the job. I show up at the apartment and her housemate answers the door. . . . I tell her I am here to speak with Ronnie; this is her job interview. Could she please knock on Ronnie's bedroom door? The girl . . . looks surprised. "Oh no," she says, "I would never do that. That would be intrusive. I'll text her." And so she sent a text message to Ronnie, no more than fifteen feet away.[7]

Immediately it becomes clear that the capacity for communication has increased exponentially through internet technologies; we talk far more than decades past. However, has such communication contributed to more robust communities? In Turkle's anecdote, communication technologies *mediated* human interaction but did not *facilitate* human community. Do online communities like many MMOs simply increase communication or do they provide community with other human beings?

Online games serve both a communicative and a communal purpose. They facilitate uncommon relationships, provide common goals between persons, and remove many of the ever-present hierarchies of human existence. In addition to offering an arena of interaction for prior friends, online games often serve a relational purpose for those unwilling or unable to cultivate such relationships within "real life." Yee notes that many married gamers who met their future spouses online admitted they would not have been attracted to one another in the real world. Frequently players confessed that had they met in real life, "they would have immediately written the other person off because of a physical trait. The other person was too young, too tall, too thin, too blue-collar, or simply not their physical 'type.'"[8] Beyond romantic possibilities, persons confined to their homes may also find that online games offer opportunities to interact with other human beings. Online games provide more than a meeting place; they also provide immediate commonality. The limited range of goals within virtual worlds allows for instant and widespread goal-overlap between players. Whether one is a killer or a socializer, there are many in the virtual game world like oneself. In a real world of constantly shifting and conflicting narratives, virtual worlds provide needed structure and purpose.

---

7. Turkle, *Alone Together*, 2.
8. Yee, *Proteus Paradox*, 132–33.

There exists a radical equality within online games; no one has access to resources or to potential development unavailable to others within the game. What inequalities do exist are overt and intelligible.[9] So many of the disparities which often inhibit community like appearance, achievement, or social status are absent from online communities. In this way, it might be said that online communities like those formed in MMOs artificially create space for freer self-expression.[10] Given both the immense variety of those who play online games and the equality of the worlds which they inhabit, it does not overstate the case to call such communities "catholic."

For philosopher of technology Albert Borgmann, such positive description of MMO communities remains ironical at best and misguided at worst. Pervasive within Borgmann's account of postmodern and technological society is his observance of the loss of the "hearth." The hearth for Borgmann is, "the symbolic center of the house" and what gives communal life its intelligibility.[11] A consequence of what Borgmann calls the "postmodern divide" is the loss of this intelligibility, following the decentralization of the "focal practices" which the hearth centers. Simply put, in the name of immediacy and ease of consumption, our technological society has lost the ability to be rooted in the real world.[12] Internet

---

9. The most obvious inequality follows from the "pay to win" approach of some MMOs. This approach encourages profit by reducing up-front buy-in from the consumer but makes elite content available for additional fees. Those who can afford to invest in video games can increase character power or playing efficiency at a far greater pace than those who play the game in its free form. For those gamers who play to beat the game, this blatant inequality removes the challenge and renders the game "pay to win."

10. Of course, this has negative as well as positive implications. While it may be true that online communities remove persons from their immediate context with its interpersonal baggage, it also means that responsibility is removed. Thus, one finds "trolls" on the internet with alarming frequency. Apart from social and political contexts that require civility and perspective, one is free to be either as respectful or disrespectful as one so chooses. Additionally, while online games or other virtual worlds allow for freedom from social limitations, they place other limitations on the player. For example, genuine self-giving is impossible in games.

11. Borgmann, *Technology and the Character*, 197.

12. Over against being rooted in the "real world," Borgmann contends that we exist in a "hyper-real" world where actions are fundamentally separated from outcomes. There is no manifestly obvious reason why, when my finger touches the "a" key on a keyboard, the letter "a" appears on the computer screen in front of me. This separation contributes to the ease of the hyper-real world; in hyper-reality I no longer need to do the hard(er) work of chopping wood, killing chickens, or impressing a metal block with the letter "a" engraved on it into ink. Instead, my thermostat turns on the heat, I open a package of chicken breasts, and press the keyboard once. Cf. Borgmann, *Crossing the Postmodern*

technologies like MMOs contribute to this malaise by providing simulacra of genuine experiences.

For Heidegger, the concept of "enframing" (*Gestell*) lies at the heart of modern technology. Enframing, as the essence of modern technology, refers to the proclivity towards ordering and revealing. Science, as one example of such a proclivity, seeks to unveil and circumscribe all that appears to human beings. At its core enframing follows from a will to power and to domination. Heidegger states,

> Modern technology too is a means to an end. This is why the instrumental conception of technology conditions every attempt to bring man into the right relation to technology. Everything depends on our manipulating technology in the proper manner as a means. We will, as we say, "get" technology "intelligently in hand." We will master it. The will to mastery becomes all the more urgent the more technology threatens to slip from human control.[13]

The internet, as perhaps the greatest organizing venue in human history, manifests the truth behind Heidegger's articulation. Human beings create the content which appears online and yet are shaped by their creation. Centrally, we are shaped not by some insidious force which the internet represents, but by the access and the presentation the internet allows. Every aspect of human existence presents itself in some form on the internet. All is available for consumption and use or, in the words of Heidegger, for mastery. There is no mystery that the internet promises in art, sex, or the Eucharist.

While for Heidegger modern technology reflects the revealing and the organizing obsession of human beings, for McLuhan the consequence of "electric technologies" is more immediate. Modern technologies form vast networks which communicate and facilitate communication at an unthinkable pace. Moreover, such networks emerge from and reinforce particular ways of thinking over against others. Electric technologies privilege speed and efficiency over thoughtfulness and patience. The effect on human beings is devastating. Writing during the social turbulence of the 1960s, McLuhan locates such diverse problems as social detachment, colonialism, and mental illness within the realm of the technological life.[14] Modern technologies shape human beings so profoundly because we understand

---

Divide, 85.

13. Heidegger, "Question Concerning Technology," 313.

14. McLuhan, "Playboy Interview," 241–43.

those technologies as *extensions of our own bodies*. While this is nothing new, given that the wheel might be considered an extension of the foot, what is new is the scope of such self-extension. For McLuhan, the television forms the height of such self-extension. He writes, "Today, television is the most significant of the electric media because it permeates nearly every home in the country, extending the central nervous system of every viewer as it works over and molds the entire sensorium with the ultimate message."[15] Relative to the television, the internet represents an even greater extension of our "central nervous systems."[16] Internet technologies allow us to engage the world in ways unimagined for our forebears (including McLuhan, who died in 1980).

There is good reason to consider carefully how churches are affected by the mediums they employ. Surely we are conditioned by our technological context. Turkle is right when she observes that "we are shaped by our tools."[17] At the same time this is not new. Human beings have shaped and been shaped by their tools since the advent of tool-making. One can imagine accounts from nomadic tribal philosophers lamenting the discovery of agriculture for compromising tribal integrity (which it certainly would)! The inexorable march of history suggests that while technological advances truly impact ways of relating and thinking, human beings are remarkably adept at adapting to their increasingly technological context. Since one cannot revert to former ways of existence, such as a world prior to the internet, perhaps the most pertinent question is not should one reject internet technologies, but how can one embrace one's world while not losing oneself within it? Attending to Dietrich Bonhoeffer's characterization of community will equip us to better consider the shape of faithful Christian participation in this technological age.

Bonhoeffer and the Burden of Community

Across arguable shifts, changes in political context and even profound personal developments, Bonhoeffer's theology remains unremittingly Christocentric. Virtually every aspect of his theology, whether early or late, proceeds from his conviction regarding the absolute priority of Jesus Christ. Particularly, Bonhoeffer shows an abiding concern for the

15. McLuhan, "Playboy Interview," 245.
16. McLuhan, "Playboy Interview," 245.
17. Turkle, *Alone Together*, x.

Christocentric character of the *Gemeinde*, or church-community.[18] For Bonhoeffer the church exceeds both voluntary associations (although it is voluntary) and social collectives (although it does form a collective). Instead, it is the very incarnation of Christ in the world. As such, the church-community reflects the concerns and the will of its Lord. The church as *Gemeinde* exists only where Christ is present. Simple collections of individuals do not a Christian community make. Crucially, the church-community as the incarnation of Christ necessarily bears the burdens of its members as Christ bears the burdens of humankind. Such burden-bearing is a fundamental mark of Christian community.

Far from being a mere gathering of like-minded individuals, for Bonhoeffer the church-community signifies the space in the concrete world where Christ presents himself in the word and the sacrament of the church. The church-community, mediated through and established by Christ, relies not on individual inclination for fellowship but on the initiative of Christ and the preservation of the Holy Spirit. By participation in the church-community the individual is transformed. More specifically, participation in Christ's body resurrects genuine relation with other members of that body. This new form of relation reveals both the scandal and the promise of Christian community; at the core of their being Christians are no longer for themselves. To be for Christ, to be obedient to Christ, is to be for and in service of the others in the community. Bonhoeffer writes, "A Christian comes into being and exists only in Christ's church-community and is dependent on it, which means on the other human being. One person bears the other in active love, intercession, and forgiveness of sins, acting completely vicariously."[19] Acting vicariously, or putting oneself in the place of the other, constitutes the consummately Christian movement, since it emulates the self-renunciation exhibited by Christ.[20] Like Christ's sacrifice, the sacrifice

---

18. Bonhoeffer distinguishes between the physical church in one's town, whether *Kirche* or *Gemeinshaft*, and the church-community as the incarnation and the body of Christ, or the *Gemeinde*. Church (*Kirche*) and the church-community (*Gemeinde*) are not entirely distinct, insofar as religious gatherings are either churches (*Kirchen*) or church-communities (*Gemeinden*). Wherever the church-community (*Gemeinde*) exists it does so in the form of a church (*Kirche*). However, the church (*Kirche*) is not necessarily a church-community (*Gemeinde*). Gatherings of people, even while experiencing some aspect of community, do not constitute the church-community (*Gemeinde*). *Gemeinde* is translated in the Bonhoeffer Works edition as "church-community," a practice followed in this paper. Cf. Bonhoeffer, *Sanctorum Communio*, 14–16.

19. Bonhoeffer, *Sanctorum Communio*, 191.

20. Cf. Bonhoeffer, *Discipleship*, 124. "Because the Son of God became a human

of the individual on behalf of others extends beyond the boundaries of both personal fulfillment and life. The capacity of the person, as a member of the body of Christ, to intercede in the life of another constitutes a critical gift from God. It is a gift because it not only imitates Jesus's own self-gift, but because in giving oneself for another true freedom is found. As disciples of Christ, freedom comes not from seeking one's own welfare, which cultivates obsession and enslavement, but from the freedom of giving one's own life away for another. There is a common life within the community, for both good and ill, and so for Bonhoeffer the concrete practice of bearing one another's burdens holds real import.

Because the vicarious action on behalf of others follows from Christ's own vicarious action on behalf of humankind, such action only happens where Christ invades the world. Wherever Christ's body is there is vicarious action on behalf of others. Wherever the church-community exists it is accompanied by disciples who share the sufferings of their neighbors.[21]

Reconsidering Internet Communities

Human beings, generally speaking, have an innate desire and even need for community. For a segment of the population this desire is filled through online computer games, or MMOs. Yet, despite the niche that MMOs occupy in terms of facilitating community among their players, there is a further question which must be asked: what *sort* of community do MMOs create? To begin to address this further question, I gave a brief account of Bonhoeffer's idea of Christian community with particular emphasis placed on the role of being-for-others within the church-community. However, why compare MMOs to Christian communities? Surely one cannot judge MMOs for not being churches. At the same time, examining MMOs may give some insight into how communities are formed by their mediums. Inherent within MMOs are constraints and values which

---

being, service to God in worship can no longer be detached from service to sisters and brothers."

21. In Bonhoeffer, *Discipleship*, 123, Bonhoeffer notes the seriousness of not living humbly for others: "Jesus' community ought to examine whether it has given a sign of Jesus' love, which preserves, supports and protects lives, to those whom the world has despised and dishonored. Otherwise the most correct form of worship, the most pious prayer, and the bravest confession will not help, but will give witness against it, because it has ceased following Jesus. . . . God does not want to be honored if a sister or a brother is dishonored."

condition how players occupy those worlds. This is no problem when the online communities find their ground in the medium itself. *World of Warcraft* players ostensibly participate in their online communities because that is the purpose of that particular online community. Places which lack the internet intrinsically lack *World of Warcraft* communities. But what about online communities which have their ground elsewhere? A subsequent consideration of online church communities reveals the force of this inquiry: does the medium condition the community in such a way as to render online church communities only marginally different than secular online communities (like MMOs)?

Broadly speaking churches employ the internet in three key ways. First, and most pervasively, churches employ websites to provide basic information regarding service times, giving, and doctrinal affiliations. The value of the internet here lies in its ability provide *information*. Second, and more substantially, some churches have waded into the practice of utilizing social media such as Facebook, Twitter, Youtube, and Vimeo. Here the internet supplies a greater service: it extends the church's online presence into the virtual world. Third, and most radically, some churches have entire segments (or all) of their congregations online. No longer does the internet serve as an *extension* of the body. Instead, it *comprises* the church body. As one reflects on the almost infinite incarnations of internet usage among churches, a disturbing question emerges: do mediums of ministry affect the content of those ministries? If Martin Heidegger and Marshall McLuhan are correct about the nature and the effect of modern technology, then the answer must be affirmative.

Still, how does this inform a discussion of internet churches, or how churches utilize internet technologies? I suggest three guiding questions for further consideration. First, what does the internet church invite people into? Second, what does the internet church say, implicitly of course, about itself? Third, what does it say about the person as a part of that community? These three related questions offer a starting point for a discussion that demands sustained reflection.

Desire, or the cultivation of desire, lies at the heart of the Christian gospel. That the gospel constitutes good news and ought to be proclaimed as such stands at the center of the New Testament witness. It is water to the thirsty, freedom for the captive, and joy for the brokenhearted. Not only a relief of desperation, the gospel presents the fullness and even infinite excess of human desire. This gospel abundance shapes one's perspective of the world; the Kingdom transforms one's gaze within creation. Fields are no longer fields but treasure houses, Samaritans are no longer outcasts but exemplars of divine charity, and God's kingdom is not empire but mustard seed. The church too reflects the exclamatory imperative of the New Testament. Like the gospel which it proclaims, the church invites all people into its midst. But what is it that they invite people towards? Purely web-based formats shape the church to be simply another internet community. While such communities can undeniably reach people irrespective of distance, they also have limitations which critically weaken their persuasive force. The distinctive character of bearing one another's suffering, the distinctive mark of Christian love, disseminates in sheer *words* of love. Internet churches can speak to the theological revolution enacted in the Incarnation, but cannot be incarnate for its members. This limitation in no way denies the benefit for some of internet church participants; there are those who simply cannot attend churches. For these the ability to be a part of any church community is life-giving. Such situations are, however, border cases insofar as the vast majority of people can attend physical church locations.[22]

The second question posed, drawing on the first, addresses the identity of the church. What do internet churches imply about themselves? Few want to describe the church as just another therapeutic institution, designed to meet the psychological needs and wants of its members. Although one may wish to say that the gospel *does* meet ultimate needs of its members, personal fulfillment is surely not the church's primary intention. Yet, internet churches lend themselves to precisely such distortions when the church's members are released from the practical service of the community. Even mundane tasks undertaken for the church community, such as groundskeeping, greeting, teaching, or cleaning, participate in the body of Christ in life-giving ways. Such service constitutes bearing the burdens of the community in a way different from bearing the burdens of individuals. In either case, Christian burden-bearing binds human beings to the

---

22. The phenomenon of the internet church relies on particularly "low" Protestant doctrines of ecclesiology. Specifically, churches that privilege the priesthood of the believer, individual capability of Scriptural interpretation, and the pure symbolism of communion translate well into online formats. Such doctrines emphasize the individual's personal inclination for or against God, over against more ecclesiastical models of church that emphasize the role of leadership in the mediation and the communication of God's gifts within the community. Although Catholicism, for example, has an internet presence, one can only with difficulty imagine a Catholic internet church.

community through Christ. The bondage of Christ liberates people from the autocracy of their own wills. Churches which foster members who simply "receive" messages or cultivate knowledge fail to realize the fullness of the community which exists for concrete service of others.[23]

Such concrete service binds human beings together in lasting ways. Friendships formed during hardship often find resources to endure beyond their immediate need. While such friendships can also be formed online, they suffer from a problem with many online institutions: people can simply "log off." Internet communities intrinsically struggle to sustain long-term engagement.[24] Two aspects of this struggle merit mention. First, internet communities often lack any discernible unity of purpose and second, they frequently cannot support or encourage their users long-term. The first instance explains the difficulty facing MMOs: there is no ultimate unity of purpose for many players. Once the immediate challenge of the game has been overcome further involvement ceases. Although players may participate in an online world with others, they lack the enduring unity of purpose which sustains stable communities. The second instance explains the difficulties facing online educational models. While online education may inculcate knowledge, it lacks the subtle suggestion that *someone is waiting for and expecting your presence*. While in some cases burdensome, as is evident in 8:00 am university courses, this expectation helps constitute communities. Internet churches occupy a strange middle ground; they have a purpose (of meeting for worship/receiving wisdom and knowledge) but they lack the expectation of presence (though not as much as the online education course). Nevertheless, the end result is that the internet church demands less of its parishioners and inadvertently renders itself just another online community to be abandoned at one's convenience.[25]

---

23. Such communities might even be called gnostic insofar as they prioritize the epistemic aspect of faith with little to no physical aspect. This does not mean that those who participate in online churches do not undertake works of faith, but only that the models themselves are gnostic. The fundamental communication of the faith is epistemic rather than performative.

24. Online educational initiatives, for example, show dramatically increased rates of attrition and drop-out. Cf. Parry, "Online 'Attrition Puzzle'"; and Jenkins, "Why Are So Many Students." Similarly, one of the greatest challenges for those creating MMOs is sustaining interest. Inevitably, users gravitate to newer games with more advanced (or simply different) content. Cf. Bartle, "Decline of MMOs."

25. Of course, no church physical or otherwise can inoculate itself against attendance attrition. Nevertheless, internet churches invite such attrition by lacking basic incentives for participation present in physical congregations, like repeated and expected physical

In addition to implicitly making claims regarding the nature and purpose of the Christian community, internet churches implicitly comment on their members. Centrally, people observing sermons or even participating in chat rooms are *not perceived as people*. Instead, they are usernames with no histories other than the ones they ascribe to themselves or ones projected upon them by their nameless and faceless peers. Either alternative discourages truthful discourse. The former promotes false self-aggrandizement and the latter transforms users into objects for manipulation.

The disembodied presence of persons on the internet reduces their humanity in the minds of other users. One need look no further than the comments section of any web page to see such dynamics in action. Without the responsibility of standing before the recipient of their words, commenters are free to post and leave, without considering how those posts will affect another. Despite the prevalence of such "trolls" one should not deduce that there are thousands of moral monsters frequenting webpages. Instead, trolls inadvertently demonstrate the moral weight of embodied communication: moderation of vitriol occurs when one stands responsible for those words. While hateful words on the internet mean less because of their medium, positive speech means less as well. Physical affirmation between friends, even as mundane as hugs or sustained eye contact, encourages better than a well-wisher's words on Facebook. There is a moral force that attends the recognition of another's humanity. Brothers and sisters, rather than users, comprise the community of faith.

People consistently fear online mediums for their duplicitous potential.[26] The online small group consists of users who freely adapt and customize their online presence. While this is intrinsic to every instance of human communication (everyone controls their "message" in terms of fashion, style of speech, etc.), online mediums exponentially extend the power of control. The internet allows for unprecedented customization of self-presentation. This has both theological and pastoral valence. There is considerable Christian precedent to suggest that, even if intermittently practiced, dealing with the concrete infirmities of others offers hope and sanctifies charity. God's kingdom is furiously and famously irrespective of hygiene, sociability, conversational skill, and physical attractiveness. Engaging and loving others in their weakness reveals God's engagement and love in one's own finitude. The harsh light of the internet, however, sanitizes encounters with other persons.

---

26. Yee, *Proteus Paradox*, 119.

one's infirmities before others. The internet medium shades the true light of graced participation in another's need.

Conclusion

The internet has revolutionized modern Western living. It has changed how and what one consumes, facilitated the spread of Western culture, and—perhaps most of all—exponentially increased communicative capacities. It comes as no surprise that exponential growth of internet technologies has garnered the attention of the Christian church. This is in itself no problem. The church has historically benefitted from a great number of communication technologies. However, there are distinctive implementations of online mediums which invite appraisal. The arrival of "internet churches" particularly begs for reflection. While such churches do indeed reach a worldwide audience, there are severe limitations to their ministries. The limitations, in the estimation of this paper, lessen the distinctiveness of their message and mission. In effect, internet churches look uncomfortably close to a number of alternative online communities that revolve around a common theme or purpose.

Albert Borgmann argues that our technological context has replaced real experiences in the world with clever simulacra. In contrast to "focal practices" which unite communities and families, this context only decenters persons like a cultural centrifuge. Martin Heidegger suggests that modern technology reveals human beings to be thoroughly consumptive; humankind persistently concerns itself with rendering the world standing-reserve (*Bestand*) for its own use. Marshall McLuhan presents "electric" technology as humankind's own self-extension and self-realization. In his account the internet might exist as the quintessential expression of humankind's desire for immediate relation.

While the church is not intrinsically opposed to modern technology, the church does privilege practices which do not align with the effects of internet technologies. A significant example of such distinctive practice exists in the priority of ecclesial bearing of one another's burdens. Exemplified in the thought of Dietrich Bonhoeffer, the church is neither an institution defined by its universal communication of its message (although it is universal) nor by its immediate relation to anything (all things are mediated by Christ). In addition, it has its own practices which form the parameters of the community. Online churches, therefore, must take care when engaging certain forms of internet technologies, unless in their desire to communicate the message they wish to lose the distinctive form of their witness.

Bibliography

Anonymous. "How Americans are Spending their Time and Money." *Nielsen*, February 9, 2012. http://www.nielsen.com/us/en/insights/news/2012/report-how-americans-are-spending-their-media-time-and-money.html.

Bartle, Richard. "The Decline of MMOs." MUD, May 2013. http://www.mud.co.uk/richard/The%20Decline%20of%20MMOs.pdf.

———. "Hearts, Clubs, Diamonds, Spades: Players Who Suit Muds." MUD, n.d. http://www.mud.co.uk/richard/hcds.htm.

Bonhoeffer, Dietrich. *Discipleship*. Dietrich Bonhoeffer Works 4. Edited by Martin Kuske and Ilse Tödt. Translated by Geffrey B. Kelley, John D. Godsey, Barbara Green, and Reinhard Krauss. Minneapolis: Fortress, 2003.

———. *Sanctorum Communio: A Theological Study of the Sociology of the Church*. Dietrich Bonhoeffer Works 1. Edited by Joachim von Soosten and Clifford J. Green. Translated by Reinhard Krauss and Nancy Lukens. Minneapolis: Fortress, 1998.

Borgmann, Albert. *Crossing the Postmodern Divide*. Chicago: University of Chicago Press, 1992.

———. *Technology and the Character of Contemporary Life: A Philosophical Inquiry*. Chicago: University of Chicago Press, 1987.

Heidegger, Martin. "The Question Concerning Technology." In *Basic Writings*, edited by David Farrell Krell, 307–42. London: Routledge, 2004.

Jenkins, Rob. "Why Are So Many Students Still Failing Online?" *Chronicle of Higher Education*, May 22, 2011. http://chronicle.com/article/why-are-so-many-students-still/127584/.

McLuhan, Marshall. "Playboy Interview: A Candid with the High Priest of Popcult and Metaphysician of Media." In *Essential McLuhan*, edited by Eric McLuhan and Eric Zingrone, 233–69. New York: Basic Books, 1995.

Parry, Marc. "The Online 'Attrition Puzzle': New Study Revisits Dropout Debate." *Chronicle of Higher Education*, June 19, 2009. http://www.chronicle.com/blogs/wiredcampus/the-online-attrition-puzzle-new-study-revisits-dropout-debate/7228.

Turkle, Sherry. *Alone Together: Why We Expect More From Technology and Less From Each Other*. New York: Basic Books, 2011.

Yee, Nick. *The Proteus Paradox: How Online Games and Virtual Worlds Change Us and How They Don't*. New Haven: Yale University Press, 2014.

Subject Index

4G Data, 117

acoustic ghosts, 46
algorithms, 119, 122
Amazon, 162
anonymity, 44, 46, 121, 132, 133, 135, 160
Apple, 162
audience of one, 65, 72
authorial metanarratives, 43
authority
    and the internet, 87, 88–89, 91–92, 99
    in the Gospel of Mark, 87, 89–91, 92, 99
    of demons, 45n31
    of humans in the Garden, 77
    of the Pope, 53

blogs, 47, 49, 67, 174
body of Christ, xvi, 10, 19, 32, 35, 36, 37, 167, 168, 170

canon, 59, 87
capital vices, 67
cell phone, 23, 154
character-formation, xiii, xv, xvii, xviii, xix, 63, 64, 65, 69, 70
community, 68, 76, 78, 83, 84, 151, 161, 163
    and the internet, 86, 96–97, 132, 162, 168–174

    as a network, 98, 99
    Bonhoeffer's theology of, 161, 166–168
    in the Gospel of Mark, 86, 97–99
Complex Emergent Developmental Linguistic Relational Neurophysiologicalism (CEDLRN), 30–32, 37
cyber-conflagration, 49
cyber-self, xv, 42, 48
cyberspace, 2, 44, 45, 46, 50, 51

database, 41, 52–61
Decemberists (the), 39
deindividuation, 46
demonology and the internet, xiv, xvii, xviii, 6, 39–51, 67, 91, 97, 128, 146n32
diakonia, 83
digital
    communion of the saints, xiv, xvi, xvii, xix, xx
    self, xiv, xvi, xvii, xviii, xix, 39–51
    world, 24, 26, 27, 31, 32, 33, 35
disembodiment, xi, xvii, 28, 44, 92, 172

Ecclesia and Ethics (conference), xi, xii, 50, 151
efficiency (of technology), 151–159

electronic media, 23, 43, 53, 151, 153, 154, 155, 156, 158
email, 118, 133, 152
embodiment, xvi, 28, 31, 35, 37, 38, 64, 66
emergent systems, 30, 31, 33, 34, 35, 36, 37, 45
ethics of seeing, xiv, 13
Eucharist, x, 10, 11, 20, 129, 165
evangelical, x, 53
excarnation, xvi, 25, 26, 28, 32
extension, xvi, xvii, 27, 28, 29, 30, 32, 33, 34, 35, 36, 37, 38, 51, 58, 91, 166

FaceBook, 12, 16, 118, 119, 121, 122, 130, 133, 158, 159, 161n5, 169, 172
fake news, 30, 119
fasting of the eyes, xiv, 2, 21
fragmentation, xv, xvi, xvii, 42, 43

geo-demographic data, 122
global village, 43, 46, 51
Google, 29n14, 30n14, 56, 58, 59, 119, 123, 140, 141n21, 142, 146, 147, 149, 162

Hades, 43, 43n13
   of HTML, 40, 41, 43, 43n13, 47, 49, 50
Hirschhorn, Thomas, 17–21

ideation, xviii, 41, 42, 43, 44, 45, 47, 48, 49, 50
identity,
   and the internet, 92–93, 99, 121, 132, 133, 135, 140n21
   communal, 162
   cultural, 107
   formation, 42, 44, 45, 92, 95
   in the Gospel of Mark, 93–95, 99
   of Israel, 103, 148
ignis sacer, 19–20
image-saturated society, 2
incarnation, xi, xvi, xvii, 25, 26, 26n4, 28, 32, 36, 37, 103, 114, 145n29, 158, 160, 167, 167n18, 169, 170

interface, xvi, xvii, xx, 23–38
internet, xi, xii, xvi, xvii, xviii, xix, xx, 17, 24, 27, 30n14, 34, 40, 41, 44, 46, 47, 62, 63, 66, 67, 68, 70, 71, 72, 73, 87, 88, 89, 92, 93, 95, 96, 98, 99, 102, 113, 117–130, 132, 133, 134, 140n21, 141, 143, 144, 145, 148, 149, 151n1, 154, 155, 156, 158, 161–66
   and Heidegger's thought on modern technology, 161–174
   churches, xvii, 162, 168–174
   cookies, 122
   phenomenality of, 145–147
inter-subjectivity, 120
iPhone, 32, 55, 162, 162n6
iPod, 25n1, 26
Isenheim Altarpiece, 19
Israel,
   Law (Torah) of, 132–50
   Temple of, 101–16

James, LeBron, 63

Kindle, 23, 32

Lady Gaga, 63
language game, 45
laptop, 23, 27, 101
Luther, Martin, 47, 56, 57

Medusa, 145, 146
mimetic desire, 127, 128, 129
moral agency, 2, 3
multiplicity, 44, 46, 133, 134

Netflix, 23, 32
Nintendo Wii, 25, 26, 27
network sociality, xiv, xv, xvi, xvii, xix, 42, 44, 46
new sacred (the), 47
NPR, 56

online personae, 45
Oryx and Crake, 1

parasocial interaction, 43
Paul's vision of embodiment, 35
phantom presence, xviii, 41, 42, 43, 43n13, 44, 46, 49
Phelps, Fred, 41
phone poltergeists, 46
photoshop, 66
podcasts, xx
pornography, 1, 2, 12, 14, 14n46, 17
PowerPoint, 154, 156
printing press, 53, 54, 132
propaganda, 104, 119
Prosperity Gospel, 55
Protestant, 53, 58, 63, 170n22
proto-genesis, 39

Queen Elizabeth, 117

reader-response hermeneutics, 40–41
Reformation, 58
remote control, 23, 24
residual narrative self, xviii, 42, 43n13, 44, 46, 48, 49

sacraments, xiv, 10, 11, 54, 129, 167
sanctification, xvi, xvii, xix
schematic clusters, 28, 37, 40, 41, 43, 43n13, 44, 45, 46, 47, 49
search engine, xviii, 40, 41, 46, 56, 133, 134, 140n21, 141, 141n21, 142, 146, 147
Simul Sanctus et Stoicheia, 47, 47n28, 49
Skype, 162
slavery, 57, 82, 137n13
social network, xvii, 25, 33, 33n20, 36, 44n15, 93, 96, 121, 122
spiritual formation, xix, 66, 70
stoicheia, 46, 47, 47n28, 49
Stoics, 49, 49n34, 50
surveillance, 15, 89, 118, 119, 121, 123, 125, 127, 128, 129, 130

television, ix, 23, 43, 117, 118, 155, 160n2, 166
Temple,
 adaptation and, 108–9
 and the internet, 113–15
 as Jesus body, 103
 innovation and, 111–12
 repudiation and, 109–11
 Solomonic Temple, 101–16
temptation of temptation, 132–50
 and Google, 140–43
 and parenting, 148–49
 and the Torah, 143–49
texting, 133, 163
The Body of the Dead Christ in the Tomb, 18
Touching Reality, 17, 18
touchscreen, 23, 24, 26
Twitter, 12, 16, 154, 169

URL, 56, 121

vainglory, xviii, 62–74
video games, 160, 161, 164n9
 Call of Duty, 160n1
 Halo, 160n1
 MMOs, 160, 161, 161n4, 161n5, 163, 164, 164n9, 165, 168, 169, 171, 171n24
 World of Warcraft, 160, 169
viral (posts), 14, 14n46, 62
virtual
 ambiguity, 133
 culture, 12,
 world, 26, 27, 45, 76, 84, 132, 133, 142, 145, 160, 161, 163, 164n10, 169
 personas, 133
 reality, 44n15, 143
virtue ethics, xvii, 63, 69
virus (computer), 50
visual
 asceticism, xix, 2, 9, 20
 discipline, 2, 11, 20
 pedagogy, 9
 piety, 11, 12

Westboro Baptist Church, 41

Wi-Fi, 117
Work
    and the dominion mandate, 76–77
    and the Fall, 77–80
    and God, 80–82
    as service to God, 82–83
    in the virtual age, 75–76, 83–85
    theology of, xv, 75–85
workplace, xv, 76, 79, 82, 84, 85
World Wide Web, 26, 148
Wright, Frank Lloyd, 102, 102n4, 114,
    114n33, 115

YOLO, 134
YouTube, 26, 119, 169

Author Index

Ackerman, Joshua M., 105n9, 115
Albertz, Rainer, 108n19, 115
Andrejevic, Mark, 123, 123nn20–23, 124, 124n24, 130
Aquinas, Thomas, 64n3, 65, 73, 126
Aristotle, 74
Arnold, Clinton, 48n31, 50
Aronowicz, Annette, 149, 150
Arvidsson, Adam, 123, 123n23, 130
Athanasius, 11, 11nn41–43, 21, 57
Athenagoras, 3, 3nn3–4, 21
Atwood, Margaret, 1, 1n2, 2, 21
Augustine, 8, 8n27, 12, 18, 18n56, 21, 68, 73

Baldwin, Robert, 19n59, 21
Ball, Kirstie, 131
Baltzly, Dirk, 49n34, 50
Bargh, John A., 46n24, 51, 105n9, 115
Barker, Rachel, 44n15, 50
Bartholomew, Craig, 61
Bartle, Richard, 161, 161n3, 171n24, 174
Beals, Corey, 149
Belloc, Hilaire, 16, 16n52, 21
Blakely, Jeffrey A., 116
Bloch-Smith, Elizabeth, 110n23, 115
Boers, Arthur P., 155, 155n5, 159
Bonhoeffer, Dietrich, x, 161, 162, 166, 167, 167nn18–20, 168, 168n21, 173, 174

Borgmann, Albert, 161, 164, 164nn11–12, 173, 174
Brooks, Neil, 142n24, 149
Brown, Warren S., 30, 31, 31nn16–18, 35n22, 37
Brown, Wendy, 124, 125, 125n28–29, 128, 130
Bruckner, Pascal, 136n9, 149
Bumiller, Elisabeth, 156, 156n6, 159

Cahill, Jane M., 106n10, 116
Callaway, Kutter, xi, xiv, xv, xvi, xvii, 26n5, 37
Campbell, Heidi A., 27n6, 33, 33n19–20, 34n21, 37, 87, 88, 88n2–5, 89nn6–12, 92nn16–19, 93nn20–23, 96, 96nn26–32, 97nn33–34, 99
Cassian, John, 11, 11n40, 21, 66, 74
Cathcart, Will, 119n8, 130
Chappell, Tom, 83, 83n12, 85
Chilton, Bruce D., 99
Chrysostom, John, 4, 4nn8–9, 5, 5n10, 10, 10nn36–38, 21
Churchill, Winston, 101, 101n1, 102, 115
Clark, Andy, 27n8, 28, 28n10, 29, 29nn11–14, 30, 30n14, 31, 37
Clement of Alexandria, xix, 9, 9nn28–35, 21
Clines, David J.A., 116

AUTHOR INDEX

Cogan, Mordechai, 104n8, 106n11, 107n17, 112n28, 115
Colson, Charles W., 81, 81n10, 85
Cone, James, 57, 57n5, 61
Coogan, Michael D., 115, 116
Crites, Stephen, 43, 43n14, 50
Crossley, Nick, 120n10, 120n12, 121n15, 130
Cyprian, 3, 3n6, 4, 4n7, 21

Davies, Philip R., 116
Detweiler, Craig, 26n4, 37, 58, 58n7, 61
DeYoung, Rebecca Konyndyk, 65nn7–8, 66nn9–11, 67, 67n13, 68nn14–16, 70n20, 72, 72n26, 72n29, 73nn30–32, 74
Dodd, C. H., 97n36, 99
Dyer, John, 155, 155n4, 156, 156n7, 159

Ellul, Jaqcues, xviii, 27n6, 47n27, 50
Ericson, V., 121n16, 130, 131
Exum, J. Cheryl, 115

Flaubert, Gustave, 15n49, 21
Fickett, Harold, 81n10, 85
Fornaciari, Federica, 43n14, 50
Foster, Richard, 72n27, 74
Foucault, Michel, 120, 120nn9–10, 130, 131
Frank, Georgia, 11n39, 21
Freedman, David Noel, 116
Frederick, John, xi, xii, xiv, xvi n1, 47n29, 50
Fuchs, Christian, 121, 122n17, 130, 131

Garner, Stephen, 27n6, 33, 33nn19–20, 34n21, 37
Geyer, Felix, 44n17, 50
Girard, René, 127, 127n43, 129n49, 130
Goheen, Michael, 61
Goldhagen, Sarah Williams, 103, 104n6, 106, 106n14, 115
Gorringe, Timothy, 125, 125n31, 126, 126nn32–39, 127, 127nn40–41, 130

Graff, Joakim, 15n48, 21
Green, Clifford J., 174
Griffiths, Paul J., 18, 18n58, 21
Grudem, Wayne, 79n5, 81n10, 85
Gutheim, Frederick, 102n4, 114n33, 115
Guzzo, Giovanni, 133n1, 149

Haggerty, Kevin D., 121n16, 130, 131
Hauerwas, Stanley, 50, 51
Haugeland, J., 27n7, 38
Hayum, Andrée, 19, 19n60, 21
Hazan, Joshua G., 140n21, 149
Higgott, Gordon, 113n30, 115
Hipps, Shane, 53, 53n1, 54n2, 61, 152, 153n2, 159
Hirschhorn, Thomas, 17, 18, 18n55, 19, 21
Hurowitz, Victor, 104n7, 110, 110n22, 115

Ignatius of Loyola, 144n27, 149
Illich, Ivan, 1, 1n1, 21
Iser, Wolfgang, 40, 40nn2–5, 51

Jenkins, Rob, 171n23, 174
John Paul II, 136n7, 150
Jones, L. Gregory, 50, 51

Kaplan, Lawrence, 150
Katz, James E., 44n17, 45n18, 51
Kearney, Richard, 20n62, 21
Kierkegaard, Søren, 15, 15nn48–49, 16n50, 21, 22
King, Philip J., 115, 116
Kleinman, Zoe, 117n2, 131
Koyama, Kosuke, 153, 154, 154n3, 159
Kuske, Martin, 174

Labberton, Mark, 54, 55nn3–4, 61
Lactantius, 3, 3n5, 22
Laytham, D. Brent, 25, 25nn1–2, 26, 26nn3–5, 27, 27n6, 28, 38
Leader, Darian, 17, 17n54, 22
Lee, Timothy B., 121n16, 131

AUTHOR INDEX

Levinas, Emmanuel, xviii, 133, 134, 134n2, 135, 135nn3–5, 136, 136nn8–10, 137nn11–13, 138, 138nn13–16, 139, 139nn17–18, 140, 140nn19–20, 141, 141n22, 142, 143, 143n26, 144, 144n28, 145, 145nn29–30, 146nn31–32, 148n33, 149, 149, 150
Linfield, Susie, 14n47, 22
Lombard, Matthew, 43, 43nn10–11, 51
Lührmann, D., 89n13, 99
Luppicini, Rocci, 50, 51
Lupton, Deborah, 125n30, 131
Lyon, David, 119n4, 131

MacDonald, Dwight, 13n44, 22
MacIntrye, Alasdair, 42n9, 51
Malbon, Elizabeth Struthers, 97n35, 99
Marche, Stephen, 159, 159n12
Markus, Hazel, 51
Marion, Jean-Luc, 150
Mathieson, Thomas, 119, 119n5, 119n7, 131
Mazar, Amihai, 106n13, 107n16, 111n24, 116
McKenna, Katelyn Y.A., 46, 46n24, 51
McLuhan, Marshall, xviii, 43, 43n12, 46, 46n25, 51, 161, 165n14, 166, 166nn15–16, 169, 173, 174
Meilander, Gilbert, 78nn2–4, 85
Merleau-Ponty, Maurice, 120, 120n10, 120nn13–14, 126, 130, 131
Meyers, Carol L., 111n25, 115n34, 116
Mierse, William E., 103n5, 107n15, 108n18, 111nn26–27, 116
Moltmann, Jürgen, 37n23, 38

Neumaier, Anna, 87, 87n1, 99
Neusner, Jacob, 99
Nocera, Christopher C., 105n9, 115

Orwell, George, 129, 129nn47–48

Palmer, G.E.H., 67n12, 71nn23–24, 72n28, 74

Parry, Marc, 171n24, 174
Pelfrey, William V., 133n1, 150
Pickup, Martin, 90n14, 99
Pieper, Josef, 72n25, 74
Pinckaers, Servais, 150
Plantinga, Alvin, 63, 64n2, 74
Polkinghorne, Donald E., 45, 45n23, 51
Powers, Bruce R., 43n12, 46n25
Pridmore, Jason, 122n18, 131

Rafferty, Rebecca, 133n1, 150
Ratan, Rabindra, 44, 44n16, 51
Ratzinger, Joseph, 20n61, 22
Ricouer, Paul, 45, 45n18, 45n22, 51

Sandel, Michael J., 124, 124nn26–27, 125, 128, 131
Sanneh, Lamin O., 157, 157nn8–11, 158, 159
Sanz, Esteve, 140n21, 150
Sartre, Jean-Paul, 120, 120nn10–11, 126, 131
Sayers, Dorothy, 78, 78n4, 81, 81n9, 85
Schams, Christine, 89n13, 100
Sheldrake, Philip, 126, 126n37, 126n39
Snider, Laureen, 131
Snodgrass, Klyne, 97n36, 100
Soltani, Ashkan, 121n16, 131
Sontag, Susan, 13, 14n45, 16, 16n53, 22
Stager, Lawrence, 107n16, 108n20, 110n21, 115, 116
Stančík, Juraj, 140n21, 150
Stevens, Paul R., 81n10, 85
Strawn, Brad D., 30, 31, 31nn16–18, 35n22, 37
Sung, Jung Mo, 127, 127n43, 128, 128nn44–46, 131

Tarler, David, 106n10, 116
Taylor, Charles, 25n2, 38
Taylor, Mark C., 37, 37n23, 38
Terranova, Tiziana, 123, 123n19, 131
Tertullian, 5, 5n11, 6, 6nn12–16, 7, 7nn17–24, 8, 8nn25–26, 12, 22
Tödt, Ilse, 174

Toth, Josh, 142n24, 149
Tracy, David, 150
Treanor, Brian, 20n62, 21
Trottier, Daniel, 119n6, 131
Turkle, Sherry, 27, 45, 45nn19–21, 51, 102, 102nn2–3, 113, 113nn31–32, 116, 162, 163, 163n7, 166, 166n17, 174
Turow, Joseph, 124n25, 131

Vander Ven, Thomas, 133n1, 150
Volf, Miroslav, 79, 79nn6–7, 80, 80n8, 85
von Soosten, Joachim, 174

Weber, Nicole, 133n1, 150
Webster, William R., 131
Whitaker, Robyn, 94n25, 100

Willard, Dallas, 64n4, 65nn5–6, 68, 69n17, 70n21, 71n22, 74
Williams, Rowan, 18, 18n57, 22, 129n48, 131
Wink, Walter, 46n26, 47, 47n30, 48, 48nn31–33, 51
Wittel, Andreas, xv, 42, 42nn6–8, 51
Wittkower, Rudolf, 112n29, 116
Wright, N.T., 43n13, 51, 58, 58n6, 61, 69, 69nn18–19, 74
Wynn, Eleanor, 44n17, 45n18, 51
Wyschogrod, Edith, 134, 134n2, 150

Yee, Nick, 160n1–2, 163, 163n8, 172n26, 174
Yngvesson, Susanne Wigorts, 120n10, 131
Younger, K. Lawson, 116

Ancient Document Index

Aetius

46A   49

Aristocles (in Eusebius)

46G   49

Athanasius

Life of Antony

67   11
87–88   11
92   11

Athenagoras

Embassy for the Christians

32   3
35   3

Augustine

Confessions

6.18.13   8

True Religion

51.100   18

Clement of Alexandria

Christ the Educator

1.6   9
2.2   9
2.9   9
2.11   9
2.13   9
3.2   9
3.11   9

Cyprian of Carthage

To Donatus

6–7	3
7	4

Diogenes Laertius

Lives of Eminent Philosophers

44B	49

Lactantius

Epitome of the Divine Institutes

63	3

John Cassian

Conferences

11.2	11

John Chrysostom

Baptismal Instructions

1.32	4
1.43	4
2.10	10
3.11	10
6.1–2	5
11.12	10
12.18	10

Homilies on the Statues

3.11	10

Tertullian

De Spectactulis

1.3	5
2.1–2	6
2.2	6
2.8	6
2.10	6
2.11	6
3.2	7
14.2–3	7
16.1–5	7
16.6	7
17.5	7
18.1	7
24.3–4	8
25.4	7
25.5—26.3	8
28.1	7

Old Testament

Genesis

1–2	80
1:2	110
1:28	77
2:2	80
2:3	80
3:17–19	76
3:24	110
4:6–7	143

Exodus

20:8–11	76
20:9	80
20:11	80
40:34–38	103

ANCIENT DOCUMENT INDEX

Numbers

3:38	110
33:52	105

Deuteronomy

12:2	105
12:5	103

1 Samuel

4:4	111

1 Kings

5	107
5:6	103
6	104
6:2	106
6:16	108
6:17	106
6:18	109
6:23	110
6:29	109
6:31–35	104
6:31, 34–35	108
7:15–22	111
7:21–22	110
7:23–24	110
7:50	108
8:6	108
8:13	111
8:27	111
12:31	105

2 Kings

21:3	105

Psalms

7:6	68
19	77
80:1	111
99:1	111
104	81
104:4–9	81
104:10–31	81
104:13	81
104:31	81

Proverbs

8:22–31	80
8:22–36	77

Ecclesiastes

1:18	142
3:13	81
3:22	81
2:17–23	82
2:24–25	81
5:18–19	81

Isaiah

2:2–4	103
2:4	77
37:16	111

Jeremiah

7:4	103

Ezekiel

47	103, 109
47:1	110

Daniel

8:8	64

Zechariah

14	103

New Testament

Matthew

4	67
5–7	64
5:14–16	65
5:28	4
5:29	1
6:2	68
6:4	69
6:9–13	70
6:14–15	70
18:20	36
23:5–7	65

Mark

1:15	97
1:17	94
1:22–28	90
1:22, 27	92
1:22	90
1:27	90
1:40–45	97
2:1–12	90, 91
2:5–7	90
2:10	90
2:14	94
2:15–16	97
3:14–15	94
3:15	91
3:34–35	98
4	126
4:11, 26, 30	97
5:1–20	97
5:21–43	97
6:1–6	98
6:6	98
6:7	91
6:30–44	98
6:34	97
7:24–30	98
8:1–10	98
8:2	97
8:27–30	93
8:33	94
8:34–37	94, 95
8:34	94
9:1, 47	97
9:33–37	94
9:35	94
9:37	94
10:14–15, 23–35	97
10:21	94, 95
10:28–30	98
10:29–30	94
10:35–40	94
10:41	94
10:43–45	95
10:45	92
11:15–19	91
11:27–33	91
11:31	91
11:33–34	91
12:34	97
13:34	91
14:25	97
15:13–14	92
15:31	90

Luke

4	67

John

1:14	36, 103
2:19	103
5:17	81

Acts

6	83

Romans

1:24	126
8:23	79
11:36	37

1 Corinthians

12:7	79
12:12–30	35
12: 12, 14, 27	35
15:28	37

2 Corinthians

1:22	79
1:23—2:4	157
8:9	73

Ephesians

2:21	103
4:11–12	79

Colossians

1:15–17	81
1:16	47
3:23	82

Hebrews

2:14	36

1 Peter

2:5	103

1 John

2:16	2